Together Again with God

Together Again with God

More Daily Devotions from a Pastoral Heart

Glenn L. Monson

RESOURCE *Publications* • Eugene, Oregon

TOGETHER AGAIN WITH GOD
More Daily Devotions from a Pastoral Heart

Resource Publications
An Imprint of Wipf and Stock Publishers
199 W. 8th Ave., Suite 3
Eugene, OR 97401

www.wipfandstock.com

PAPERBACK ISBN: 978-1-6667-8176-2
HARDCOVER ISBN: 978-1-6667-8177-9
EBOOK ISBN: 978-1-6667-8178-6

VERSION NUMBER 09/12/23

This book is dedicated to my wife, Ruth, whose undying love and support are among God's greatest gifts to me.

Contents

Acknowledgements

I had the encouragement of many people as I wrote this second volume of daily devotions in the second year of the coronavirus pandemic. Members of my former congregations, St. John's Lutheran Church of Williams Township in Easton, Pennsylvania and Our Savior's Lutheran Church in Austin, Minnesota, as well as members of my current congregation, Mount Olive Lutheran Church in Rochester, Minnesota, have all been important in encouraging this second volume. My wife, Ruth, our daughters, Abby and Catherine, along with their spouses, and my extended family members, friends, and colleagues have also been valuable supporters of this book. As in any work of this kind, my teachers and mentors in college, seminary, and graduate school have also been vital sources of insight and wisdom from which I have drawn much in these reflections. Thank you, all.

Abbreviations

OT

Genesis	Gen
Exodus	Exod
Leviticus	Lev
Numbers	Num
Deuteronomy	Deut
Joshua	Josh
Judges	Judg
Ruth	Ruth
1 Samuel	1 Sam
2 Samuel	2 Sam
1 Kings	1 Kgs
2 Kings	2 Kgs
1 Chronicles	1 Chr
2 Chronicles	2 Chr
Ezra	Ezra
Nehemiah	Neh
Esther	Esth
Job	Job
Psalms	Ps (Pss)
Proverbs	Prov
Ecclesiastes	Eccl
Song of Solomon	Song
Isaiah	Isa
Jeremiah	Jer
Lamentations	Lam
Ezekiel	Ezek
Daniel	Dan
Hosea	Hos
Joel	Joel
Amos	Amos
Obadiah	Obad
Jonah	Jon
Micah	Mic
Nahum	Nah
Habakkuk	Hab
Zephaniah	Zeph
Haggai	Hag
Zechariah	Zech
Malachi	Mal

NT

Matthew	Matt
Mark	Mark
Luke	Luke

John	John
Acts	Acts
Romans	Rom
1 Corinthians	1 Cor
2 Corinthians	2 Cor
Galatians	Gal
Ephesians	Eph
Philippians	Phil
Colossians	Col
1 Thessalonians	1 Thess
2 Thessalonians	2 Thess
1 Timothy	1 Tim
2 Timothy	2 Tim
Titus	Titus
Philemon	Phlm
Hebrews	Heb
James	Jas
1 Peter	1 Pet
2 Peter	2 Pet
1 John	1 John
2 John	2 John
3 John	3 John
Jude	Jude
Revelation	Rev

Introduction

It was Pentecost Sunday, May 23, 2021, and we were gathering for in-person, indoor worship for the first time since the coronavirus unleashed its fury upon the world fourteen months earlier in March of 2020. Joyful anticipation, mixed with lots of questions about protocol, filled our minds. Who would come? How would everyone adjust to the still-evolving COVID parameters like self-screening for symptoms, mask-wearing, sitting at distance from one another, new communion practices to eliminate contamination, no handshaking, and so on and so on? And how would it be to worship together again after so many months apart?

Those fourteen months of online worship, and, for an adventurous few, parking lot worship even during the cold of a Minnesota winter, had been trying. While, prior to the vaccine rollout, the virus was undeniably dangerous and even, for some, deadly, isolation was also proving to be deadly. I remember very well preaching week after week into a camera while standing in an empty sanctuary; how exhausting that was. At times I wondered how long I could endure that situation. I knew, too, as a pastor, that the imposed isolation was taking its toll on our congregation. While people were being spared from getting sick from the virus, their spirits were flagging. Without regular opportunities for service and fellowship, worship, and gathering, we were drying up spiritually. News reports of lonely people as well as creative efforts to overcome that loneliness supported my observations.

But now the day had arrived: worship indoors together in person was again permissible. We announced that "The Spirit was Blowing Anew" and all were welcome to worship once again. The energy I experienced that day stays with me to this day. We were Together Again with God! To hear the congregation singing together, albeit through masks, brought tears to my eyes, as it did to others'. To be able to preach to actual people, not just a camera, was dramatically different. The synergy was palpable. We were together again as the Body of Christ! Even though it would be months before something approaching "normal" would be in place, I could feel the weariness of those months apart melting away.

At the same time, the pandemic was far from over. It would be another year before most people were fully vaccinated, and the protocols we instituted on that Pentecost Sunday were only gradually lifted as the virus released its grip on our lives. In view of the ongoing stress of the pandemic, the congregation of Mount Olive asked that another series of devotions be written, and so in Advent of 2021 I began writing the reflections that eventually became this volume. Once again, they were designed to support people in their ongoing life with God and the people of God, combining the wisdom of Scripture with the challenges and opportunities of everyday life amidst the waning pandemic.

Members of the congregation have regularly thanked me for sharing this second collection of devotions as we made our way through the pandemic. I now offer them to a wider readership, hoping that, as the first readers were blessed, so others will find comfort, encouragement, challenge, and blessing in these words. Soli Deo Gloria!

—Glenn Monson

The First Week of Advent

Monday

Neh 9:6–8

> [6] And Ezra said: "You are the LORD, you alone; you have made
> heaven, the heaven of heavens, with all their host, the earth and
> all that is on it, the seas and all that is in them. To all of them you
> give life, and the host of heaven worships you. [7] You are the LORD,
> the God who chose Abram and brought him out of Ur of the
> Chaldeans and gave him the name Abraham; [8] and you found
> his heart faithful before you, and made with him a covenant to
> give to his descendants the land of the Canaanite, the Hittite, the
> Amorite, the Perizzite, the Jebusite, and the Girgashite; and you
> have fulfilled your promise, for you are righteous."

Nehemiah was a servant of the court in Persia during the Jews' exile there, and is credited, along with Ezra the priest, with leading the people of Israel once they returned home from exile. In the ninth chapter of the book of Nehemiah, we have an account of what is sometimes called a "national confession." This is the story of the whole people of Israel standing before God, confessing their sins. But notice that the beginning of this confession, in the passage we read today, is a hymn of praise extolling the mighty works of God. This goes on well beyond these verses. One of my seminary professors, Gerhard Forde, used to remind us that the reason we begin worship with confession is because we are coming into the presence of a holy God, and we are not holy. So perhaps the Israelites began their confession with praise to remind themselves of how majestic God is and how little they were compared with God. What would it look like if our confessions started this way as well?

Prayer

Almighty God, as we begin this new season of the Church year, we give you praise. We praise you for your mighty works of creation, your compassion shown in Christ, and your abundance poured out upon us in the Holy Spirit. Grant that every day we might be found giving you praise, and in so doing, we might be caught up in joyful service in your name to all we encounter. In the name of Christ, we pray. AMEN.

Tuesday

1 Thess 5:8–11

> [8] But since we belong to the day, let us be sober, and put on the breastplate of faith and love, and for a helmet the hope of salvation. [9] For God has destined us not for wrath but for obtaining salvation through our Lord Jesus Christ, [10] who died for us, so that whether we are awake or asleep we may live with him. [11] Therefore encourage one another and build up each other, as indeed you are doing.

It is hard for us to imagine, but the people of Thessalonica, to whom St. Paul first wrote this letter, were living in expectation of the Lord's return in their own lifetime. That's right; they thought that Christ would return any day. Even so, Paul was practical in his advice to them. He knew that in their waiting they might find their faith weakening and they might become vulnerable to Satan's lies. One of Satan's favorite lies to God's people is, "You are destined for wrath. You are a sinner, and there is no mercy for you." Ironically people of faith, who are sometimes more aware of their own sins, can be more susceptible to this lie. But Paul assures us, "You are not destined for wrath, but for obtaining salvation through our Lord Jesus Christ." There is a story often told of Martin Luther as he sat alone in his room in the Wartburg castle. As the story goes, Satan was tempting him to despair, to doubt his salvation. Suddenly, Luther stood up and shouted, "I am baptized!," and threw his ink well at the castle wall. It is said that you can still see the stain on the wall. Luther was reiterating what St. Paul tells us here: You are destined for obtaining salvation. You have been baptized. You have been claimed by God, and nothing shall ever separate you from that love.

Prayer

God of Great Mercy, how blessed we are to be called your own. Through no merit of our own, you have claimed us as your children and even made us co-heirs with Christ of an eternal inheritance. All thanks and praise to you. Let us never doubt such a great salvation but rejoice in it each day, living lives of faith and gratitude. In Jesus' name, we pray. AMEN.

Wednesday

Num 17:1–8

> The LORD spoke to Moses, saying: 2 Speak to the Israelites,
> and get twelve staffs from them, one for each ancestral house,
> from all the leaders of their ancestral houses. Write each man's
> name on his staff, 3 and write Aaron's name on the staff of
> Levi. For there shall be one staff for the head of each ances-
> tral house. 4 Place them in the tent of meeting before the cov-
> enant, where I meet with you. 5 And the staff of the man whom
> I choose shall sprout; thus I will put a stop to the complaints of
> the Israelites that they continually make against you. 6 Moses
> spoke to the Israelites; and all their leaders gave him staffs, one
> for each leader, according to their ancestral houses, twelve staffs;
> and the staff of Aaron was among theirs. 7 So Moses placed the
> staffs before the LORD in the tent of the covenant. 8 When Moses
> went into the tent of the covenant on the next day, the staff of
> Aaron for the house of Levi had sprouted. It put forth buds,
> produced blossoms, and bore ripe almonds.

Needless to say, this is a strange story. We do not generally go around choosing our leaders according to which staff sprouts. Laying that aside, what is important to know is that, just prior to this episode, there is a very serious revolt amongst God's people. The leaders of that revolt had even assembled an army of several hundred men to oppose Moses and Aaron. In short, the whole future of the nation of Israel was at stake. This story highlights the importance of leadership. We have learned this over and over throughout history, and it is no less important today than it was in the time of Moses. When wicked leaders are allowed to gain power, destruction is assured. When fools are put in charge of complex systems, chaos results. Even when good-hearted but unprepared people of faith are given responsibility far beyond their ability, things do not go well.

Leadership is important. These days, we need to be praying for our leaders—the leaders of our communities, our churches, our nation, and even our globe. Be assured that when we rally behind a leader who follows in the footsteps of Christ, we will be blessed.

Prayer

God of Wisdom, thank you for the example of Christ. As he led his disciples in the way of wisdom, compassion, and love, let us do so as well. Grant that those who lead and those who follow might all have the mind of Christ so that together we might find our way to your will for us all. We are in your hands, Gracious God. Hear us, we pray. In Christ's name. AMEN.

Thursday

2 Pet 3:8–13

> 8 But do not ignore this one fact, beloved, that with the Lord
> one day is like a thousand years, and a thousand years are like
> one day. 9 The Lord is not slow about his promise, as some think
> of slowness, but is patient with you, not wanting any to perish,
> but all to come to repentance. 10 But the day of the Lord will
> come like a thief, and then the heavens will pass away with a
> loud noise, and the elements will be dissolved with fire, and the
> earth and everything that is done on it will be disclosed. 11 Since
> all these things are to be dissolved in this way, what sort of
> persons ought you to be in leading lives of holiness and godli-
> ness, 12 waiting for and hastening the coming of the day of God,
> because of which the heavens will be set ablaze and dissolved,
> and the elements will melt with fire? 13 But, in accordance with
> his promise, we wait for new heavens and a new earth, where
> righteousness is at home.

This passage in the second letter of St. Peter reminds us of two things that could rightly be called "law" and "gospel". The *law* here reminds us that the day of the Lord will come. What we confess in the Apostles' Creed, that Christ will someday come "to judge the living and the dead," is assured. This should cause us to live with a due sense of responsibility, not allowing ourselves to be drawn into patterns that suggest that nothing is expected of us as people of God. As St. Peter says, we ought to lead lives of "holiness and godliness."

Having said this, the *gospel* in this passage reminds us that the Lord is not "wanting any to perish, but all to come to repentance." It is God's will that *all* know grace, *all* know Christ's love, and *all* are brought to the place where they rejoice in Christ's coming. Because of this, we have the joyful duty of proclaiming this Good News to the world. Our message is: "Christ's love is for all! God has no favorites! Sins are forgiven. Christ lives. Rejoice in the goodness of God!" This message also has the effect of bringing us joy, for we live, confident that when Christ appears, we will receive him with joy.

Prayer

Gracious God, make us bearers of the good news. Inspire us to share your love with those around us, telling the good news that Christ has come for all. Grant us also the good sense to live lives of holiness and godliness, not presuming upon your mercy. We are your children. Guide us, we pray. In the Name of Christ. AMEN.

Friday

2 Sam 7:18–22

> 18 Then King David went in and sat before the LORD, and said,
> "Who am I, O Lord God, and what is my house, that you have
> brought me thus far? 19 And yet this was a small thing in your
> eyes, O Lord God; you have spoken also of your servant's
> house for a great while to come. May this be instruction for the
> people, O Lord God! 20 And what more can David say to you?
> For you know your servant, O Lord God! 21 Because of your
> promise, and according to your own heart, you have wrought
> all this greatness, so that your servant may know it. 22 There-
> fore you are great, O LORD God; for there is no one like you,
> and there is no God besides you, according to all that we have
> heard with our ears."

This passage is the beginning of a prayer of thanksgiving that David offers after God's covenant has been renewed with David's family. God has assured him that his family would forever lie in God's embrace, and that David's house and kingdom would stand forever. In this promise we, Christians, hear the promise of Christ. To this great gift, David offers this prayer. Note David's incredulous posture before God: "Who am I to have received all this?" In his gratefulness, David can only refer to himself as "your servant," again emphasizing that all his blessings come not because of his deserving, but despite his undeserving. When we examine our lives as people of faith, as citizens of this land, as recipients of so much abundance, David's posture commends itself to us. Certainly none of us can claim that all that we have comes to us because we deserve it. Indeed, if we are honest with ourselves, we know that we often fall short of God's will for us, and yet God has blessed us. We, too, are simply servants in the Lord's house, recipients of God's grace.

Prayer

We are your servants, Lord God. We are those whose only claim is that you have seen fit to call us your own and call us to tasks that give us purpose and joy. Help us to live lives of gratitude and service, always remembering that your grace is what has brought us all this abundance. We ask this in Christ's name. AMEN.

The Second Week of Advent

Monday

Luke 1:67, 76–79

67 Then his father Zechariah was filled with the Holy Spirit and spoke this prophecy:
76 "And you, child, will be called the prophet of the Most High;
for you will go before the Lord to prepare his ways,
77 to give knowledge of salvation to his people
by the forgiveness of their sins.
78 By the tender mercy of our God,
the dawn from on high will break upon us,
79 to give light to those who sit in darkness and in the shadow of death,
to guide our feet into the way of peace."

We hear from John the Baptizer in Advent more than in any other season. John is the one who calls out to us, "Prepare the way of the Lord! Make his paths straight!" In the passage above, we hear John's father responding to those who are asking, at John's birth, "What then will this child become?" From all the miraculous happenings surrounding John's birth, they know that his life will be special, but they have no idea how. Here, Zechariah, filled with the Holy Spirit, tells them: "He will be a prophet of God, preparing the Lord's way, giving the knowledge of salvation to all people. He will announce God's tender mercy to those who sit in despair and the shadow of death." At first glance, this seems to be at odds with the John we know, the one who calls for repentance, announcing God's judgment. Could it be that John did both? The answer lies in the different ways John's words were received. His message sounded like judgment to some people, while to others, that same word sounded like good news. Those who had used their power to tramp people down heard a call to repentance. Those who had been trampled heard the good news that God had come to deliver them. This is how God's word works. It both comforts and convicts, in whatever way we need it.

Prayer

Gracious God, thank you for your Everlasting Word, the word that comforts and convicts. Give us ears to hear your word of comfort when we despair, and an openness to repentance when your word convicts us. In both, we know we find life. In Jesus' name. AMEN.

Tuesday

Mal 3:5–7

> 5 Then I will draw near to you for judgment; I will be swift
> to bear witness against the sorcerers, against the adulterers,
> against those who swear falsely, against those who oppress
> the hired workers in their wages, the widow and the orphan,
> against those who thrust aside the alien, and do not fear me,
> says the LORD of hosts. 6 For I the LORD do not change; there-
> fore you, O children of Jacob, have not perished. 7 Ever since
> the days of your ancestors you have turned aside from my stat-
> utes and have not kept them. Return to me, and I will return to
> you, says the LORD of hosts.

The prophet Malachi is another voice that comes to us in the season of Advent. Like John the Baptizer, Malachi, too, calls us to repentance. The name Malachi literally means "my messenger." It is not thought to be a proper name, but simply the title of the one who speaks for God. In this case, Malachi speaks primarily against a corrupt priesthood who has led the people astray. Notice what sins are lifted up: sorcery, adultery, lying, oppressing workers and the vulnerable, and failing to care for the foreigner. All of these sins, Malachi says, come from a fundamental failure to fear God. What Malachi seems to be saying is that a healthy reverence for God can keep us from falling into sin. When we realize that God is faithful, that just might lead us to be more faithful. When we realize God is compassionate to the vulnerable, we might become more compassionate ourselves. When we realize that God cares about the life of the foreigner amongst us, we might be more likely to do the same. Malachi's lesson: Fear God, for in this posture there is life for us and for all those we encounter.

Prayer

God of All Righteousness, grant us a healthy sense of awe in your presence. Keep us from presumption and disregard for your holiness. Remind us that you are a God who loves righteousness and hates wickedness, so that in all our days we might be faithful to you. We pray this in Christ's name. AMEN.

Wednesday

Phil 1:12–18

> [12] I want you to know, beloved, that what has happened to me has actually helped to spread the gospel, [13] so that it has become known throughout the whole imperial guard and to everyone else that my imprisonment is for Christ; [14] and most of the brothers and sisters, having been made confident in the Lord by my imprisonment, dare to speak the word with greater boldness and without fear. [15] Some proclaim Christ from envy and rivalry, but others from goodwill. [16] These proclaim Christ out of love, knowing that I have been put here for the defense of the gospel; [17] the others proclaim Christ out of selfish ambition, not sincerely but intending to increase my suffering in my imprisonment. [18] What does it matter? Just this, that Christ is proclaimed in every way, whether out of false motives or true; and in that I rejoice.

The Apostle Paul is the ultimate maker of lemonade when handed lemons. In this letter, Paul is in prison, and not only is he not complaining about it, he is saying that his situation is actually furthering the ministry of the gospel. He goes on to say that it does not matter to him *why* people proclaim Christ, just that they do it. What an example Paul is for us. I had a friend in college who told me about a book he was reading that explained that life can be seen as a series of miracles. Blue miracles were the events that happened in life that would likely be seen as positive developments. Red miracles were those events that would be seen by most as negative developments. In other words, no matter what happened, it was a miracle. Now, it's fair to say that this theology isn't without its problems, but be that as it may, there's no doubt that having such a mindset is commendable. The result is expecting God to be at work (i.e. perform miracles) in *everything*, and that is a grand place to be. We could even call it a spirit of "holy anticipation." Now, doesn't that sound like Advent?

Prayer

Fill us with holy anticipation, O God. Give us faith to see you at work in all times and places, continually expecting your reign to break in. You are the God who delights in breaking into our world with a word of hope and love. Help us to be those who hear this good word and live in it. In your holy name, we pray. AMEN.

Thursday

Ps 126

1 When the LORD restored the fortunes of Zion,
we were like those who dream.
2 Then our mouth was filled with laughter,
and our tongue with shouts of joy;
then it was said among the nations,
"The LORD has done great things for them."
3 The LORD has done great things for us,
and we rejoiced.
4 Restore our fortunes, O LORD,
like the watercourses in the Negeb.
5 May those who sow in tears
reap with shouts of joy.
6 Those who go out weeping,
bearing the seed for sowing,
shall come home with shouts of joy,
carrying their sheaves.

A couple of winters ago, my wife and I spent some time in Tucson with relatives. It was lovely to get away from the snow and cold of Minnesota for a few days and take in the warmth and sunshine of Arizona in January. Near the place we stayed was a watercourse, or what Arizonans call a "wash." It is a river bed that is dry most of the time, but it holds the water when the occasional downpour happens. In the Negeb desert of Israel, there were watercourses, too. When the psalmist asks God to restore their fortunes "like the watercourses in the Negeb," the picture is of a watercourse filled to overflowing following a rain. What has been bone-dry for a long time is suddenly overflowing with water. In other words, the psalmist is asking not just for a few drips of blessing, but a torrent of abundance that will proclaim to the whole world the goodness of God. Let us be, says the psalmist, like "those who go out weeping" but after experiencing God's abundance, return home "with shouts of joy," carrying the fruits of the harvest. We too can pray this prayer, trusting that even if our days seem to be in the midst of a drought, God is faithful, and a thunder shower of blessing is not far off.

Prayer

We praise you, Faithful One, for the promise of your blessing. Our days are sometimes filled with sorrow; we need your comfort. Our days are often filled with anxiety; we need your peace. Our days are regular reminders of our mortality; we need your eternal spirit. Bless us, O God. Grant us your favor, that we might take joy in you in all our days. In your precious name, we pray. AMEN.

Friday

Isa 40:1–5

Comfort, O comfort my people,
    says your God.
2 Speak tenderly to Jerusalem,
    and cry to her
that she has served her term,
    that her penalty is paid,
that she has received from the LORD's hand
    double for all her sins.

3 A voice cries out:
"In the wilderness prepare the way of the LORD,
make straight in the desert a highway for our God.
4 Every valley shall be lifted up,
and every mountain and hill be made low;
the uneven ground shall become level,
and the rough places a plain.
5 Then the glory of the LORD shall be revealed,
and all people shall see it together,
for the mouth of the LORD has spoken."

I cannot read these words of Isaiah without hearing the music of Handel's Messiah in my head. I remember first hearing this marvelous piece of music as a boy, and being absolutely mesmerized. The tenor soloist is the first voice to sing, and his opening notes are pure comfort. In the words of King James English he sings forth: "Comfort ye." The music is like a gentle spring rain running over your head. And why should we be comforted? Because the penalty for our sins has been paid, even double for all our sins. And then, in joyous praise at this announcement, the whole chorus chimes in, singing, "Every valley shall be lifted up," and we, the listeners, are lifted up as well. There is great mystery in the way music and words lift our spirits. How can a certain combination of words and music cause us to laugh, to cry, to feel ecstasy or despair? We don't know. Martin Luther once said that, next to God's word, there is no greater gift to humankind than music. I believe this, too. Do yourself a favor: listen to Handel's Messiah this Advent season and experience the comfort and joy that God gives.

Prayer

Lord Christ, you are the Savior of the world. You are the One who brings us comfort, for indeed, in you, all our sins are forgiven. Make us bearers of comfort to others, as well. Make us proclaimers of the good news that sins are forgiven, hope is alive, and Christ is coming again. We praise you forever. AMEN.

The Third Week of Advent

Monday

Isa 19:19–25

> [19] On that day there will be an altar to the LORD in the center of
> the land of Egypt, and a pillar to the LORD at its border. [20] It will
> be a sign and a witness to the LORD of hosts in the land of Egypt;
> when they cry to the LORD because of oppressors, he will send
> them a savior, and will defend and deliver them. [21] The LORD will
> make himself known to the Egyptians; and the Egyptians will
> know the LORD on that day, and will worship with sacrifice and
> burnt offering, and they will make vows to the LORD and per-
> form them. [22] The LORD will strike Egypt, striking and healing;
> they will return to the LORD, and he will listen to their supplica-
> tions and heal them.[23] On that day there will be a highway from
> Egypt to Assyria, and the Assyrian will come into Egypt, and the
> Egyptian into Assyria, and the Egyptians will worship with the
> Assyrians.[24] On that day Israel will be the third with Egypt and
> Assyria, a blessing in the midst of the earth, [25] whom the LORD of
> hosts has blessed, saying, "Blessed be Egypt my people, and As-
> syria the work of my hands, and Israel my heritage."

If you know anything at all about the history of Israel, you know that this passage is really remarkable. Who were Israel's fiercest enemies in much of its history? Egypt and Assyria. Egypt in the Exodus story, and Assyria as the nation that hauled the Israelites off into exile. Yet here, in this passage, the prophet envisions them as "a blessing in the midst of the earth." What a reversal! I remember a set of twins I once had in a confirmation class. They were an unholy terror. They egged each other on to see which one could wreak the most havoc. Those two were solely responsible for me taking a course in classroom management during my ministry. What a pair! Years after I had left the congregation where those two boys had tormented me, I happened to ask one of the secretaries at that church, "Whatever became of those boys?" She said, "I know you will find this hard to believe, but they became leaders in our church youth group. They were some of the best and most faithful young people we ever had." I was stunned. Yes, God does sometimes use our tormentors to bless the world. What a God we have!

Prayer

God of surprises, thank you for using all sorts of people for your glory. Forgive the small-mindedness that keeps us from seeing the potential in each person. Grant us wisdom to see even our tormentors as those whom you can use for blessing the world. In Christ's name, we pray. AMEN.

Tuesday

2 Pet 1:3–9

> 3 His divine power has given us everything needed for life and
> godliness, through the knowledge of him who called us by his
> own glory and goodness. 4 Thus he has given us, through these
> things, his precious and very great promises, so that through
> them you may escape from the corruption that is in the world
> because of lust, and may become participants of the divine
> nature. 5 For this very reason, you must make every effort to
> support your faith with goodness, and goodness with knowl-
> edge, 6 and knowledge with self-control, and self-control with
> endurance, and endurance with godliness, 7 and godliness with
> mutual affection, and mutual affection with love. 8 For if these
> things are yours and are increasing among you, they keep you
> from being ineffective and unfruitful in the knowledge of our
> Lord Jesus Christ. 9 For anyone who lacks these things is short-
> sighted and blind, and is forgetful of the cleansing of past sins.

These are remarkable verses. First, the writer makes clear that we have been given everything needed "for life and godliness." Second, we are told *why* we have received these things: "So that through [the promises of God]we may escape from the corruption that is in the world . . . and become participants of the divine nature." Third, the writer gives us a charge: we are to "make every effort to support our faith" with all sorts of attributes and efforts. Finally, why must we do this? The answer is stated clearly: so that we are not "ineffective and unfruitful in the knowledge of our Lord Jesus Christ." It's important to note that we are not asked to supplement our faith with all these attributes and efforts in order to avoid *losing* our faith or our salvation. Instead, we are exhorted to these things so that we might be effective and fruitful in the ministry to which God has called us. Once again, we see that God has blessed us to be a blessing.

Prayer

God of All, your vision for the world is so much grander than ours. How often we get caught up in thinking that we are blessed for our own benefit alone. Forgive us for this small, self-centered thinking. Give us a glimpse of your vision for the world, and make us effective and fruitful servants. In the name of Christ, we pray. AMEN.

Wednesday

Luke 7: 18–23

> [18] The disciples of John reported all these things [that Jesus
> had been doing]to him. So John summoned two of his dis-
> ciples [19] and sent them to the Lord to ask, "Are you the one
> who is to come, or are we to wait for another?" [20] When the
> men had come to him, they said, "John the Baptist has sent
> us to you to ask, 'Are you the one who is to come, or are we to
> wait for another?'" [21] Jesus had just then cured many people of
> diseases, plagues, and evil spirits, and had given sight to many
> who were blind. [22] And he answered them, "Go and tell John
> what you have seen and heard: the blind receive their sight,
> the lame walk, the lepers are cleansed, the deaf hear, the dead
> are raised, the poor have good news brought to them. [23] And
> blessed is anyone who takes no offense at me."

Have you ever been asked to be a reference for someone looking for employment? If so, you know how it goes. The hiring manager calls you and asks all sorts of questions. "So tell me about this person. What kind of work habits do they have? Are they reliable? Do they get along well with others?" And so forth. But if a prospective employer is really savvy, they won't just ask your opinion. They will want to hear some concrete examples of behavior to illustrate the traits they are looking for. They might inquire about the track record of a person over time, which will reveal much about the person's character. In today's scripture passage, John the Baptist is asking for Jesus' credentials. Is he the Messiah or not? Is he the One for whom they have waited or should they seek another? In answer, Jesus doesn't produce a resume. Instead, he simply says, "Tell John what you see. My actions will tell him what he needs to know." Someone once asked the question, "If being a Christian was a crime, would there be enough evidence to convict you?" I pray that for each of us, there would be.

Prayer

Lord Jesus, you are the One for whom the world has waited. You are the healer of all our ills, the wisdom for all our confusion, and the resurrected Lord over all that is dead and dying in our lives. Grant us faith to see you as Lord, and give us tongues to proclaim your deliverance to all. In your holy name, we pray. AMEN.

Thursday

2 Cor 8:1–7

> We want you to know, brothers and sisters, about the grace of
> God that has been granted to the churches of Macedonia; 2 for
> during a severe ordeal of affliction, their abundant joy and their
> extreme poverty have overflowed in a wealth of generosity on
> their part. 3 For, as I can testify, they voluntarily gave accord-
> ing to their means, and even beyond their means, 4 begging
> us earnestly for the privilege of sharing in this ministry to the
> saints— 5 and this, not merely as we expected; they gave them-
> selves first to the Lord and, by the will of God, to us, 6 so that
> we might urge Titus that, as he had already made a beginning,
> so he should also complete this generous undertaking among
> you. 7 Now as you excel in everything—in faith, in speech, in
> knowledge, in utmost eagerness, and in our love for you—so we
> want you to excel also in this generous undertaking.

In this passage, the Apostle Paul is writing to his beloved congregation in Corinth, exhorting them to take up a collection for the members of the fledgling congregation in Jerusalem who are enduring a famine. In this appeal, he lifts up another congregation in Macedonia which has been going through a "severe ordeal of affliction." We do not know the exact nature of this ordeal; perhaps they were being persecuted, perhaps inner strife was tearing them apart, or maybe some calamity had befallen them. In any case, while in the midst of this, they had given generously to provide aid to the starving saints in Jerusalem, even "begging . . . earnestly for the privilege of sharing in this ministry." This is an example to which we might aspire. How likely we are to say to ourselves, "*Someday*—when all my bills are paid, when my job situation is secure, when my retirement portfolio is in better shape—*then* I will give generously to those in need and to the ministry of Christ." St. Paul shows us another way—the Macedonian way. Even in times of difficulty, be generous. God wants us to excel not only in faith and knowledge and love, but in generosity.

Prayer

Generous God, how apt we are to let fear control our giving. How apt we are to trust only in our bank account and not in your provision. Fill us with faith so that we might excel in generosity, and know the joy of living by faith. You are our source of life. Help us to trust your good will for our lives. In Jesus' name, we pray. AMEN.

Friday

Amos 6:1, 4–7

Alas for those who are at ease in Zion,
　　and for those who feel secure on Mount Samaria,
the notables of the first of the nations,
　　to whom the house of Israel resorts!
4 Alas for those who lie on beds of ivory,
　　and lounge on their couches,
and eat lambs from the flock,
　　and calves from the stall;
5 who sing idle songs to the sound of the harp,
　　and like David improvise on instruments of music;
6 who drink wine from bowls,

and anoint themselves with the finest oils,
but are not grieved over the ruin of Joseph!
7 Therefore they shall now be the first to go into exile,
and the revelry of the loungers shall pass away.

The prophet Amos was not popular with the corrupt, wealthy leaders of Israel. He saw their indifference to the decline in the nation, and he called them on it. "Why are you not grieved over the ruin of Joseph?" he shouted. (By *Joseph*, he meant the nation of Israel.) "How can you lounge about on your couches and eat and drink like there's no tomorrow when people are dying in the streets?" Amos knew all too well that these leaders were in a position to help those in distress, and yet they did not raise a finger to help. We, who are in positions of wealth and access to power would do well to heed this warning. How are we responding to the needs of the poor? How are we showing our care for the most vulnerable? How are we making use of our resources to bring relief to those without an advocate in our community? These are terribly important questions, for us and for those who need our aid. Amos gives a warning: "[Those rich who neglect the poor]shall be the first to go into exile, and the revelry of the loungers shall pass away."

Prayer

God of Mercy and Compassion, we are sorry for the times we have not heeded your call to care for the vulnerable. We are sorry for the ways we have turned a blind eye and closed our ears to the desperate situations around us. Grant us clear vision and the will to do what we can to benefit those who suffer. Help us to discern our part in your ministry of compassion, trusting that we all have a part to play in this ministry. In the name of Jesus, we pray. AMEN.

The Fourth Week of Advent

Monday

Isa 12:2–6

[2] Surely God is my salvation;
I will trust, and will not be afraid,
for the LORD God is my strength and my might;
he has become my salvation.
[3] With joy you will draw water from the wells of salvation. [4] And
you will say in that day:
Give thanks to the LORD,
call on his name;
make known his deeds among the nations;
proclaim that his name is exalted.
[5] Sing praises to the LORD, for he has done gloriously;
let this be known in all the earth.
[6] Shout aloud and sing for joy, O royal Zion,
for great in your midst is the Holy One of Israel.

In 2009, I was fortunate to travel to the Central African Republic to witness the dedication of a hospital our congregation helped to build. As part of the building project, a new well was dug near the campus where anyone could come and gather water. People did come, from the nearby village and all around, mostly young girls with buckets on their heads. They came and filled those buckets to overflowing, put them on their heads, and walked back home, which in some cases was miles away. The well that served those folks was a gushing fountain, a pipe coming out of the hillside that flowed day and night. It brought clean, cold, clear water day after day, as well as supplying the hospital with all its needs. It was indeed a "well of salvation." The Word of God is like that fountain for us. It gushes forth wisdom and grace day and night, never ceasing to provide all that thirsty souls need. We come day after day, filling our buckets to overflowing. Sometimes the well is in worship as we hear the Word preached. Sometimes it is in our daily devotions as God speaks to us there. Sometimes it comes to us through song, or a prayer, or a conversation with another child of God. Indeed, it is the well of salvation.

Prayer

How we thank you, Gracious God, for giving us your Word which fills us day after day. We need your Word to strengthen, to rebuke, to heal, to convict, to correct, and to give us courage. Grant that each day we might receive what we need and be found faithful to you. In your holy name, we pray. AMEN.

Tuesday

Luke 1:57–66

> 57 Now the time came for Elizabeth to give birth, and she bore a son. 58 Her neighbors and relatives heard that the Lord had shown his great mercy to her, and they rejoiced with her. 59 On the eighth day they came to circumcise the child, and they were going to name him Zechariah after his father. 60 But his mother said, "No; he is to be called John." 61 They said to her, "None of your relatives has this name." 62 Then they began motioning to his father to find out what name he wanted to give him. 63 He asked for a writing tablet and wrote, "His name is John." And all of them were amazed. 64 Immediately his mouth was opened and his tongue freed, and he began to speak, praising God. 65 Fear came over all their neighbors, and all these things were talked about throughout the entire hill country of Judea. 66 All who heard them pondered them and said, "What then will this child become?" For, indeed, the hand of the Lord was with him.

We don't often think of it, but Luke spends a lot of time in his gospel telling us about John the Baptizer. In fact, his birth and the people and divine encounters associated with, it take up the entire first chapter of Luke—80 verses!

Why all this attention to John? Jesus tells us: "Among those born of women no one is greater than John" (Luke 7:28). John prepared the way for Christ. He pointed to Jesus. But before we think that John was extraordinary in ways that are beyond us, listen to what Jesus goes on to say: "Among those born of women no one is greater than John; *yet the least in the kingdom of God is greater than he.*" Apparently, God has designed *each of us* to point to Christ, each in our own way. Can you speak for Christ? Then speak. Can you serve others in the name of Christ? Then serve. Can you pray that others might find the peace and joy of Emmanuel—God with us—in this darkest time of the year? Then pray. Point to Christ. That's what Christians do.

Prayer

God of All, we give you thanks for John the Baptizer and others down through the ages who have preached the good news. We give thanks also for those who have served silently through humble acts of generosity and service. Help us to find our place as we seek each day to point to Christ, the Light of the World, in whose name we pray. AMEN.

Wednesday

Acts 28:23–27

23 After [the Jewish leaders in Rome]had set a day to meet with
[Paul], they came to him at his lodgings in great numbers. From
morning until evening he explained the matter to them, testify-
ing to the kingdom of God and trying to convince them about
Jesus both from the law of Moses and from the prophets. 24 Some
were convinced by what he had said, while others refused to
believe. 25 So they disagreed with each other; and as they were
leaving, Paul made one further statement: "The Holy Spirit was
right in saying to your ancestors through the prophet Isaiah,

26 'Go to this people and say,
You will indeed listen, but never understand,
and you will indeed look, but never perceive.
27 For this people's heart has grown dull,
and their ears are hard of hearing,
and they have shut their eyes;
so that they might not look with their eyes,

and listen with their ears,
and understand with their heart and turn—
and I would heal them.'

You can hear Paul's frustration and disappointment in his words here to the Jewish leaders in Rome. They are his people. They are his blood. He spent his entire youth as a faithful member of the synagogue in Jerusalem. He longs for those he loves to love Jesus as he does. Some do. Some don't. His life ends without him knowing whether the Way of Jesus would survive and flourish or die out. Perhaps you, too, have people you love who do not seem the least bit interested in Jesus. It is a hard thing, when for us, the Person of Christ is the Living Water from which we drink each day. We can do two things: We can continue to love these people in word and deed, and we can pray for them that Christ reveals himself to them. They are God's children. God will not abandon them. We can trust in that promise.

Prayer

We long for your Spirit to inspire those we love, O God. We long for them to drink from the Living Water which is Christ. Give to all our loved ones your protection and healing. And in your time, grant them also faith and peace. In the name of Christ, we pray. AMEN.

Thursday

Heb 10:11–18

[11] And every priest stands day after day at his service, offering
again and again the same sacrifices that can never take away
sins. [12] But when Christ had offered for all time a single sacrifice
for sins, "he sat down at the right hand of God," [13] and since then
has been waiting "until his enemies would be made a footstool
for his feet." [14] For by a single offering he has perfected for all
time those who are sanctified. [15] And the Holy Spirit also testi-
fies to us, for after saying,

[16] "This is the covenant that I will make with them
after those days, says the Lord:
I will put my laws in their hearts,
and I will write them on their minds," [17] he also adds,

> "I will remember their sins and their lawless deeds no more."
> [18] Where there is forgiveness of these, there is no longer any offering for sin.

Here's a strangely comforting image: God with amnesia. God says, "I will remember their sins and their lawless deeds no more." I don't know about you, but forgetting things is something that happens to me all the time. I forget a name. I forget that I promised I was going to do something. I forget where I put my keys. Sometimes I even forget where I put the list of things that I wrote down so that I wouldn't forget! For us, forgetting is a pain. For God, however, forgetting must be a joy. When we say to God, "I hope you aren't going to be too hard on me for all those sins I keep committing," God says, "What sins? I don't remember any sins." And when we say, "I am so sorry that I keep coming to you confessing the same sins over and over," again God says, "What sins?" God forgets. God remembers them no more. The Psalmist says that God throws our sins as far as the east is from the west. That's pretty far. And St. John says that whenever we confess our sins, God is faithful and just and forgives *all* our sins [even the ones we forgot to confess]. How great it is to have such a forgetful God!

Prayer

We praise you, O God, for your amazing grace. Even though we remember our sins, you do not. Even though we commit the same sins again and again, they are new to you and you forgive them anew over and over. How gracious you are! Grant us faith and joy in believing. In your Son, Jesus' name, we pray. AMEN.

Friday

Ps 112:1–9

1 Praise the LORD!
    Happy are those who fear the LORD,
    who greatly delight in his commandments.
2 Their descendants will be mighty in the land;
    the generation of the upright will be blessed.
3 Wealth and riches are in their houses,

and their righteousness endures forever.
4 They rise in the darkness as a light for the upright;
they are gracious, merciful, and righteous.
5 It is well with those who deal generously and lend,
who conduct their affairs with justice.
6 For the righteous will never be moved;
they will be remembered forever.
7 They are not afraid of evil tidings;
their hearts are firm, secure in the LORD.
8 Their hearts are steady, they will not be afraid;
in the end they will look in triumph on their foes.
9 They have distributed freely, they have given to the poor;
their righteousness endures forever;
their horn is exalted in honor.

When I was growing up, Christmas Eve was a special family time. We all got cleaned up and dressed in nice clothes for Christmas dinner. After dinner, we heard the Christmas story and sang some carols, and then *finally*, we got to open our presents around the Christmas tree. What fun it was! I still remember one Christmas when my dad opened his present from me—a hammer. He needed a hammer, and when he opened it up, it was clear that it was just what he wanted. How happy that made me. I almost never bought just the right gift for my dad, but that time I did. Getting special gifts is certainly a joy, but getting just the right gift for another is even more memorable. Perhaps that's why the psalmist reminds us that those who fear the Lord are also those who "have distributed freely, they have given to the poor, their righteousness endures forever; their horn is exalted in honor." Giving generously brings us joy; there is no doubt about that. And, as St. Paul says, "Not only does [our generosity]supply the needs of the saints, but overflows in many thanksgivings to God". Happy are they who fear the Lord, who greatly delight in God's commands, who give generously to those in need.

Prayer

Grant us generous hearts, O God. We have been given so much. Our lives are overflowing with your abundance. Accept our grateful praises. AMEN.

The First Week of Christmas

Monday

Ps 147:12–20

12 Praise the LORD, O Jerusalem!
Praise your God, O Zion!
13 For he strengthens the bars of your gates;
he blesses your children within you.
14 He grants peace within your borders;
he fills you with the finest of wheat.
15 He sends out his command to the earth;
his word runs swiftly.
16 He gives snow like wool;
he scatters frost like ashes.
17 He hurls down hail like crumbs—
who can stand before his cold?
18 He sends out his word, and melts them;
he makes his wind blow, and the waters flow.
19 He declares his word to Jacob,
his statutes and ordinances to Israel.
20 He has not dealt thus with any other nation;
they do not know his ordinances.
Praise the LORD!

In my house growing up, it was always expected that we write thank-you notes. When we opened a gift at Christmas, my mother would dutifully write down what we had received and who it was from. Then, sometime shortly after Christmas, we were expected to write a thank you to Grandma and Grandpa or anyone else not in our immediate family who had given us a gift. Ps 147 is kind of like a thank you note to God. If you read the entire psalm, you will see that there are many more gifts listed beyond the ones in these eight verses. Here's an exercise to do this week, by yourself or with another person: sit down and make a list of all the gifts you have gotten from God in recent days. Perhaps you can even consider writing a thank you note to God. I'll bet God likes getting thank you notes as much as you do.

Prayer

We thank you, Generous God, for gifting us with life and breath and everything we need from day to day. We thank you for the relationships we enjoy, the abilities we've been given, and the callings that are ours. Grant that we might ever be found grateful. In Christ's name, we pray. AMEN.

Tuesday

Acts 6:1–7

> Now during those days, when the disciples were increasing in
> number, the Hellenists complained against the Hebrews because
> their widows were being neglected in the daily distribution of
> food. 2 And the twelve called together the whole community of
> the disciples and said, "It is not right that we should neglect the
> word of God in order to wait on tables. 3 Therefore, friends, se-
> lect from among yourselves seven men of good standing, full
> of the Spirit and of wisdom, whom we may appoint to this
> task, 4 while we, for our part, will devote ourselves to prayer and
> to serving the word." 5 What they said pleased the whole com-
> munity, and they chose Stephen, a man full of faith and the Holy
> Spirit, together with Philip, Prochorus, Nicanor, Timon, Parme-
> nas, and Nicolaus, a proselyte of Antioch. 6 They had these men
> stand before the apostles, who prayed and laid their hands on
> them.7 The word of God continued to spread; the number of the
> disciples increased greatly in Jerusalem, and a great many of the
> priests became obedient to the faith.

In the sixth chapter of Acts, we have one of the first reports of dissension in the early Christian community in Jerusalem. Sure enough, as often seems to be the case, the issue is beginning to cause a split in the community. Notice, however, how the leaders of the community handle the situation: they realize that, with the growing community, they do not have time to do the daily distribution of food as perhaps they had done with a smaller group of people. They need to delegate this responsibility to others. But not to just anybody. They invite *the people* to select folks "of good standing, full of the Spirit and of wisdom" who will fulfill this task. Notice how the disciples do *not* select the persons themselves, but instead trust the people to do this based on some simple criteria: those in good standing in the community who are wise and full of God's Spirit. This, in some ways, is how the Church continues to operate today. Pastors teach and preach and counsel and pray, while many others serve in ways needed for the well-being of the community. Wise, Spirit-filled people, well-thought of in the community, are essential to the work of the church. No advanced degrees are required, only a heart for God and for one another.

Prayer

We praise you, O God, for wise, compassionate, Spirit-filled people who do the work of ministry. We praise you that you use *all* of us, in whatever ways you have gifted us, to bring the gospel to the world. Grant us faith to believe that you use each one of us, each day, to do the work of ministry. In your name, we pray. AMEN.

Wednesday

Prov 8:32–36

32 "And now, my children, listen to me:
happy are those who keep my ways.
33 Hear instruction and be wise,
and do not neglect it.
34 Happy is the one who listens to me,
watching daily at my gates,
waiting beside my doors.
35 For whoever finds me finds life

and obtains favor from the Lord;
[36] but those who miss me injure themselves;
all who hate me love death."

The person speaking in this section of Proverbs is Wisdom, often portrayed as a wise woman. She is speaking like a mother to her children. Notice how many times she urges them to listen. She insists that listening closely to her will bring blessing. Indeed, she says that whomever finds wisdom finds life, and those who fail to find wisdom injure themselves. Finally, she gives a warning: "All who hate wisdom, love death." This is a stern reminder that our choices have consequences. Almost nobody would say that they love death, and yet, Wisdom tells us, "If you hate me, you are necessarily embracing your own destruction." Today, wisdom is more important than ever. With the advent of the internet, information and *mis*information, and even purposeful *dis*information is readily available on any subject. Wisdom, on the other hand, is even harder to come by since we have to sift through so much nonsense. We need to take heed to Wisdom's call and be good listeners, asking God to give us the discernment we need.

Prayer

All-Wise God, grant us wisdom. Keep us from wrong paths and foolish ways. Give us wise counselors, helpful leaders, and people who will steer us in the way of life. Fill us with your Holy Spirit, the Counselor, that in all our words and deeds, we might follow in the ways of wisdom and grace. In your holy name, we pray. AMEN.

Thursday

1 Cor 3:10–15

[10] According to the grace of God given to me, like a skilled mas-
ter builder I laid a foundation, and someone else is building on
it. Each builder must choose with care how to build on it. [11] For
no one can lay any foundation other than the one that has been
laid; that foundation is Jesus Christ. [12] Now if anyone builds on
the foundation with gold, silver, precious stones, wood, hay,
straw— [13] the work of each builder will become visible, for the
Day will disclose it, because it will be revealed with fire, and

> the fire will test what sort of work each has done. [14] If what has been built on the foundation survives, the builder will receive a reward. [15] If the work is burned up, the builder will suffer loss; the builder will be saved, but only as through fire.

The metaphor St. Paul is using here is one of building. He is talking specifically about the building up of the Church, the people of God. Notice that he says the "foundation [of the Church]is Jesus Christ." Paul was trying to deal with a division in the congregation at Corinth that had arisen because of people's preference for a certain leader. Some church members said they belonged to Paul, and others said they belonged to another preacher named Apollos. Paul reminds them that they *all* belong to Christ, and the foundation of the Church is *not* a preacher, but Jesus. This is so important for us to remember. Jesus is our foundation, our base, and our center. Preachers come and go, but Jesus is forever. We can be free to like one preacher's style better than another, or prefer one's personality over that of another, but when it really comes down to it, Jesus Christ is the *only one* who deserves our praise, our adoration, and our love.

Prayer

Thank you, Loving God, for faithful pastors, teachers, deacons, and other leaders of faith. Thank you for their faithful work and witness. Grant them your blessing always. As we go forward together, help us keep our eyes on Jesus, our rock and our salvation. In your holy name, we pray. AMEN.

Friday

Mark 13:32–37

> [32] "But about that day or hour no one knows, neither the an-
> gels in heaven, nor the Son, but only the Father. [33] Beware, keep
> alert for you do not know when the time will come. [34] It is like
> a man going on a journey, when he leaves home and puts his
> slaves in charge, each with his work, and commands the door-
> keeper to be on the watch. [35] Therefore, keep awake—for you
> do not know when the master of the house will come, in the
> evening, or at midnight, or at cockcrow, or at dawn, [36] or else he
> may find you asleep when he comes suddenly. [37] And what I say
> to you I say to all: Keep awake."

If you were around at the turn of the last century, you might remember the Y2K moment. That was what we called the stroke of midnight when the year 2000 commenced. Leading up to that date, there was massive worry that the computer systems in our electric grid, our utilities, our government, our banking system, and every other large interlocked system would crash at the stroke of midnight. The thinking was that when the calendar turned over, the computers would think it was the year 1900, because the year would simply read "00" in the system. Whether we avoided a catastrophic shutdown because of a massive effort to fix the problem or because it never merited panic in the first place, I don't know. I do know that we stayed up late that night to see what would happen. I remember watching on TV as a man tried to use an ATM at midnight, and rejoicing with him that it still worked! According to Jesus' words near the end of the gospel of Mark, there is a lot more at stake in the coming of the Lord than making sure an ATM works. He says, "Stay awake—for you do not know when the master of the house will come." If you know this metaphor, you know that, as servants of the Master, we need simply to be focused on the work the Master expects of us: caring for one another and the creation, speaking the truth in love, and living as Christ commanded. To do this is to remain awake.

Prayer

Be near us, Lord Jesus, we ask you to stay close by us forever, and love us we pray. Bless all your dear children in your tender care, and fit us for heaven, to live with you there. AMEN.

The Second Week of Christmas

Monday

Job 42:10–12a, 17

> [10] And the LORD restored the fortunes of Job when he had prayed
> for his friends; and the LORD gave Job twice as much as he had
> before. [11] Then there came to him all his brothers and sisters and
> all who had known him before, and they ate bread with him in
> his house; they showed him sympathy and comforted him for all
> the evil that the LORD had brought upon him; and each of them
> gave him a piece of money and a gold ring. [12] The LORD blessed
> the latter days of Job more than his beginning.
>
> [17] And Job died, old and full of days.

While the story of Job's suffering is well-known, the end of his story is often forgotten. Job's story ends in a return to prosperity; indeed "the Lord gave Job twice as much as he had before." Not only that, but the family and friends who had been trying to pin the blame for his troubles on Job himself, now, we learn, show him sympathy and comfort, and bring him gifts. It is only after Job has finally silenced all his critics and declared once and for all that "the Lord gave, and the Lord has taken away; blessed be the name of the Lord" (1:21) that his advisors at long last understand his wisdom. What Job learned, and what we can learn from the book of Job, is that we live by virtue of the abundant mercy of God. Neither abundance nor lack come to us as a direct result of our actions. Yes, there are wise and foolish ways to do things, as well as virtuous and wicked ways to live our lives, and undoubtedly we are called to wisdom and virtue. But neither wisdom nor virtue will guarantee us a pain-free life. We will simply have to declare with Job that whether God gives or God takes away, our trust is in God, the Maker of all things, our Strength, and our Redeemer.

Prayer

Help us to count our days, O Lord. Help us to trust you in good times and in bad. Help us to live in gratitude for all you have given us, and in faith, that, come what may, you are a God of Love and Mercy and Compassion. We are your people. Accept our grateful praises. AMEN.

Tuesday

Isa 6:1–5

> In the year that King Uzziah died, I saw the Lord sitting on a
> throne, high and lofty; and the hem of his robe filled the tem-
> ple. 2 Seraphs were in attendance above him; each had six wings:
> with two they covered their faces, and with two they covered
> their feet, and with two they flew. 3 And one called to another
> and said:
>
> "Holy, holy, holy is the LORD of hosts;
> the whole earth is full of his glory."
>
> 4 The pivots on the thresholds shook at the voices of those who
> called, and the house filled with smoke. 5 And I said: "Woe is
> me! I am lost, for I am a man of unclean lips, and I live among
> a people of unclean lips; yet my eyes have seen the King,
> the LORD of hosts!"

It has always been curious to me why the prophet Isaiah bothered to date his vision of God in the temple. Why did he think it important to write that his vision came "in the year that King Uzziah died"? Was it perhaps because that date was etched in the people's minds, King Uzziah having reigned for 52 years? Or was it because King Uzziah's death from leprosy (see 2 Chr 26) was considered God's judgment against him for his pride? Whatever the reason, Isaiah was clear in his vision: to come into the presence of a holy God is a fearsome thing! Sometimes people ask, "Why do we Lutherans so often begin our worship with the Order of Confession and Forgiveness?" Here, Isaiah gives us the answer: it is because we who are *not* holy are entering into worship with a God who *is* holy. Knowing this, it is only right that we should begin worship by asking for God to cleanse us from our sins so that we might freely and joyfully worship God.

Prayer

We confess our unholiness, Holy God. We confess that our lives often fall short of all that we know and want as your people. As St. Paul says, "Even what we do not want, that we do." How gracious you are to accept our confession again and again. Keep us near, we pray. In Jesus' name. AMEN.

Wednesday

John 1:9–14

> 9 The true light, which enlightens everyone, was coming into
> the world.[b]
>
> 10 He was in the world, and the world came into being through
> him; yet the world did not know him. 11 He came to what was
> his own, and his own people did not accept him. 12 But to all
> who received him, who believed in his name, he gave power to
> become children of God, 13 who were born, not of blood or of
> the will of the flesh or of the will of man, but of God.
>
> 14 And the Word became flesh and lived among us, and we have
> seen his glory, the glory as of a father's only son, full of grace
> and truth.

During this Christmas season, of which this is the last day, we celebrate many things. We celebrate the story of Christ's birth in the manger, the song of the angels, the visitation of the shepherds, and the faith of Mary. We celebrate one another as well, as we both give and receive gifts, gather for feasts and parties, and send cards and greetings to all our loved ones. For me, the most profound gift in all of this is stated here in John's gospel: "The Word became flesh and lived among us." This is what makes the Christian story so hopeful. The Creative Word, the Person who was with God and who *was* God in the beginning, and who has no beginning or end, *that One*, has become flesh and blood. And at the same time, that Word continues to be divine in all of its majesty. What a mystery this is, and yet so hopeful; God has decided to be one with us, so surely we have no reason to despair. There is hope for this world, and for all our lives, because the Word dwells with us. Thanks be to God!

Prayer

O Great Mystery, how can we thank you for the sacrifice you have made for our salvation? You have become one of us. You have taken on pain and poverty, cold and heat, life and death, and you know our every temptation. Because you are with us, we do not despair. We live, knowing that you live too, beside, above, and within us. Grant us your peace, we pray. In the Name of Christ. AMEN.

Thursday

Matt 2:1–8

> In the time of King Herod, after Jesus was born in Bethlehem
> of Judea, wise men from the East came to Jerusalem, 2 asking,
> "Where is the child who has been born king of the Jews? For we
> observed his star at its rising,and have come to pay him hom-
> age." 3 When King Herod heard this, he was frightened, and all
> Jerusalem with him; 4 and calling together all the chief priests
> and scribes of the people, he inquired of them where the Mes-
> siah was to be born. 5 They told him, "In Bethlehem of Judea; for
> so it has been written by the prophet:
>
> 6 'And you, Bethlehem, in the land of Judah,
> are by no means least among the rulers of Judah;
> for from you shall come a ruler
> who is to shepherd my people Israel.'"
>
> 7 Then Herod secretly called for the wise men and learned from
> them the exact time when the star had appeared. 8 Then he sent
> them to Bethlehem, saying, "Go and search diligently for the
> child; and when you have found him, bring me word so that I
> may also go and pay him homage."

This is the Day of Epiphany, the beginning of the liturgical season when we celebrate the appearances of God amongst us. I often think of it as the season when we celebrate the "aha" moments God gives us. Of course, it goes without saying that "aha" moments can be either wonderful or terrifying. When King Herod had his "aha" moment it was terrifying. He suddenly realized that his power was shaky, to say the least. The whole city of Jerusalem also had an "aha" moment with the wise men's inquiry, for they all knew that when King Herod wasn't happy, they were at risk. "Aha" moments, however, can also be wonderful. Perhaps we suddenly realize that we are not alone in our pain—that someone cares or that God cares. Perhaps we have an emerging sense that we do not need to prove ourselves to anyone anymore—that we are just fine as God made us. Perhaps a person we respect and admire tells us we are gifted and we finally believe it. These are "aha" moments worth celebrating. They are epiphanies that can change the trajectory of our lives.

Prayer

Dear Jesus, give us wonderful "aha" moments in this New Year, we pray. Help us to realize how much you love us, how deeply we are blessed in Christ, and how profound is the calling we have as your beloved. Help us to also be a source of inspiration to others. In your blessed name we pray. AMEN.

Friday

Eph 5:15–20

> [15] Be careful then how you live, not as unwise people but as
> wise, [16] making the most of the time, because the days are
> evil. [17] So do not be foolish, but understand what the will of the
> Lord is. [18] Do not get drunk with wine, for that is debauchery;
> but be filled with the Spirit, [19] as you sing psalms and hymns and
> spiritual songs among yourselves, singing and making melody to
> the Lord in your hearts, [20] giving thanks to God the Father at all
> times and for everything in the name of our Lord Jesus Christ.

I have always liked the J.B. Phillips' translation of the first 2 verses of this passage: "Live life, then, with a due sense of responsibility, not as [those] who do not know the meaning of life but as *those who do*." He suggests what I think the original writer means: that our whole life needs to be governed by our relationship with God. We are those who know the meaning of life is " to serve and enjoy God forever," as the reformer John Calvin put it. And so our lives reflect that. No decision, no task, no relationship is outside of this influence. Our lives are caught up in the abundance of being called children of God, and our calling is to be a light and a blessing to others, and so we live with this "due sense of responsibility," joyfully serving others. Making the most of the time we have does not mean making the most money, or achieving the most awards or accolades, or attaining the most degrees. Instead, it means living out our calling as co-heirs with Christ of all the riches of God's grace. What could be better than that?

Prayer

We wish to be found faithful, Gracious God. We wish to live our lives in joyful service. Grant us your Holy Spirit, that we might be inspired every day to do just that. We ask this in the name of your Son, Jesus Christ, our Lord. AMEN.

The First Week After Epiphany

Monday

Luke 1:67–68, 76–80

[67] Then his father Zechariah was filled with the Holy Spirit and
spoke this prophecy: [68] "Blessed be the Lord God of Israel,

for he has looked favorably on his people and redeemed them.

[76] And you, child, will be called the prophet of the Most High;

for you will go before the Lord to prepare his ways,

[77] to give knowledge of salvation to his people

by the forgiveness of their sins.

[78] By the tender mercy of our God,

the dawn from on high will break upon us,

[79] to give light to those who sit in darkness and in the shadow of death,

to guide our feet into the way of peace."

[80] The child grew and became strong in spirit, and he was in the
wilderness until the day he appeared publicly to Israel.

The passage immediately preceding the above verses describes the scene at the circumcision of the infant John the Baptizer, who was, at this point, only 8 days old. Can't you just see Zechariah holding up his infant son and announcing to all those assembled that this son of his will be a prophet of God? Last year, my wife and I were reminded of how precious the birth of a little one is when our first grandchild was born. We were there on the day of his baptism, and as the water was poured over him, all of our hopes and dreams for this little guy were also pouring out. We pray that he might be wise and strong, compassionate and loving, and filled with faith and love. We hold him up in prayer every day, thanking God for him, and asking for God's blessing.

Prayer

Heavenly Father, be with our children, we pray. Grant them wisdom and understanding, strength of mind, body, and spirit, and a faith that is strong. Guide them into the ways of peace. Give them light when they are lost in darkness. Give them hope when they near despair. In all times and places, grant them your grace. In the Name of Jesus, your Son, our Lord. AMEN.

Tuesday

Ps 29:3–9

3 The voice of the LORD is over the waters;
the God of glory thunders,
the LORD, over mighty waters.
4 The voice of the LORD is powerful;
the voice of the LORD is full of majesty.
5 The voice of the LORD breaks the cedars;
the LORD breaks the cedars of Lebanon.
6 He makes Lebanon skip like a calf,
and Sirion like a young wild ox.
7 The voice of the LORD flashes forth flames of fire.
8 The voice of the LORD shakes the wilderness;
the LORD shakes the wilderness of Kadesh.
9 The voice of the LORD causes the oaks to whirl,
and strips the forest bare;
and in his temple all say, "Glory!"

In this psalm, the psalmist is contemplating God's power, apparently while watching a thunderstorm. The thunder is described as God's voice sounding forth, while God's actions are compared to the lightning ("flashes forth flames of fire"), and the wind ("causes the oaks to whirl and strips the forest bare"). When the psalmist sees all this, all he can say is, "Glory!" This psalm reminds us of how awesome God is. God is unimaginably greater than us. God's power is immeasurably greater than ours. God is simply beyond us. We do well to remember this. Sometimes we gravitate towards more intimate images of God (Father, Good Shepherd, Healer of our Every Ill) that assure us of God's love for us and knowledge of us. This is right to do, but it is also good to balance it with a healthy appreciation for God's majesty. We, too, need to simply say, "Glory!"

Prayer

You are the God of Creation and Lord of All. You are the God of Heavenly Armies, the One who has always been and always will be. You are worthy of all praise. We do praise you, Awesome God. Receive our grateful praises. AMEN.

Wednesday

Eccl 1:2–9

2 Vanity of vanities, says the Teacher,
vanity of vanities! All is vanity.
3 What do people gain from all the toil
at which they toil under the sun?
4 A generation goes, and a generation comes,
but the earth remains forever.
5 The sun rises and the sun goes down,
and hurries to the place where it rises.
6 The wind blows to the south,
and goes around to the north;
round and round goes the wind,
and on its circuits the wind returns.
7 All streams run to the sea,
but the sea is not full;
to the place where the streams flow,
there they continue to flow.
8 All things are wearisome;
more than one can express;

the eye is not satisfied with seeing,
    or the ear filled with hearing.
9 What has been is what will be,
    and what has been done is what will be done;
    there is nothing new under the sun.

These opening words from the book of Ecclesiastes are seemingly some of the most depressing verses in the Bible. They seem to indicate that life is basically one thing after another until you die. But if we look further into this book, we realize that the writer's aim is to have us quit placing our hopes for an abundant life in the accumulation of wealth, power, or prestige. *This*, the writer explains, is what leads to despair. True abundance is found in life with God, life filled with service, worship, works of compassion, and the pursuit of true wisdom. Such a life as this is not just one day after another but filled with possibility and hope. During this pandemic time, when it does seem like every day is simply a battle with the virus and its effects, we do well to remember that God is still the source of the abundant life. Start the day in prayer, read a bit of God's word, listen to God's voice, and then get up and do the things that bring blessing to others and fill you with joy.

Prayer

Thank you, Gracious God, for granting us the way to abundant life. Thank you for giving us Jesus, whose words and deeds show us the way. Guide us each day into such a life. In your holy name, we pray. AMEN.

Thursday

1 Cor 1:18–25

18 For the message about the cross is foolishness to those who
are perishing, but to us who are being saved it is the power of
God. 19 For it is written, "I will destroy the wisdom of the wise,
and the discernment of the discerning I will thwart." 20 Where
is the one who is wise? Where is the scribe? Where is the de-
bater of this age? Has not God made foolish the wisdom of the
world? 21 For since, in the wisdom of God, the world did not
know God through wisdom, God decided, through the foolish-
ness of our proclamation, to save those who believe. 22 For Jews

> demand signs and Greeks desire wisdom, [23] but we proclaim Christ crucified, a stumbling block to Jews and foolishness to Gentiles, [24] but to those who are the called, both Jews and Greeks, Christ the power of God and the wisdom of God. [25] For God's foolishness is wiser than human wisdom, and God's weakness is stronger than human strength.

I have always been struck by the opening verse in this passage as St. Paul describes two kinds of people: "those who are perishing" and "us who are being saved." Though these two groups seem to be opposites, it strikes me that they are similar in their lack of agency. Those "being saved" are at the mercy of someone greater than them—a Savior. We might think of those who are "perishing" as being swept along by flood waters or trapped in a burning building. They also are not in control. I have also always wondered if these roles are fixed, or if they can change with time. Can person who is perishing yet be saved and the person being saved yet be lost? It is unclear. I always pray that, finally, God's almighty love and compassion will prevail and *all* will be saved. Let us pray that it is so.

Prayer

Save us, dear Lord, from being swept away from you. Save us from foolishness and wickedness that might lead us to destruction. Grant that always we might be found as those who are safe in your arms, fully embraced by our Savior, in whose name we pray. AMEN.

Friday

Eccl 3:1–8

> For everything there is a season, and a time for every matter under heaven:
>
> [2] a time to be born, and a time to die;
>
> a time to plant, and a time to pluck up what is planted;
>
> [3] a time to kill, and a time to heal;
>
> a time to break down, and a time to build up;
>
> [4] a time to weep, and a time to laugh;
>
> a time to mourn, and a time to dance;

5 a time to throw away stones, and a time to gather stones together;
a time to embrace, and a time to refrain from embracing;
6 a time to seek, and a time to lose;
a time to keep, and a time to throw away;
7 a time to tear, and a time to sew;
a time to keep silence, and a time to speak;
8 a time to love, and a time to hate;
a time for war, and a time for peace.

This well-known passage, as you might remember, is part of a famous song. Pete Seeger wrote it in the 1950s and it was made popular by the Byrds in the 1960s. It is another example of the style of the writer of Ecclesiastes, whose philosophical bent is obvious. This passage reminds us that life is normally filled with ups and downs, happy days and sad days, wins and losses. In our ultra-competitive world, we are often told that the only life worth living is the one where we are always winning, always getting stronger, always laughing, always enjoying life. In other words, the only life worth living is one that no one has or can possibly have. This makes the pursuit of such a life a fool's errand, or even worse, a cause for despair. How much better to remember what the Teacher says here: that life has seasons. Seasons of planting and seasons of harvesting, seasons of growing and seasons of decline, seasons of quiet and seasons of boisterous celebration. Each season has its gifts. Perhaps wisdom is seeking the gift of each of life's seasons.

Prayer

Grant us wisdom, O God. Help us to see the gifts in all the seasons of life. Give us faith to believe that in every season, you walk with us. In Christ's name. AMEN.

The Second Week After Epiphany

Monday

Ps 106:43–48

43 Many times he delivered them,
but they were rebellious in their purposes,
and were brought low through their iniquity.
44 Nevertheless he regarded their distress
when he heard their cry.
45 For their sake he remembered his covenant,
and showed compassion according to the abundance of his steadfast love.
46 He caused them to be pitied
by all who held them captive.
47 Save us, O LORD our God,
and gather us from among the nations,
that we may give thanks to your holy name
and glory in your praise.
48 Blessed be the LORD, the God of Israel,
from everlasting to everlasting.
And let all the people say, "Amen."
Praise the LORD!

Ps 106 is an historical psalm; it recounts many of the most significant points in Israel's history, highlighting the cycle of rebellion, repentance, and restoration that characterized Israel's life. If you haven't read the whole psalm, it is worth doing. This psalm reminds me of our regular pattern in worship, where we come together every week and begin with Confession and Forgiveness. Like the Israelites, we are also regularly part of this cycle of rebellion, repentance, and restoration: We sin, we feel remorse and confess it, and God forgives and restores every time. We might ask, "Isn't this a futile exercise given that we seem to return again and again to the same pattern?" The answer is no. Forgiveness does one very important thing: it cleanses us. That's right, whenever we confess our sin, we are cleansed of it; God forgives and forgets, and we are restored. If we do not seek forgiveness, the sin remains, and it eats away at us spiritually. Eventually, this sin that remains in us can give us untold burdens: anger, guilt, depression, despair. So come to the waters of your baptism every day, confess, and be cleansed.

Prayer

Thank you, Forgiving God, for your unending mercy. Each time we come to you in confession, you cleanse us. You never turn us away. Grant us confidence in your never-failing mercy and love, and cleanse us every day that we might walk as free and joyful people of God. We ask this in the name Christ, our Savior. AMEN.

Tuesday

Num 27:1–8

> Then the daughters of Zelophehad came forward. Zelophehad was son of Hepher son of Gilead son of Machir son of Manasseh son of Joseph, a member of the Manassite clans. The names of his daughters were: Mahlah, Noah, Hoglah, Milcah,
> and Tirzah. [2] They stood before Moses, Eleazar the priest, the leaders, and all the congregation, at the entrance of the tent of
> meeting, and they said, [3] "Our father died in the wilderness; he was not among the company of those who gathered themselves together against the LORD in the company of Korah, but died for
> his own sin; and he had no sons. [4] Why should the name of our father be taken away from his clan because he had no son? Give to us a possession among our father's brothers."
>
> [5] Moses brought their case before the LORD. [6] And the LORD spoke
> to Moses, saying: [7] The daughters of Zelophehad are right in what they are saying; you shall indeed let them possess an inheritance among their father's brothers and pass the inheritance

of their father on to them. [8] You shall also say to the Israelites, "If a man dies, and has no son, then you shall pass his inheritance on to his daughter."

Here is an old church joke: The Seven Last Words of the Church are, "We have never done it that way." Of course, this joke is funny because it pokes fun at our tendency to resist change. When we are comfortable with a certain way of doing things, we often prefer to just keep doing things that way, even if it no longer makes any sense. In today's reading, we see a different approach. The father of the family has died without any sons to pass his legacy onto. According to Hebrew law, daughters could not be the recipients of an inheritance. These five daughters are not satisfied with this arrangement, so they come before the leaders of Israel and plead their case. They want to be the recipients of their father's inheritance. What do the leaders do? They apparently assign Moses the task of asking the Lord for wisdom, and the Lord's answer is clear: "You shall indeed give them the inheritance of their father." What do you know? God's people *can* change! Perhaps God is calling you to a change. As Jesus said, "Let those who have ears, listen."

Prayer

God of All Creation, we know you have set certain patterns in nature and we are blessed and sustained by them. We also know that patterns *we* set up may not always be life-giving. Help us to discern between those patterns that are life-giving and those that are not. We ask this in Jesus' name. AMEN.

Wednesday

Luke 11:33–36

[33] "No one after lighting a lamp puts it in a cellar, but on the
lampstand so that those who enter may see the light. [34] Your
eye is the lamp of your body. If your eye is healthy, your whole
body is full of light; but if it is not healthy, your body is full of
darkness. [35] Therefore consider whether the light in you is not
darkness. [36] If then your whole body is full of light, with no part
of it in darkness, it will be as full of light as when a lamp gives
you light with its rays.

This passage seems to be a collection of different sayings of Jesus on the subject of light. The first one is familiar from the Sermon on the Mount where Jesus encourages listeners to "let your light shine so that others may see your good works and glorify your Heavenly Father." When we let our light shine, we are often a blessing to others, bringing a word of Christ to those we encounter. The second saying speaks of the eye as the entrance through which outside influences enter our innermost parts. It is important, Jesus says, to keep your eye healthy so that those things that God wishes to show you may be seen. Keeping our spiritual eyes healthy is an ongoing task as we spend time in prayer, reflection on God's word, worship, healthy conversation with others, and acts of love. Examples of having unhealthy eyes (spiritual blindness) are when sin, guilt, anger, or shame keep us from seeing what God would have us do. Jesus says that it is even possible that what we *think* is light (understanding and wisdom) is actually darkness (deceptions and lies). Jesus wants you to be "as full of light [i.e., truth]as when a lamp gives you light with its rays."

Prayer

Keep us from living in darkness, Gracious God. Take away from us those blinders that steal our joy and cause us to stumble about in fear and guilt. Grant us clear vision to see the paths to which you call us and avoid those that lead to destruction. In all our days, be our guide, that we may glorify you. AMEN.

Thursday

Acts 8:14–24

> [14] Now when the apostles at Jerusalem heard that Samaria
> had accepted the word of God, they sent Peter and John to
> them. [15] The two went down and prayed for them that they
> might receive the Holy Spirit [16] (for as yet the Spirit had not
> come upon any of them; they had only been baptized in the
> name of the Lord Jesus). [17] Then Peter and John laid their hands
> on them, and they received the Holy Spirit. [18] Now when Si-
> mon saw that the Spirit was given through the laying on of the
> apostles' hands, he offered them money, [19] saying, "Give me also
> this power so that anyone on whom I lay my hands may receive
> the Holy Spirit." [20] But Peter said to him, "May your silver perish

> with you, because you thought you could obtain God's gift with money! [21] You have no part or share in this, for your heart is not right before God. [22] Repent therefore of this wickedness of yours, and pray to the Lord that, if possible, the intent of your heart may be forgiven you. [23] For I see that you are in the gall of bitterness and the chains of wickedness." [24] Simon answered, "Pray for me to the Lord, that nothing of what you have said may happen to me."

In this 8th chapter of Acts, we meet a man called Simon the magician. He apparently is quite skilled in his craft, but when he sees the miracles the apostles perform, he is utterly astonished. He becomes a believer and is even baptized. In the course of events, he witnesses the giving of the Spirit through the laying on of hands by the apostles Peter and John, and suddenly reverts back to his magician days. He offers money to the apostles if they will just give him the same power that they have. Peter's rebuke is clear: "May your silver perish with you, because you thought you could obtain God's gift with money!" Throughout the history of the church, countless people have somehow gotten the notion that money is the key to God's storehouse of spiritual gifts. Today, so-called "prosperity gospel preachers" are still at it, telling people that if they only give a certain sum of money, they will gain God's favor or power. Inevitably, the money those preachers receive fails to elicit any blessing from God and only results in further requests for even more money. Today this practice is called simony after Simon the Magician. Be skeptical when anyone promises you God's blessing in exchange for cold, hard cash.

Prayer

Blessed One, you have given us all things for our enjoyment, and provided us with everything we need from day to day. Keep us from greed and from ways of thinking that are contrary to your will. Thwart the plans of the wicked, and protect your people from all who would prey upon them. By your power, keep us safe. In the Name of Christ, we pray. AMEN.

Friday

Rom 12:9–21

9 Let love be genuine; hate what is evil, hold fast to what is
good; 10 love one another with mutual affection; outdo one an-
other in showing honor. 11 Do not lag in zeal, be ardent in spirit,
serve the Lord. 12 Rejoice in hope, be patient in suffering, per-
severe in prayer. 13 Contribute to the needs of the saints; extend
hospitality to strangers.

14 Bless those who persecute you; bless and do not curse
them. 15 Rejoice with those who rejoice, weep with those who
weep. 16 Live in harmony with one another; do not be haughty,
but associate with the lowly; do not claim to be wiser than you
are. 17 Do not repay anyone evil for evil, but take thought for
what is noble in the sight of all. 18 If it is possible, so far as
it depends on you, live peaceably with all. 19 Beloved, never
avenge yourselves, but leave room for the wrath of God; for it is
written, "Vengeance is mine, I will repay, says the Lord." 20 No,
"if your enemies are hungry, feed them; if they are thirsty, give
them something to drink; for by doing this you will heap burn-
ing coals on their heads." 21 Do not be overcome by evil, but
overcome evil with good.

In some Bibles, this passage is called "Marks of the True Christian." There are 30 commands in this passage, every one of them a challenge to fulfill faithfully. I dare say that if this list is a mark of a true Christian, no one will measure up. Only Jesus could meet the qualifications of this job description. And that is exactly the point. This list of virtues can only become characteristics of our life as we are filled more and more with the Spirit of Jesus. Only by inviting Christ to come into our hearts each day and fill us with his Spirit do we have a chance of living like a true Christian. Only by dying to ourselves every day, and letting Christ be our life, can we begin to look like a true believer. But in Christ, we can! As St. Paul said, "It is no longer I who live, but Christ who lives in me; and the life I now live in the flesh I live by faith in the Son of God who loved me and gave himself for me" (Gal 2:20).

Prayer

You are our Righteousness, O Jesus. You are our Strength and our Song. You are the Goodness we desire, the Love that we share, the Hope that dwells within us. Help us die every day to our own ego and sin, and come live within us, so that we might bear the marks of a true Christian, bringing glory to you and blessing to others. In your precious name, we pray. AMEN.

The Third Week After Epiphany

Monday

1 Cor 1:3–9

> 3 Grace to you and peace from God our Father and the Lord
> Jesus Christ.
>
> 4 I give thanks to my God always for you because of the grace
> of God that has been given you in Christ Jesus, 5 for in every
> way you have been enriched in him, in speech and knowledge of
> every kind— 6 just as the testimony of Christ has been strength-
> ened among you— 7 so that you are not lacking in any spiritual
> gift as you wait for the revealing of our Lord Jesus Christ. 8 He
> will also strengthen you to the end, so that you may be blameless
> on the day of our Lord Jesus Christ. 9 God is faithful; by him you
> were called into the fellowship of his Son, Jesus Christ our Lord.

This is the opening greeting of the Apostle Paul's first letter to the Christians in Corinth. I love the J.B. Phillips translation of verse 5. It reads: "For, as the Christian message has become established among you, [Christ]has enriched your whole lives, from the words on your lips to the understanding in your hearts." Isn't this so? Because of God's gift of faith to us in Christ, our lives have been enriched in every way, not only with knowledge and understanding, but with relationships with others, with opportunities for service, and, as Paul says here, *with every spiritual gift*. Where would we be apart from the grace of God? The Bible describes that state as "lost," and that seems to sum it up quite clearly. Lost in the wilderness, lost at sea, without a home, utterly alone, away from home, in despair—all of those scenarios might describe us apart from God's grace. But the good news is that grace has come to us. We are held in God's eternal embrace. It is our great privilege to celebrate this grace and share it with all we encounter.

Prayer

We praise and thank you, Gracious God, for your abundant grace to us. In the mystery of your will, you have granted us faith, and we are ever grateful. Help us live in humble gratitude all our days, seeking to be a blessing to all we meet and a glory to you. In the Name of Christ, we pray. AMEN.

Tuesday

Isa 61:1–4

The spirit of the Lord God is upon me,
    because the LORD has anointed me;
he has sent me to bring good news to the oppressed,
    to bind up the brokenhearted,
to proclaim liberty to the captives,
    and release to the prisoners;
2 to proclaim the year of the LORD's favor,
    and the day of vengeance of our God;
    to comfort all who mourn;
3 to provide for those who mourn in Zion—
    to give them a garland instead of ashes,
the oil of gladness instead of mourning,
    the mantle of praise instead of a faint spirit.
They will be called oaks of righteousness,
    the planting of the LORD, to display his glory.
4 They shall build up the ancient ruins,
    they shall raise up the former devastations;
they shall repair the ruined cities,
    the devastations of many generations.

This ongoing pandemic has left many of us identifying with those to whom Isaiah is writing in this passage: oppressed, brokenhearted, captive, prisoners. I have talked to more than one household that has reported,

"We don't go anywhere!" That's hard. It's hard to stay away from those you love. It's hard to live in isolation. It's hard feeling like you just can't be safe from the virus anywhere. I wonder if this pandemic time won't be what the Great Depression was for our forbearers; it changed them in profound ways, giving them a mindset that stayed with them forever. The prophet Isaiah is reminding all of us that the time will come when we will experience again "a garland instead of ashes, the oil of gladness instead of mourning." The time will come when what has been lost will be regained, and what has been broken down will be built up again. God has not abandoned us, and God's favor is from everlasting to everlasting. We live in hope, because our God is faithful.

Prayer

Grant us strength and faith, O God, in these trying days. Remind us of your faithfulness. Give us glimpses of your goodness, and help us to be witnesses of your love and grace each day. We pray in the Name of Jesus. AMEN.

Wednesday

Rom 12:3–8

> [3] For by the grace given to me I say to everyone among you not
> to think of yourself more highly than you ought to think, but to
> think with sober judgment, each according to the measure of
> faith that God has assigned. [4] For as in one body we have many
> members, and not all the members have the same function, [5] so
> we, who are many, are one body in Christ, and individually we
> are members one of another. [6] We have gifts that differ according
> to the grace given to us: prophecy, in proportion to faith; [7] min-
> istry, in ministering; the teacher, in teaching; [8] the exhorter, in
> exhortation; the giver, in generosity; the leader, in diligence; the
> compassionate, in cheerfulness.

In this passage, the Apostle Paul encourages us to "think with sober judgment, each according to the measure of faith that God has assigned." This advice has been interpreted in various ways, of course, but the original language suggests that Paul is simply advising us to "be reasonable." He explicitly warns us against being haughty, but being "reasonable" also means being clear-headed about our own abilities. That's what the second part of the passage is about. Paul is reminding us that everyone has a gift, everyone has a role, and none is more or less essential than the other. Reinhold Niebuhr, the great 20th century American theologian, famously insisted that our sinful nature is, at its most basic level, simply pride. While this is undoubtedly true, feminist theologians have long responded to Niebuhr by pointing out that self-denial is a sin that is equally as destructive as pride. It is as deadly to say, "I am worth nothing," as it is to say, "I am worthy of all praise." Sober judgment. Clear-headed thinking. Reasonableness. This is what God calls us to.

Prayer

Grant us clarity of mind, All-Wise God, as we judge ourselves. Help us to be neither haughty nor self-doubting, but clear that we have gifts, as do all of God's children. Help us to be graceful with ourselves and with others, seeing all people as you do. In Christ's Name, we pray. AMEN.

Thursday

Ps 119:89–96

89 The LORD exists forever;
  your word is firmly fixed in heaven.
90 Your faithfulness endures to all generations;
  you have established the earth, and it stands fast.
91 By your appointment they stand today,
  for all things are your servants.
92 If your law had not been my delight,
  I would have perished in my misery.
93 I will never forget your precepts,
  for by them you have given me life.
94 I am yours; save me,
  for I have sought your precepts.
95 The wicked lie in wait to destroy me,
  but I consider your decrees.
96 I have seen a limit to all perfection,
  but your commandment is exceedingly broad.

The 119th Psalm is an acrostic psalm. This means there is a discernible pattern according to the beginning letter of each stanza. The pattern in this psalm is that the first word of each 8-verse stanza begins with a letter of the Hebrew alphabet. There being 22 letters in the Hebrew alphabet, there are 22 stanzas in this psalm. This form served as a memory device, helping students of scripture memorize the entire psalm in praise of God's Word. This 12th stanza (vss. 89-96) includes a vow to be devoted to the study of God's Word. This vow, however, is not merely a ceremonial rite. Rather, the writer says, "I will never forget your precepts, *for by them you have given me life.*" This is our testimony as well. As the disciple Peter said, when asked if he would abandon Jesus, "Lord, to whom can we go? You have the words of eternal life." The Word of God is food for our soul. We are sustained by its message. We do not abandon God's word, for by it, God has given us life. As another verse in this psalm says, "Thy Word is a lamp unto my feet and a light unto my path."

Prayer

We praise you, Glorious God, for your wisdom and grace in providing your Word for us. Through this Word you feed our souls and we are satisfied. Through this Word you give us holy drink and our thirst is quenched. All thanks and praise to you, Gracious God. AMEN.

Friday

2 Chr 34:1–7

> Josiah was eight years old when he began to reign; he reigned
> thirty-one years in Jerusalem. 2 He did what was right in the
> sight of the LORD, and walked in the ways of his ancestor Da-
> vid; he did not turn aside to the right or to the left. 3 For in
> the eighth year of his reign, while he was still a boy, he began
> to seek the God of his ancestor David, and in the twelfth year
> he began to purge Judah and Jerusalem of the high places, the
> sacred poles, and the carved and the cast images. 4 In his pres-
> ence they pulled down the altars of the Baals; he demolished the
> incense altars that stood above them. He broke down the sacred
> poles and the carved and the cast images; he made dust of them
> and scattered it over the graves of those who had sacrificed to
> them. 5 He also burned the bones of the priests on their altars,

> and purged Judah and Jerusalem. [6] In the towns of Manasseh, Ephraim, and Simeon, and as far as Naphtali, in their ruins all around, [7] he broke down the altars, beat the sacred poles and the images into powder, and demolished all the incense altars throughout all the land of Israel. Then he returned to Jerusalem.

Today's account of King Josiah gives us a remarkable picture of this boy king. At age 8, he begins his reign (albeit with counselors, we assume). By age 16, he begins to pursue a life of faith in the manner of King David, and by age 20 he has begun a series of reforms that will result in the total elimination of the pagan practices which had sprung up during the reign of his forbearers. If we look back at the other account of Josiah's reign in the book of 2 Kings, we see that the impetus for these reforms was likely the discovery of God's law. King Josiah apparently had an epiphany when the Law was read to him, and he acted on that growing awareness, putting away pagan practices, and leading the people once again in following the God of the patriarchs and matriarchs, of Moses and Miriam, and all those who had followed God faithfully. We who are leaders are given an example in King Josiah. We are inspired by his witness to spend time listening to God's Word, and then living and leading in response to that Word. When we do this, we find, as Josiah did, that God's people are blessed.

Prayer

Be with the leaders of your Church, O God. Guide pastors and bishops, deacons and musicians, counselors and teachers, to be faithful followers of your Son. Give them open ears to hear your Word, open hearts to receive it, and courageous spirits to live as you inspire. Bless your people with strong leaders and build up your Church, we pray. In the Name of Christ. AMEN.

The Fourth Week After Epiphany

Monday

Acts 10:44–48

> 44 While Peter was still speaking, the Holy Spirit fell upon all
> who heard the word. 45 The circumcised believers who had come
> with Peter were astounded that the gift of the Holy Spirit had
> been poured out even on the Gentiles, 46 for they heard them
> speaking in tongues and extolling God. Then Peter said, 47 "Can
> anyone withhold the water for baptizing these people who have
> received the Holy Spirit just as we have?" 48 So he ordered them
> to be baptized in the name of Jesus Christ. Then they invited
> him to stay for several days.

This passage comes at the end of the wonderful story of Cornelius, a Roman centurion. Cornelius received a vision from God regarding a visitor named Simon Peter who had something to share with him. If you have not read this amazing story, it is well worth it. At the end of this story, when it becomes clear to Peter the disciple and his cohort that the Spirit has been given to Cornelius and his household as surely as it has been given to them, we read that "the circumcised believers [i.e., Jews]who had come with Peter *were astounded* that the gift of the Holy Spirit had been poured out even on the Gentiles." The Greek word for "astounded" is defined as "the feeling of astonishment mingled with fear, caused by events which are miraculous, extraordinary, or difficult to understand." In this case, the last part of the definition seems most appropriate. The early believers were all Jews, of course, and as such, they assumed that as others became followers of Christ, they too would come from the Jewish fold. In other words, they would be people like them. This seems to be an affliction to which we are still prone today.

When we think of who we are most likely to invite to worship or Bible study or some other event of spiritual formation, we probably think of people like ourselves. How freeing it is to realize that God has no such parameters. God invites all. Maybe we should follow God's lead.

Prayer

Forgive us, Lord, for being astonished that people unlike us might believe and be baptized. Forgive us for our narrow thinking. Forgive us for our blind eyes and deaf ears to those who differ from us. Give us generous spirits, full of wonder at those you will call next. In your holy name, we pray. AMEN.

Tuesday

2 Chr 35:20–24

> 20 After all this, when Josiah had set the temple in order, King
> Neco of Egypt went up to fight at Carchemish on the Euphra-
> tes, and Josiah went out against him. 21 But Neco sent envoys
> to him, saying, "What have I to do with you, king of Judah? I
> am not coming against you today, but against the house with
> which I am at war; and God has commanded me to hurry.
> Cease opposing God, who is with me, so that he will not de-
> stroy you." 22 But Josiah would not turn away from him, but
> disguised himself in order to fight with him. He did not listen
> to the words of Neco from the mouth of God, but joined battle
> in the plain of Megiddo. 23 The archers shot King Josiah; and
> the king said to his servants, "Take me away, for I am badly
> wounded." 24 So his servants took him out of the chariot and
> carried him in his second chariot and brought him to Jerusa-
> lem. There he died, and was buried in the tombs of his ances-
> tors. All Judah and Jerusalem mourned for Josiah.

This little-known account of the death of Josiah—one of Judah's faithful, righteous kings—has an important lesson in it. King Neco of Egypt reports to Josiah that he has received a word from God that he is to be granted safe passage through Judah on his way to fight at Carchemish. He tells Josiah straight out that his quarrel is not with him and that if he opposes him he will be opposing God. Josiah refuses to heed this word, is wounded, and dies as a result. In this story we see once again, as in yesterday's passage from Acts 10, that God is very capable of speaking to and working through those who are not from our tribe. If we really think about this, we realize it is ridiculous to believe God only speaks to and works with those like us; yet this is so often what we assume. Not too many years ago, in 2012, Christian author and theologian Brian McLaren wrote a book entitled *Why Did Jesus, Moses, the Buddha, and Mohammed Cross the Road?* In this book, McLaren argued that being a strong Christian isn't fulfilled by us strong-arming someone into believing as we do, but rather by us showing "vigorous hospitality toward, interest in, and collaboration with 'the other.'" In fact, God might actually speak through "the other" to us!

Prayer

Speak to us, Gentle Lord, through the words of our neighbors. Speak to us in ways that we can hear, so that we will learn that you speak many languages, and through many voices. Grant us open ears and open hearts to hear from those least like us, so that your will—that *all* be delivered from sin and death—might come on earth as in heaven. In your precious name, we pray. AMEN.

Wednesday

Acts 19:1–7

> While Apollos was in Corinth, Paul passed through the interior regions and came to Ephesus, where he found some disciples. 2 He said to them, "Did you receive the Holy Spirit when you became believers?" They replied, "No, we have not even heard that there is a Holy Spirit." 3 Then he said, "Into what then were you baptized?" They answered, "Into John's baptism." 4 Paul said, "John baptized with the baptism of repentance, telling the people to believe in the one who was to come after him, that is, in Jesus." 5 On hearing this, they were baptized in the name of the Lord Jesus. 6 When Paul had laid his hands on them, the Holy Spirit came upon them, and they spoke in tongues and prophesied— 7 altogether there were about twelve of them.

This passage has often confused readers because it seems to suggest there are two baptisms necessary for "real" conversion. Indeed, some traditions have adopted this practice, although most churches have not. What this story lifts up is the fact that different followers of Jesus have different understandings and different experiences of what conversion is. Some experience a quiet, inner peace upon receiving the gift of faith, while others literally jump for joy in ecstatic celebration. Some understand faith as primarily a journey of the mind, while for others it is a journey of the heart. Some feel the practice of faith is best expressed through lives of service, while others need to express their faith in worship and praise. Some believers insist that sharing the good news through preaching and song is the only way to evangelize, while others let their lives do the talking. The fact is, there is great variety in how faith in Christ is expressed in people's lives, and it is likely that any practice, done in love for God and neighbor, is acceptable to God. So be at peace, for God is with you.

Prayer

We praise you, Gracious God, for accepting our meager acts of faithfulness in whatever shape they manifest themselves. Forgive us for judging those whose practices differ from ours. Give us your generous heart. Humble us with your merciful example, and lead us in the way of life. In the name of Jesus, we pray. AMEN.

Thursday

John 1:43–49

> 43 The next day Jesus decided to go to Galilee. He found Philip
> and said to him, "Follow me." 44 Now Philip was from Bethsaida,
> the city of Andrew and Peter. 45 Philip found Nathanael and
> said to him, "We have found him about whom Moses in the law
> and also the prophets wrote, Jesus son of Joseph from Naza-
> reth." 46 Nathanael said to him, "Can anything good come out
> of Nazareth?" Philip said to him, "Come and see." 47 When Jesus
> saw Nathanael coming toward him, he said of him, "Here is truly
> an Israelite in whom there is no deceit!" 48 Nathanael asked him,
> "Where did you get to know me?" Jesus answered, "I saw you
> under the fig tree before Philip called you." 49 Nathanael replied,
> "Rabbi, you are the Son of God! You are the King of Israel!"

I love Jesus' response to Nathanael's snarky attitude: "Here is truly an Israelite in whom there is no deceit." Jesus could have called Nathanael out. He could have said to him, "What do you mean by saying, 'Can anything good come out of Nazareth?' You have insulted me and my hometown." Instead, Jesus interprets his attitude generously, claiming that Nathanael is simply a person who tells it like it is. I wonder how we might learn from Jesus here. Perhaps you know someone who finds it easy to criticize others or, it seems, most everything. Maybe you could say, "Here is truly a person with an eye for detail." Or perhaps you know someone who is disorganized or kind of messy. Maybe you could say, "Here is truly someone who doesn't waste time worrying about impressing others." There is always a way to describe another person's actions that lifts them up, rather than belittles them. And isn't that how we hope other people will interpret *our* quirks and bad habits? As Luther said in his *Small Catechism*, when answering the question of the meaning of the 8th commandment: "We are to fear and love God, so that we do not betray, slander, or lie about our neighbor, but defend them, speak well of them, and explain their actions in the kindest way."

Prayer

Forgive us, Almighty God, for not having the mind of Christ when describing the actions of others. Forgive us for being willing to believe the lie that when we tear others down, we lift ourselves up. Grant us a fresh spirit of humility, O God, and lead us in the way of mercy and peace. In your gracious name, we pray. AMEN.

Friday

Ps 56:1–4, 8–11

1 Be gracious to me, O God, for people trample on me;
all day long foes oppress me;
2 my enemies trample on me all day long,
for many fight against me.
O Most High, 3 when I am afraid,
I put my trust in you.
4 In God, whose word I praise,
in God I trust; I am not afraid;
what can flesh do to me?
8 You have kept count of my tossings;

put my tears in your bottle.
Are they not in your record?
9 Then my enemies will retreat
in the day when I call.
This I know, that God is for me.
10 In God, whose word I praise,
in the LORD, whose word I praise,
11 in God I trust; I am not afraid.
What can a mere mortal do to me?

The Psalmist, King David, is an example for us here. David says that two things sustain him in the day of trouble: God's Word, and prayer. In verse 4, David testifies to his trust in God's Word. In verse 9, he testifies to God's sure answer to prayer "in the day when I call." In both cases, David ends with the phrase, "What can flesh, or a mere mortal do to me, if I trust in God?" When we are assailed by enemies from within or without, by voices that oppress us or call our worth into question, we too can turn to God's Word and prayer. There are scores of verses that declare God's love for us. Setting one or two of them to memory and making them a prayer mantra is one way of fighting off these enemies. Generations of believers have found Ps 23:1 to be just such a mantra: "The Lord is my Shepherd; I shall not want." Others have memorized 1 Pet 5:7: "Cast all your anxieties on God, for he cares about you." Find your own favorite verse and carry it with you in your heart. Then, in your day of trouble, you too will be able to say, with David, "In God I trust; I am not afraid. What can a mere mortal do to me?"

Prayer

We are in your hands, Gracious God. We are with you from the rising of the sun to its setting, from our first day to our last. You have promised us eternal life, and a love that is beyond measure. Give us faith to believe your good promises and to live in joy all our days. In the Name of Christ, we pray. AMEN.

The Fifth Week after Epiphany

Monday

1 Kgs 17:8–16

> [8] Then the word of the LORD came to [Elijah], saying, [9] "Go now to Zarephath, which belongs to Sidon, and live there; for I have commanded a widow there to feed you." [10] So he set out and went to Zarephath. When he came to the gate of the town, a widow was there gathering sticks; he called to her and said, "Bring me a little water in a vessel, so that I may drink." [11] As she was going to bring it, he called to her and said, "Bring me a morsel of bread in your hand." [12] But she said, "As the LORD your God lives, I have nothing baked, only a handful of meal in a jar, and a little oil in a jug; I am now gathering a couple of sticks, so that I may go home and prepare it for myself and my son, that we may eat it, and die." [13] Elijah said to her, "Do not be afraid; go and do as you have said; but first make me a little cake of it and bring it to me, and afterwards make something for yourself and your son. [14] For thus says the LORD the God of Israel: The jar of meal will not be emptied and the jug of oil will not fail until the day that the LORD sends rain on the earth." [15] She went and did as Elijah said, so that she as well as he and her household ate for many days. [16] The jar of meal was not emptied, neither did the jug of oil fail, according to the word of the LORD that he spoke by Elijah.

St. Paul famously stated that, as followers of Christ, we "walk by faith, not by sight." This story from 1 Kings is an excellent example of this concept. The widow of Zarephath has a choice to make: will she trust the promise of God that comes to her through the words of Elijah, or will she trust only what her own eyes can see and what she fears most? This makes clear what is always true about "walking by sight"—it is based on fear and a feeling of scarcity. We don't give generously not because we are inherently stingy but because we are *afraid* that we might not have enough. We don't reach out to a new person not because we are generally unfriendly, but because we are *afraid* we might be rejected or might be thought a fool. It turns out that, when we think about it, walking by faith is simply refusing to allow fear to control us. We choose, as the widow of Zarephath did, to trust God and follow God's call, even when we are afraid. In that, not only are we blessed, but many others are as well.

Prayer

Grant us faith and courage to follow your call, O God. Forgive us when we fall back in fear. Forgive us when we lack the courage that will lead us to new life. Fill us with your Holy Spirit so that all our days might be lived in joy and hope. In Christ's name. AMEN.

Tuesday

1 Cor 2:1–9

> When I came to you, brothers and sisters, I did not come proclaiming the mystery of God to you in lofty words or wisdom. 2 For I decided to know nothing among you except Jesus Christ, and him crucified. 3 And I came to you in weakness and in fear and in much trembling. 4 My speech and my proclamation were not with plausible words of wisdom, but with a demonstration of the Spirit and of power, 5 so that your faith might rest not on human wisdom but on the power of God. 6 Yet among the mature we do speak wisdom, though it is not a wisdom of this age or of the rulers of this age, who are doomed to perish. 7 But we speak God's wisdom, secret and hidden, which God decreed before the ages for our glory. 8 None of the rulers of this age understood this; for if they had, they would not have crucified the Lord of glory. 9 But, as it is written,
>
> "What no eye has seen, nor ear heard,
> nor the human heart conceived,
> what God has prepared for those who love him"—

The Greek word for wisdom is *sophia*. You can easily see, in that word, the basis for the word "sophistication." In this first letter to the Corinthians, the Apostle Paul was arguing against those who believed that sophisticated thinking was the pathway to faith, and even more than that, the shortcut to God's favor. Disagreement had arisen in this early congregation, with some believing that only those with superior knowledge of divine things and the ability to communicate with divine beings were favored by God. Paul would have none of this. We who have studied much, and might even have seminary diplomas hanging on our walls, are prone to the thinking Paul rejected. Indeed, any of us who delight in learning and discovering new things could fall victim to this error. While learning is to be celebrated and encouraged, we must be careful to remember that God's wisdom is greater than human wisdom, and faithfulness in God's eyes does not include an IQ test. As St. Paul says, "No one can even imagine 'what God has prepared for those who love him.'"

Prayer

Grant us humility of spirit, O God, as we go about our studies. Give us open ears to be taught by others, especially those whose ways of knowing are different from our own. Grant us faith that is based on trust in you and not on our own understanding. In all things give us peace. In your holy name, we pray. AMEN.

Wednesday

2 Kgs 5:1–5, 9–14

> 1 Naaman, commander of the army of the king of Aram, was
> a great man and in high favor with his master, because by
> him the LORD had given victory to Aram. The man, though
> a mighty warrior, suffered from leprosy. 2 Now the Arameans
> on one of their raids had taken a young girl captive from the
> land of Israel, and she served Naaman's wife. 3 She said to her
> mistress, "If only my lord were with the prophet who is in Sa-
> maria! He would cure him of his leprosy." 4 So Naaman went in
> and told his lord just what the girl from the land of Israel had
> said. 5 And the king of Aram said, "Go then, and I will send
> along a letter to the king of Israel."

> 9 So Naaman came with his horses and chariots, and halted at
> the entrance of Elisha's house. 10 Elisha sent a messenger to him,
> saying, "Go, wash in the Jordan seven times, and your flesh shall
> be restored and you shall be clean." 11 But Naaman became angry
> and went away, saying, "I thought that for me he would surely
> come out, and stand and call on the name of the LORD his God,
> and would wave his hand over the spot, and cure the leprosy!
> 12 Are not Abana and Pharpar, the rivers of Damascus, better
> than all the waters of Israel? Could I not wash in them, and be
> clean?" He turned and went away in a rage. 13 But his servants
> approached and said to him, "Father, if the prophet had com-
> manded you to do something difficult, would you not have done
> it? How much more, when all he said to you was, 'Wash, and be
> clean'?" 14 So he went down and immersed himself seven times
> in the Jordan, according to the word of the man of God; his flesh
> was restored like the flesh of a young boy, and he was clean.

This ancient tale of Naaman the Syrian general and Elisha the prophet illustrates a tendency we all have to believe God's ways are always difficult, if not heroic. Perhaps, like Naaman, we might think, "Missionaries who travel to distant lands are what God requires; my pot of stew for the neighbor doesn't amount to much." Or, we might think, "Pastors who spend years studying the Bible are certainly more blessed in God's eyes than those of us who humbly come to Bible study week after week." In thinking these things, we miss the point that Jesus came to teach us: common folks, doing common acts of compassion, using common means are what the kingdom of God consists of. Yes, there are those who are called to difficult journeys or difficult settings, but even *they* must learn to minister through common means. Holy Communion and Baptism both teach us this as they, through common stuff, bring blessing to many.

Prayer

Thank you for using common folks like us, Lord, to do uncommon things. Thank you for promising that even when we give a cup of cool water to a small child, that act will not be without its reward. Grant us faith each day to see you at work in our world. In Jesus' name. AMEN.

Thursday

Luke 19:41–44

> As [Jesus]came near and saw the city [of Jerusalem], he wept over it, [42] saying, "If you, even you, had only recognized on this day the things that make for peace! But now they are hidden from your eyes. [43] Indeed, the days will come upon you, when your enemies will set up ramparts around you and surround you, and hem you in on every side. [44] They will crush you to the ground, you and your children within you, and they will not leave within you one stone upon another; because you did not recognize the time of your visitation from God."

In this passage, Jesus is coming toward Jerusalem, approaching the path down from the Mount of Olives, mounted on a donkey, listening as the crowds surrounding him call out, "Hosanna. Blessed is the king who comes in the name of the Lord!" As he gets nearer and nearer to the city he does something unexpected: he begins to weep. That is not usually something you do when you are being lauded as the next king of Israel. But Jesus knows how quickly these cries of Hosanna will turn to "Crucify him." He knows that their desire for a king comes only from the hunger in their bellies, and their desire to humble their oppressors; they do not want a king such as he is, who will call them to follow him to the Cross. We too are apt to want Jesus only on our terms. We want what he can provide us, not what he calls us to. We might well ask ourselves: how are *we* able to recognize "the things that make for peace?" How can *we* be sure to recognize "the time of *our* visitation from God?"

Prayer

We are prone, Lord Jesus, to fail to see you as you are: suffering servant, crucified and condemned, a man of sorrows and acquainted with grief. We would rather see you as glorious king, triumphant ruler, Lord of all. Give us clarity to see you as you are, dear Lord. Help us to recognize you as Savior, and give us faith to follow you, even to the Cross. In your precious name, we pray. AMEN.

Friday

Ps 138:1–6

1 I give you thanks, O LORD, with my whole heart;
before the gods I sing your praise;
2 I bow down toward your holy temple
and give thanks to your name for your steadfast love and your faithfulness;
for you have exalted your name and your word
above everything.
3 On the day I called, you answered me,
you increased my strength of soul.
4 All the kings of the earth shall praise you, O LORD,
for they have heard the words of your mouth.
5 They shall sing of the ways of the LORD,
for great is the glory of the LORD.
6 For though the LORD is high, he regards the lowly;
but the haughty he perceives from far away.

This 6th verse from Ps 138 is one I memorized years ago. It is a verse that contains both a warning and a promise. The promise is that God pays attention to those the world often does not even notice. If you have ever walked along a busy sidewalk in a large city like Chicago or New York, you know that it is not uncommon to come upon someone begging. They are usually ill-clad, dirty, and disheveled. They are also usually invisible to those who walk past them. It is as if they don't exist. But for God, they do. God sees them, for God regards the lowly. But God has a different view of the "high and mighty." God *perceives* them, says the psalmist. That is to say, God knows that they are there, but they are seen as far away, distant, located in a far country. As such they are not close to God, but have only a fleeting relationship with the Most High. So then, we learn that those who view themselves as people of consequence, are, paradoxically, of little consequence in God's eyes. What a reversal this is! This reminds of Jesus' words in the Beatitudes: "Blessed are the poor in spirit, for theirs is the kingdom of God. Blessed are those who mourn, for they will be comforted. Blessed are the meek, for they will inherit the earth."

Prayer

Help us to see those you see, O God. Help us to notice those you notice. Help us to have a heart for those for whom your heart bleeds, O God. And give us a measured view of the world's values. Lead us in the way of life each and every day. In the Name of Jesus, Lover of the lowly. AMEN.

The Sixth Week after Epiphany

Monday

Num 20:22–29

22 They set out from Kadesh, and the Israelites, the whole congre-
gation, came to Mount Hor. 23 Then the LORD said to Moses and
Aaron at Mount Hor, on the border of the land of Edom, 24 "Let
Aaron be gathered to his people. For he shall not enter the land
that I have given to the Israelites, because you rebelled against
my command at the waters of Meribah. 25 Take Aaron and his
son Eleazar, and bring them up Mount Hor; 26 strip Aaron of
his vestments, and put them on his son Eleazar. But Aaron shall
be gathered to his people, and shall die there." 27 Moses did as
the LORD had commanded; they went up Mount Hor in the
sight of the whole congregation. 28 Moses stripped Aaron of his
vestments, and put them on his son Eleazar; and Aaron died
there on the top of the mountain. Moses and Eleazar came down
from the mountain. 29 When all the congregation saw that Aaron
had died, all the house of Israel mourned for Aaron thirty days.

In our culture, we have many ways of speaking about death. Some are silly, some profound: he kicked the bucket; she passed away; he bought the farm; she went to heaven; he met his Savior; she went to her eternal reward; he cashed in his chips, and so forth. Somehow, saying that someone *died* seems harder to say than that someone *passed*. In the story of Aaron's death, we hear another way of speaking about death: he was "gathered to his people." I like that. It speaks of death as a reuniting with loved ones. I remember so well a moment at the close of a funeral for a man who had died when he was well into his nineties. His wife of 65+ years stood in front of the coffin and said, "Mike, I'll see you soon. Don't worry, I won't be long." She clearly believed that Mike was being "gathered to his people," as would she someday. Our Lord indicated such a gathering while he was dying. His words to the man dying next to him speak of a gathering as well: "Truly, I tell you, today you shall be with me in paradise."

Prayer

We praise you, Lord Christ, for your power over death. We praise you that death does not have the last word, nor does it have the power to keep us from being gathered with you and all God's people. Grant us faith to live in the sure knowledge of your gathering, and give us joy as we await your coming. In your powerful name, we pray. AMEN.

Tuesday

Acts 9:19b–25

> For several days [Saul, who would become Paul]was with the disciples in Damascus, [20] and immediately he began to proclaim Jesus in the synagogues, saying, "He is the Son of God." [21] All who heard him were amazed and said, "Is not this the man who made havoc in Jerusalem among those who invoked this name? And has he not come here for the purpose of bringing them bound before the chief priests?" [22] Saul became increasingly more powerful and confounded the Jews who lived in Damascus by proving that Jesus was the Messiah. [23] After some time had passed, the Jews plotted to kill him, [24] but their plot became known to Saul. They were watching the gates day and night so that they might kill him; [25] but his disciples took him by night and let him down through an opening in the wall, lowering him in a basket.

Have you ever switched teams? Have you ever taken one side on an issue, only to decide later that you needed to be on the other side? This was the experience of St. Paul. If you have never read the entire 9th chapter of Acts, where Paul's conversion on the Road to Damascus is recorded, you should do so. Paul was on the way to Damascus to arrest people who were following Jesus. On the way he ran straight into Jesus in the form of a voice from heaven, who blinded him and caused him to rethink his whole purpose in life. In not so many days, he began to exhibit a complete reversal of his loyalties: instead of persecuting Christians who were proclaiming Christ as Messiah, he himself began proclaiming Christ as Messiah. Instead of using his education, status, and eloquence to convict Christians of breaking the law, he used his considerable gifts to convict people of sin and invite them to the forgiveness Christ offers. All who heard Paul were astonished at his transformation. Christians were at first skeptical, but soon were protecting him and embracing him. Those whom he had led in his zeal against Christians were furious, so much so that they sought his life. St. Paul is an example of the utter transformation that can come to one whom God touches.

Prayer

Giver of Life, we know people who fight against your Church. We know people whose hatred for the gospel fuels their anger and violence. Protect your Church from such enemies, O God and transform those who rage in this way. Grant them the miracle of St. Paul, to see you as you really are, and grant them repentance and life evermore. In your holy name, we pray. AMEN.

Wednesday

Luke 4:38–44

> 38 After leaving the synagogue [Jesus]entered Simon's house.
> Now Simon's mother-in-law was suffering from a high fever, and
> they asked him about her. 39 Then he stood over her and rebuked
> the fever, and it left her. Immediately she got up and began to
> serve them.40 As the sun was setting, all those who had any who
> were sick with various kinds of diseases brought them to him;
> and he laid his hands on each of them and cured them. 41 De-
> mons also came out of many, shouting, "You are the Son of
> God!" But he rebuked them and would not allow them to speak,
> because they knew that he was the Messiah. 42 At daybreak he
> departed and went into a deserted place. And the crowds were
> looking for him; and when they reached him, they wanted to
> prevent him from leaving them. 43 But he said to them, "I must
> proclaim the good news of the kingdom of God to the other
> cities also; for I was sent for this purpose." 44 So he continued
> proclaiming the message in the synagogues of Judea.

Do you ever get the sense that Jesus was tired? I do. Just think about the day that is being described here. He healed Simon's mother-in-law and, it seems, had a bit of down time—maybe an afternoon nap. But then as darkness was approaching, suddenly the word got out that miracles of healing were happening at his hands and people showed up in droves. Some came with sicknesses and others needed exorcism. He showed compassion to all. He must have gone to bed exhausted. And then, in the early morning, just when he thought he could get away for a little time by himself, he is found out, and once again, the crowds are pressing in on him. I know young parents like this. Their work schedule is brutal, and when they get home it doesn't stop. Dinner needs to be made, clothes need to be washed, the kids need to have their homework checked, and who knows what else. Finally, everyone is in bed and the house is quiet and there is finally time to rest, and they think, "Oh, do I need this." Perhaps this story shows us that Jesus also knows what it is to be stretched thin. We read in Hebrews that he was tempted in every way we are, and maybe, just maybe that can mean that when we are running on empty, Jesus understands.

Prayer

Lord Jesus, we come to you in our exhaustion. This pandemic has left us "running on fumes" many days, and even on those days when we are not as taxed, all we want to do is sleep. Help us to be good to ourselves, dear Lord. Help us to be OK with being tired and know that it is no sin to be exhausted. Grant us rest. Grant us peace. Grant us your strength for these days. In your loving name, we pray. AMEN.

Thursday

Judg 3:7–11

> [7] The Israelites did what was evil in the sight of the LORD,
> forgetting the LORD their God, and worshiping the Baals and
> the Asherahs. [8] Therefore the anger of the LORD was kindled
> against Israel, and he sold them into the hand of King Cushan-
> rishathaim of Aram-naharaim; and the Israelites served
> Cushan-rishathaim eight years. [9] But when the Israelites cried
> out to the LORD, the LORD raised up a deliverer for the Israel-
> ites, who delivered them, Othniel son of Kenaz, Caleb's younger

brother. [10] The spirit of the LORD came upon him, and he judged
Israel; he went out to war, and the LORD gave King Cushan-
rishathaim of Aram into his hand; and his hand prevailed over
Cushan-rishathaim. [11] So the land had rest forty years. Then
Othniel son of Kenaz died.

In the history of Israel there is a veritable revolving door of leaders following the death of Moses and then Joshua. Some leaders are wicked; some are faithful. Some are remembered; some are forgotten. Othniel, brother of Caleb and one of the heroes in Israel's history, was apparently one who was faithful. We aren't told much about his reign, only that he defeated in war the people that had oppressed Israel. What is telling is how his reign is described: "So the land had rest forty years." This is always the case when faithful leadership is in place. Rest comes to a people. Their anxiety is lessened. Their tendency towards violence is stifled. Their compassion is multiplied. Conversely, unfaithful leadership is concerned with gathering power instead of empowering others, and hears every strong voice as a threat. Fear is heightened. Greed is applauded. Power-grabbing is encouraged. All this leads to more strife and less rest for all. How we need leaders like Othniel who will give the land rest. How we need to remember that with faithfulness comes peace.

Prayer

Raise up faithful leaders in our land, Lord God. Thwart the plans of those who would gather all power, all wealth, and all honor only to themselves. Grant wisdom to all who govern, all who serve the common good, and all who are called to seats of authority. Grant that your Church would also be a source of wisdom for this world. In the name of Jesus, we pray. AMEN.

Friday

1 Tim 3:1–7

The saying is sure: whoever aspires to the office of bishop desires
a noble task. [2] Now a bishop must be above reproach, married
only once, temperate, sensible, respectable, hospitable, an apt
teacher, [3] not a drunkard, not violent but gentle, not quarrel-
some, and not a lover of money. [4] He must manage his own
household well, keeping his children submissive and respectful

> in every way— [5] for if someone does not know how to manage his own household, how can he take care of God's church? [6] He must not be a recent convert, or he may be puffed up with conceit and fall into the condemnation of the devil. [7] Moreover, he must be well thought of by outsiders, so that he may not fall into disgrace and the snare of the devil.

The so-called "pastoral letters" include many instances of St. Paul giving instructions to his younger pastors, Timothy and Titus, who were apparently his mentees. He often gives them advice on how to organize and manage the church. You will notice in this passage that he speaks of bishops. That word simply means "overseers." It is unlikely that the early Church had bishops in the sense we do today, but as the Church grew, it undoubtedly needed oversight. The ones to whom this responsibility fell are those whom Paul addresses. What he demands of an overseer could well be used as qualifications for any Christian leader. All of the characteristics called for are essential for anyone in authority in Christ's Church, especially those who are called to represent the Church in the wider world. We all know the terrible price the Church has paid when its leaders have been involved in misconduct. Not only is the mission and ministry of the Church stopped in its tracks, but the witness the world sees is tarnished and many amends need to be made. It is not surprising that the last advice Paul has regarding overseers is that they "be well thought of by outsiders." Paul knows that the witness of the gospel is at stake. For Christian leaders, even more than lay people, "walking the walk" and not just "talking the talk" is essential.

Prayer

Give your Church faithful leaders, dear Lord, who will serve with humility and honor, who will guide with wisdom and compassion, and who will live their lives in ways that bring honor to you and blessing to your people. Protect them from the snares of the devil, from temptations that would destroy them and scandalize your Church. In all ways, guide and strengthen them to be faithful to their call. In Christ's name, we pray. AMEN.

The Seventh Week after Epiphany

Monday

Ps 1

1 Happy are those
   who do not follow the advice of the wicked,
or take the path that sinners tread,
   or sit in the seat of scoffers;
2 but their delight is in the law of the LORD,
   and on his law they meditate day and night.
3 They are like trees
   planted by streams of water,
which yield their fruit in its season,
   and their leaves do not wither.
In all that they do, they prosper.
4 The wicked are not so,
   but are like chaff that the wind drives away.
5 Therefore the wicked will not stand in the judgment,
   nor sinners in the congregation of the righteous;
6 for the LORD watches over the way of the righteous,
   but the way of the wicked will perish.

When I was a teenager, I used to work at our local golf course, mowing the fairways on a small Ford tractor. I would sit out on that tractor for hours in the baking sun, in nothing but a pair of cutoff jeans; no hat, no shirt, no shoes. When I'd come in after an afternoon of mowing, my sweaty back would be covered with chaff from the grass I'd been mowing. All that dry grass just clung to my skin until it looked as though I had grown a winter coat. As I recall, one of the best ways to get rid of it was to jump into the lake below our house and just let the cool, swirling water wash me clean. The psalmist compares chaff to the ways of the wicked. He says that the way of the wicked, just like chaff, will perish. Thankfully, we know of One who came to deal with the chaff in our life, Jesus our Savior. He said that whoever is born anew of water and the Spirit is freed from all sin. Or as St. John said, "Whenever we confess our sins, God is faithful and just, and will forgive our sins and cleanse us from all unrighteousness." The chaff in our lives does not need to continue to cling to us; we can wash it off each day by returning to the promises of our baptism, and feeling the cool waters cleanse us again and again.

Prayer

Grant us forgiveness, Gracious Lord, whenever we come to you in confession. Grant us peace whenever we come to you needing reconciliation. Grant us faith in your promises, so that we may live in hope and joy all our days. In Christ's name we pray. AMEN.

Tuesday

1 Pet 1:18

> 18 You know that you were ransomed from the futile ways inherited from your ancestors, not with perishable things like silver or gold, 19 but with the precious blood of Christ, like that of a lamb without defect or blemish. 20 He was destined before the foundation of the world, but was revealed at the end of the ages for your sake. 21 Through him you have come to trust in God, who raised him from the dead and gave him glory, so that your faith and hope are set on God.
>
> 22 Now that you have purified your souls by your obedience to the truth so that you have genuine mutual love, love one another deeply from the heart. 23 You have been born anew, not of perishable but of imperishable seed, through the living and enduring word of God.

The writer here says that through Christ "we have come to trust in God." This means that Jesus is the *means* whereby we have faith in God; he is the *avenue* through which faith is created. This speaks to the fact that, though we cannot see God, we can see pictures of Jesus in Scripture. We can see Jesus healing and helping those who are sick, casting out demons from those in bondage, and even raising the dead. We can also see him embracing children, refusing to condemn sinners, while at the same time rebuking the self-righteous and any who are oppressing others. In all these ways we can see Jesus, and seeing him, we see God, for as our Lord said, "Whoever has seen me, has seen the Father." Knowing then, that what is true of Jesus is true of God, we know we can trust God. God is a healing and helping God. God is one who has power over those things that hold us in bondage, and even over death itself. God is one who embraces children, forgives sinners, and rebukes oppressors and any who believe in their own righteousness. In this way, Christ is the means through which we come to trust in God.

Prayer

Grant us faith, O God, in your goodness and love. Help us to see that as Jesus is, so are you. As the poor soul cried out to Jesus in Scripture, so we cry out to you, "I believe, Lord. Help my unbelief." In Jesus' name. AMEN.

Wednesday

1 Cor 15:20–26

> 20 But in fact Christ has been raised from the dead, the first fruits
> of those who have died. 21 For since death came through a hu-
> man being, the resurrection of the dead has also come through
> a human being; 22 for as all die in Adam, so all will be made
> alive in Christ. 23 But each in his own order: Christ the first
> fruits, then at his coming those who belong to Christ. 24 Then
> comes the end, when he hands over the kingdom to God the
> Father, after he has destroyed every ruler and every authority
> and power. 25 For he must reign until he has put all his enemies
> under his feet. 26 The last enemy to be destroyed is death.

This last line is packed with power. First of all, it recognizes that death is the enemy of Christ. Christ says that he has come so that we might have life and have it to the full. He has called himself the Living Water, the Bread of Life, the Resurrection and the Life—all descriptors of one who is the enemy of death. We also know that with Christ comes faith, but with death comes fear. Fear and faith are mutually opposed. When death sends fear our way, we falter in our faith, wondering if Christ really does have the power to defeat death. But the writer here makes it clear that not only does Christ have power over death, he has the power to *destroy, to utterly annihilate* death. As St. John says in his revelation, "Death will be no more; mourning and crying and pain will be no more, for the first things have passed away." How good it is to know that our Lord has power over the Last Enemy. Because we know this, we live in faith and hope, and even joy.

Prayer

We praise you, Lord Christ, for your majesty and power. None is your equal. You are the Lord of hosts, the Victor over all your enemies, the One who defeats even Death itself. Grant us faith to believe in your power and love, and to live our days in courageous love. In your strong name we pray. AMEN.

Thursday

Ps 120

1 In my distress I cry to the Lord,
  that he may answer me:
2 "Deliver me, O Lord,
  from lying lips,
  from a deceitful tongue."
3 What shall be given to you?
  And what more shall be done to you,
  you deceitful tongue?
4 A warrior's sharp arrows,
  with glowing coals of the broom tree!
5 Woe is me, that I am an alien in Meshech,
  that I must live among the tents of Kedar.
6 Too long have I had my dwelling
  among those who hate peace.
7 I am for peace;
  but when I speak,
  they are for war.

The prayer of the psalmist could well be the prayer of us all these days: "Deliver me, O Lord, from lying lips, from a deceitful tongue." I saw recently that added to the scourges of humanity (e.g., hunger, disease, war, poverty) is *disinformation.* Disinformation is distinguished from misinformation by the fact that disinformation is false information that is distributed with *the intention* of deceiving others, while misinformation is simply false or inaccurate information. As we know, the internet, with all of its benefits, has proven to be a Pandora's Box from which disinformation is constantly flowing in overwhelming volume. These lies, some spread by single individuals and some spread by whole networks of people seeking wealth and power, confuse and weaken us, causing us to be pitted one against another. More than ever, we need discerning hearts and minds these days to hear the truth and recognize it when we see it. The Church, as the mouthpiece of God, is more essential than ever as we seek to be a people who "speak the truth in love" and follow in the way of Christ. The Living Word, even Jesus our Lord, is more precious than ever.

Prayer

Deliver us from lying lips, O Lord, and from those who practice deceit. Thwart the ways of the wicked, and bring to nothing the plans of those who seek only to kill and destroy. Grant that your Church might be a place where truth is told, where compassion is practiced, and where all God's people are honored and loved. In the Name of Christ we pray. AMEN.

Friday

Ezra 1:1–4

> In the first year of King Cyrus of Persia, in order that the word of the Lord by the mouth of Jeremiah might be accomplished, the Lord stirred up the spirit of King Cyrus of Persia so that he sent a herald throughout all his kingdom, and also in a written edict declared:
>
> [2] "Thus says King Cyrus of Persia: The Lord, the God of heaven, has given me all the kingdoms of the earth, and he has charged me to build him a house at Jerusalem in Judah. [3] Any of those among you who are of his people—may their God be with them!—are now permitted to go up to Jerusalem in Judah, and

> rebuild the house of the LORD, the God of Israel—he is the God who is in Jerusalem; [4] and let all survivors, in whatever place they reside, be assisted by the people of their place with silver and gold, with goods and with animals, besides freewill offerings for the house of God in Jerusalem."

What a day this must have been when it was announced to the people of Israel that they were free to go home to rebuild Jerusalem. It was undoubtedly Emancipation Day in every sense of the word. What is interesting is how the priest, Ezra, tells us of this event. He says that "the Lord stirred up the spirit of King Cyrus," and God did this "in order that the word of the Lord by the mouth of Jeremiah might be accomplished." In other words, even though powerful King Cyrus might have thought *he* was deciding all of these things on his own, it was *God's* decision to stir up Cyrus. This was done so that the Scripture might be fulfilled, not so that Cyrus could accomplish some great project. I don't know about you, but I like the idea that God could be at work in just about anyone and anything. We might look at a certain person and think, "God could certainly never use him or her!" Or we might observe the chaos in our Congress and say, "God could never be at work there!" Ezra reminds us that God can be at work in anyone and in any event. As St. Paul boldly claims, "All things work together for good, for those who love God and are called according to God's purposes."

Prayer

Remind us of your creative power, O God, whenever we despair. Remind us that you can take the most chaotic situation and use it for your glory and for the blessing of the world. Keep us from despair. Help us walk in faith, trusting that you are at work in even the most unexpected people and places. In Jesus' name we pray. AMEN.

The Week after the Transfiguration of our Lord

Monday

Rom 8:1–6

> There is therefore now no condemnation for those who are in
> Christ Jesus. 2 For the law of the Spirit of life in Christ Jesus
> has set you free from the law of sin and of death. 3 For God has
> done what the law, weakened by the flesh, could not do: by send-
> ing his own Son in the likeness of sinful flesh, and to deal with
> sin, he condemned sin in the flesh, 4 so that the just requirement
> of the law might be fulfilled in us, who walk not according to the
> flesh but according to the Spirit. 5 For those who live according
> to the flesh set their minds on the things of the flesh, but those
> who live according to the Spirit set their minds on the things of
> the Spirit. 6 To set the mind on the flesh is death, but to set the
> mind on the Spirit is life and peace.

These opening verses in the eighth chapter of St. Paul's letter to the Romans are perhaps some of the most glorious words in all of Scripture. The announcement is clear: Any who are in Christ are not doomed! Not now. Not ever! What is doomed is "sin in the flesh." Jesus dealt with sin on the Cross and made sure it was condemned for all time. That means that sin has no power over any sinner who is in Christ. Not now. Not ever. When I was in junior high school, there was a boy on my bus who used to bully me. He was considerably bigger than I was, and I would often do anything I could to avoid him. One day on the bus ride home from school he began picking on me, and as we got off the bus we got into a tussle. Down I went onto the concrete curb, giving me a nice gash in my scalp. My head was soon a mat of hair and blood. Funny thing was, from that day on, he never picked on me again. Christ's blood was a lot more than that. His blood stopped sin forever. Sin will never again have power over us.

Prayer

Dearest Jesus, Savior of the World, we do not fully understand how your blood condemned the sin within us, but we thank and praise you that it did. We often feel so helpless in the face of our sins. We seem to be powerless to resist them. We try to avoid them, but we cannot. Forgive us, Lord. Deliver us from the power of sin. Help us to set our minds on you and the things of the Spirit that bring us life. In your holy name we pray. AMEN.

Tuesday

1 John 2:7–11, 15–17

> 7 Beloved, I am writing you no new commandment, but an old
> commandment that you have had from the beginning; the old
> commandment is the word that you have heard. 8 Yet I am writ-
> ing you a new commandment that is true in him and in you,
> because the darkness is passing away and the true light is al-
> ready shining. 9 Whoever says, "I am in the light," while hating
> a brother or sister, is still in the darkness. 10 Whoever loves a
> brother or sister lives in the light, and in such a person there is
> no cause for stumbling. 11 But whoever hates another believer is
> in the darkness, walks in the darkness, and does not know the
> way to go, because the darkness has brought on blindness.
>
> 15 Do not love the world or the things in the world. The love
> of the Father is not in those who love the world; 16 for all that
> is in the world—the desire of the flesh, the desire of the eyes,
> the pride in riches—comes not from the Father but from the
> world. 17 And the world and its desire are passing away, but those
> who do the will of God live forever.

Many years ago now, a friend of mine from Bible study came up with an unforgettable way of remembering verse 16 in this passage. He thought of it this way: the desire of the flesh is the desire to *indulge*; the desire of the eyes is the desire to *possess*; and the pride in riches is the desire to *impress*. As I have thought about it over the years, this continues to make sense to me. The way of the world, which St. John says is passing away, is all about indulging, possessing, and impressing. There are many things that we are tempted to indulge in: food, drink, sex, foolish talk. There are also constant temptations to try to possess more and more of everything: a fatter bank account, a bigger house, fancier clothes, more extravagant toys. And the temptation to impress is constant, with voices everywhere encouraging us to inflate our own egos even at the expense of everyone else's. While giving in to these temptations can feel good for a moment, we always end up poorer and sadder when all is said and done. Why? Because the world and its temptations pass away, "but those who do the will of God live forever."

Prayer

Gracious God, save us from temptations. We are so easily seduced by all that makes us feel good for a moment, but finally leaves us empty. Fill us with your Spirit so that real life, life to the full, the kind of life that does not pass away, will be ours. In your holy name we pray. AMEN.

Wednesday

Gen 33:1–11

> 1 Now Jacob looked up and saw Esau coming, and four hundred
> men with him. So he divided the children among Leah and Ra-
> chel and the two maids. 2 He put the maids with their children
> in front, then Leah with her children, and Rachel and Joseph
> last of all. 3 He himself went on ahead of them, bowing himself
> to the ground seven times, until he came near his brother. 4 But
> Esau ran to meet him, and embraced him, and fell on his neck
> and kissed him, and they wept. 5 When Esau looked up and saw
> the women and children, he said, "Who are these with you?"
> Jacob said, "The children whom God has graciously given your
> servant." 6 Then the maids drew near, they and their children,
> and bowed down; 7 Leah likewise and her children drew near
> and bowed down; and finally Joseph and Rachel drew near, and
> they bowed down. 8 Esau said, "What do you mean by all this
> company that I met?" Jacob answered, "To find favor with my
> lord." 9 But Esau said, "I have enough, my brother; keep what
> you have for yourself." 10 Jacob said, "No, please; if I find favor

> with you, then accept my present from my hand; for truly to see your face is like seeing the face of God—since you have received me with such favor. [11] Please accept my gift that is brought to you, because God has dealt graciously with me, and because I have everything I want." So he urged him, and he took it.

The story of the two brothers, Jacob and Esau, is a long and conflicted one. Their conflict begins when they are boys, and lingers long into their adulthood. Finally, after each man has acquired much wealth and a large family, they meet at the river Jabbok. Jacob is clearly fearful that his brother, Esau, is yet holding a grudge against him. He comes to this meeting bowing on the ground, referring to himself before Esau as "your servant." Esau, for his part, has no interest in revenge or continued estrangement. On the contrary, he longs for reconciliation. Jacob, well aware of his own sins toward his brother, is overcome with emotion at this graciousness. He says, "Truly to see your face is like seeing the face of God—since you have received me with such favor." This story reminds us, though we often forget it, that reconciliation is always like this; it is sweet beyond words. When we find our way to reconciliation with someone we have wronged, or with someone who has wronged us, it is always a win-win situation. Everyone is blessed, for as the psalmist says, "Though weeping may continue for the night, joy comes in the morning."

Prayer

Gracious and Loving God, your reconciliation with us through Christ is sweet indeed. Our separation from you is over, our sins are forgiven, and we are able to start again. Give us courage to seek reconciliation with all from whom we are estranged, whether by our hand or theirs. As we have been forgiven, so let us forgive. In your precious name we pray. AMEN.

Thursday

1 Sam 24:1–10

> When Saul returned from following the Philistines, he was told,
> "David is in the wilderness of En-gedi." [2] Then Saul took three
> thousand chosen men out of all Israel, and went to look for
> David and his men in the direction of the Rocks of the Wild

> Goats. [3] He came to the sheepfolds beside the road, where there
> was a cave; and Saul went in to relieve himself. Now David and
> his men were sitting in the innermost parts of the cave. [4] The men
> of David said to him, "Here is the day of which the LORD said to
> you, 'I will give your enemy into your hand, and you shall do to
> him as it seems good to you.'" Then David went and stealthily
> cut off a corner of Saul's cloak. [5] Afterward David was stricken
> to the heart because he had cut off a corner of Saul's cloak. [6] He
> said to his men, "The LORD forbid that I should do this thing
> to my lord, the LORD's anointed, to raise my hand against him;
> for he is the LORD's anointed." [7] So David scolded his men se-
> verely and did not permit them to attack Saul. Then Saul got
> up and left the cave, and went on his way.[8] Afterwards David
> also rose up and went out of the cave and called after Saul, "My
> lord the king!" When Saul looked behind him, David bowed
> with his face to the ground, and did obeisance. [9] David said to
> Saul, "Why do you listen to the words of those who say, 'David
> seeks to do you harm'? [10] This very day your eyes have seen how
> the LORD gave you into my hand in the cave; and some urged
> me to kill you, but I spared you. I said, 'I will not raise my hand
> against my lord; for he is the LORD's anointed.'

This story from Israel's history is taken from that period when King Saul was furiously hunting for David, who had been anointed as the next king of Israel. Saul, intensely jealous of David, was bent on killing him, and searched for him furiously. David, however, did not respond in kind. In this passage, David's own men urge him to kill Saul when he can, but he refuses, even feeling remorse at the humiliation he has caused Saul. He knows that he had been anointed king of Israel, but he refuses to disobey God's law, "You shall not kill," in order to claim the promised throne. David is an example for us whenever we are tempted to take matters into our own hands when it comes to our own promotion. Perhaps we have been told we will receive a promotion at work, or an honor at school, or some distinction in the community. While it may be tempting to "enhance" the timing of this good fortune through wrongdoing and unfair play, this story shows this is not the way of God. As the psalmist reminds us, "Not from the east or from the west and not from the wilderness comes lifting up; but it is God who executes judgment, putting down one and lifting up another" (Ps 75).

Prayer

Give us faith and patience, Almighty God, to await your blessing. In whatever state we find ourselves, help us to be faithful and humble. Keep us from temptations to put down others or cause their failure. Instead, lead us to support all those in authority and to trust that in our own time, you will bless us. In the name of Jesus, we pray. AMEN.

Friday

Luke 17:1–4

> Jesus said to his disciples, "Occasions for stumbling are bound
> to come, but woe to anyone by whom they come! 2 It would
> be better for you if a millstone were hung around your neck
> and you were thrown into the sea than for you to cause one of
> these little ones to stumble. 3 Be on your guard! If another dis-
> ciple sins, you must rebuke the offender, and if there is repen-
> tance, you must forgive. 4 And if the same person sins against
> you seven times a day, and turns back to you seven times and
> says, 'I repent,' you must forgive."

Ash Wednesday, which we observed this week, begins the season of Lent, a season of repentance. In Lent we are particularly mindful of the suffering and death of Christ, and how Christ's sacrifice leads to our forgiveness. In this brief passage, we are reminded that Christ's willingness to forgive is also meant to be an example for us. Here, Jesus says, "If a person sins against you seven times a day, and turns back to you seven times and says, 'I repent,' you must forgive." In effect, what Jesus is saying is "Your forgiveness must have no limits." This is hard for us to believe. "Certainly, there must be limits!" we insist. "Certainly, if a person just keeps sinning against me, over and over, there comes a point when I must refuse to reconcile!" "No," says Jesus. "No, there is no limit, because there was no limit when I forgave you." Lest we misunderstand this passage to encourage abuse of women or children or employees or any without power, we must understand that forgiveness can be given even while we refuse to allow those who sin against us to continue. The two are not incompatible. More than once have I seen an abused spouse end the relationship by saying to their abuser, "I forgive you, but I will no longer allow you to hurt me." Yes, this is difficult, and yet, as always, forgiveness is the way of life.

Prayer

Lord of all life, grant us faith and courage in the face of those who sin against us. Fill us with your Spirit so that we might forgive as we have been forgiven, and yet live as you would have us live. Protect all who are victims of abuse. Bring all abusers to repentance. Grant your grace and pardon to all. In the Name of Christ, we pray. AMEN

The First Week in Lent

Monday

Exod 5:15–23

> 15 Then the Israelite supervisors came to Pharaoh and cried, "Why
> do you treat your servants like this? 16 No straw is given to your
> servants, yet they say to us, 'Make bricks!' Look how your ser-
> vants are beaten! You are unjust to your own people." 17 He said,
> "You are lazy, lazy; that is why you say, 'Let us go and sacrifice to
> the LORD.' 18 Go now, and work; for no straw shall be given you,
> but you shall still deliver the same number of bricks." 19 The Is-
> raelite supervisors saw that they were in trouble when they were
> told, "You shall not lessen your daily number of bricks." 20 As
> they left Pharaoh, they came upon Moses and Aaron who were
> waiting to meet them. 21 They said to them, "The LORD look
> upon you and judge! You have brought us into bad odor with
> Pharaoh and his officials, and have put a sword in their hand
> to kill us." 22 Then Moses turned again to the LORD and said,
> "O LORD, why have you mistreated this people? Why did you
> ever send me? 23 Since I first came to Pharaoh to speak in your
> name, he has mistreated this people, and you have done nothing
> at all to deliver your people."

This passage is part of the account of the slavery of the Israelites in Egypt during the time of Moses. If you know the story, you know Moses arrived very late in this story, after the Israelites had been in slavery for many years. His call from God was to announce to Pharoah that the Israelites needed to be freed. Predictably, this fell on deaf ears. What happened, as we read in today's passage, is that Pharoah responded to Moses' request by pushing the Israelites even harder. The Israelites responded with anger toward Moses, for the one they thought would be their champion was now the one responsible for making their life even harder. Finally, Moses turned his frustration toward God, complaining that it was a mistake for him to ever have entered into this situation, thinking he could make a difference. This story reminds us of what often happens when we begin the process of confronting a system that mistreats or harms vulnerable people. The ones responsible often do not take kindly to our overtures, and may even visit their annoyance at our suggestions with increased harm. This is bound to be discouraging if we feel God is calling us to stand up for these people. We might even complain to God, as Moses did. But remember the end of this story: God's people were eventually freed from slavery. It was not an easy road, but freedom came.

Prayer

Almighty God, your call sometimes includes the work of confronting evil in our midst. We know this is so, and yet we often are reluctant to heed this call. Even when we do, we are easily discouraged. Grant us courage. Grant us wisdom. Use us to bring your kingdom on earth, we pray. In Christ's Name. AMEN.

Tuesday

John 12:23–28

> 23 Jesus answered them, "The hour has come for the Son of
> Man to be glorified. 24 Very truly, I tell you, unless a grain of
> wheat falls into the earth and dies, it remains just a single
> grain; but if it dies, it bears much fruit. 25 Those who love their
> life lose it, and those who hate their life in this world will keep
> it for eternal life. 26 Whoever serves me must follow me, and
> where I am, there will my servant be also. Whoever serves me,
> the Father will honor.
>
> 27 "Now my soul is troubled. And what should I say—'Father,
> save me from this hour'? No, it is for this reason that I have
> come to this hour. 28 Father, glorify your name." Then a voice
> came from heaven, "I have glorified it, and I will glorify it again."

In the book of John, Jesus regularly refers to his dying as the place where he will be glorified. This is hard for us to wrap our heads around because we associate glory with triumph, strength, and victory, not with defeat and dying. Jesus helps us understand what this looks like by giving us the image of a grain of wheat. If you have ever planted a garden, you know how this works. The first thing that must happen for new life to come is that a seed must be buried in the soil and give up its own life. A seed that remains only a seed, never buried in the soil and never planted, remains for all practical purposes, useless. But when it is buried and it loses its own life, life springs forth. A stalk appears. Buds appear. Fruit is borne. This is how it is with Jesus. His death and burial begin the process of new life for the world. His death begins the process of his glorification. His death begins the process whereby we also die to ourselves and are born again in Him. As we live in Christ and Christ lives in us, more and more we die to our own egos and agendas, and more and more we are drawn into the life of Christ. This, then, leads to fruit borne in us—fruits of the Spirit: love, joy, peace, patience, kindness, goodness, faithfulness, gentleness, and self-control. This is the glory Christ bears in us.

Prayer

How can we thank you, Lord Christ, for your willingness to go to the Cross for us? Your love for us is beyond anything we can imagine. Grant us faith to follow you, to lose our lives for your sake, so that we might bear the fruit that brings you glory. In your holy name, we pray. AMEN.

Wednesday

1 John 2:1–6

My little children, I am writing these things to you so that you
may not sin. But if anyone does sin, we have an advocate with
the Father, Jesus Christ the righteous; [2] and he is the atoning
sacrifice for our sins, and not for ours only but also for the sins
of the whole world.

[3] Now by this we may be sure that we know him, if we obey his
commandments. [4] Whoever says, "I have come to know him,"
but does not obey his commandments, is a liar, and in such a
person the truth does not exist; [5] but whoever obeys his word,
truly in this person the love of God has reached perfection. By
this we may be sure that we are in him: [6] whoever says, "I abide
in him," ought to walk just as he walked.

It is a simple concept: if we say that we are followers of Jesus, we should resemble Jesus. This is not to say that we can be perfect as Jesus was, only that those things that characterized Jesus should at least be recognizable in us. Sadly, in recent years it has become the practice of some to claim the name "Christian" and yet be willing to inflict violence on others. Indeed, pollsters have discovered that many people in our country who claim the title "evangelical" only understand that as a political affiliation, not a religious identity. We in the Evangelical Lutheran Church understand that the word "evangelical" means "good news," and so those who call themselves by that name, as we do, must be those who bear good news to others. It is not simply a political category. It is an identity. And what does it mean to bear good news to others? St. John tells us: to act and speak in the way that Jesus would—with compassion, wisdom, patience, and humility. How desperately the world needs evangelicals to bear good news!

Prayer

Forgive us, Lord, whenever we have claimed to be your disciples and then lived as those who do not know you. We are heartily sorry for the times in which we have done this. Forgive us and grant us a new start, a new way forward, following in your way. In your holy name we pray. AMEN.

Thursday

Ps 17:8–13

8 Guard me as the apple of the eye;
hide me in the shadow of your wings,
9 from the wicked who despoil me,
my deadly enemies who surround me.
10 They close their hearts to pity;
with their mouths they speak arrogantly.
11 They track me down; now they surround me;
they set their eyes to cast me to the ground.
12 They are like a lion eager to tear,
like a young lion lurking in ambush.
13 Rise up, O Lord, confront them, overthrow them!
By your sword deliver my life from the wicked.

In this psalm, we hear the psalmist asking God to regard him as "the apple of the eye." Perhaps you have heard this term before. This phrase comes from the notion that if you look closely into someone's eye you can see your own reflection there. This then translates into a metaphor for one whose favor we enjoy. The psalm goes on to ask for deliverance from enemies who regard him without pity, enemies too great for him. There are times in all of our lives when we might pray such a prayer. Perhaps we literally are surrounded by those who wish us ill. Or perhaps our circumstances have become so difficult that it seems like the world is closing in on us. It is during times like this that we are encouraged to call out to God for deliverance. When we do, we can trust that God hears us and will respond. We are God's children. Our God is never more than a prayer away.

Prayer

Thank you for being our deliverer, O God. Thank you for protecting and guarding us when we are beset by enemies within or without,. Grant us relief in times of trouble. Give us faith that you stand with us. Bless us with your presence, we pray. In the name of Christ. AMEN.

Friday

Luke 21:29–36

> 29 Then he told them a parable: "Look at the fig tree and all the
> trees; 30 as soon as they sprout leaves you can see for yourselves
> and know that summer is already near. 31 So also, when you see
> these things taking place, you know that the kingdom of God is
> near. 32 Truly I tell you, this generation will not pass away until
> all things have taken place. 33 Heaven and earth will pass away,
> but my words will not pass away.
>
> 34 "Be on guard so that your hearts are not weighed down
> with dissipation and drunkenness and the worries of this life,
> and that day does not catch you unexpectedly, 35 like a trap.
> For it will come upon all who live on the face of the whole
> earth. 36 Be alert at all times, praying that you may have the
> strength to escape all these things that will take place, and to
> stand before the Son of Man."

Just the other day, I noticed that there are buds on the young maple tree in our front yard. We typically adorn this tree with white lights for Christmas, and now that the snowbanks have somewhat melted, I was able to work on taking them down. Even though I was still wearing my winter coat, hat, and gloves, there was no mistaking the fact that buds had already formed. Spring is on its way. Jesus reminds us that his coming is like this. Someday, he will return to claim his place as Creator, Redeemer, and Sanctifier of the whole earth. It will be a day when life in all of its fullness is restored. He also tells us that signs of this day are all around us. Whenever acts of love, compassion and faith break through, those are like buds on the tree, reminding us of Christ's imminent return. Whenever the powers of evil and disorder are defeated, those are like buds on the tree as well, reminding us again of the emerging way of Christ. So we look for signs of spring in the world around us, in our own lives, and in the people of God, rejoicing whenever we find them.

Prayer

Thank you, Creating God, for signs of spring and signs of life amongst us. Thank you for the warm sun of your love, shining down on us every day. Thank you for people of faith who give us hope and encouragement. Grant your whole creation new life and wholeness as we await your coming. In the Name of Christ we pray. AMEN.

The Second Week in Lent

Monday

Ps 27:1–3

1 The LORD is my light and my salvation;
    whom shall I fear?
The LORD is the stronghold of my life;
    of whom shall I be afraid?
2 When evildoers assail me
    to devour my flesh—
my adversaries and foes—
    they shall stumble and fall.
3 Though an army encamp against me,
    my heart shall not fear;
though war rise up against me,
    yet I will be confident.

In reading this psalm, all I can think about is the people of Ukraine, under attack from the massive forces of Putin's Russian army. An army is literally encamped against them, war rising up all around them. Are they able at this time to pray this prayer? I don't know. It sounds like something a bold commander could say in order to instill courage in the hearts of the troops. One thing is clear, the psalmist's confidence is not in the self, but in God. *The Lord* is my light and my salvation. *The Lord* is the stronghold of my life. And the last line translated as "I will be confident' is more precisely translated, "I am trusting [*God*]". Yes, the confidence of this one under siege is in the Lord. We ought to pray fervently these days for our Ukrainian siblings in the human family across the globe, in Kjiv, Odessa, and elsewhere. We ought to also be reminded by these bold words that *our* trust, *our* stronghold, *our* light and salvation is the Lord. The Lord is the one who can prevail over enemies. The Lord is the one who can bring peace.

Prayer

Gracious and almighty God, bring peace to our troubled world. Give a will to make peace to those privileged enough to have a place at the table. Give protection and strength to all those who are under attack. Give healing and help to the injured, comfort to the grieving, peace to the dying, and faith in your eternal love to all who call out to you. In Christ's name, we pray. AMEN.

Tuesday

Gen 13:2–9

> 2 Now Abram was very rich in livestock, in silver, and in
> gold. 3 He journeyed on by stages from the Negeb as far as
> Bethel, to the place where his tent had been at the beginning,
> between Bethel and Ai, 4 to the place where he had made
> an altar at the first; and there Abram called on the name of
> the LORD. 5 Now Lot, who went with Abram, also had flocks
> and herds and tents, 6 so that the land could not support both
> of them living together; for their possessions were so great that
> they could not live together, 7 and there was strife between the
> herders of Abram's livestock and the herders of Lot's livestock.
> At that time the Canaanites and the Perizzites lived in the land.
> 8 Then Abram said to Lot, "Let there be no strife between you
> and me, and between your herders and my herders; for we are
> kindred. 9 Is not the whole land before you? Separate yourself
> from me. If you take the left hand, then I will go to the right; or
> if you take the right hand, then I will go to the left."

In this story, Abram is modeling for us what St. Paul will later call "dying to oneself." Abram has a choice: he can either insist on a certain piece of land, or he can let go of his right to have the first choice of the land. He chooses the latter. He lets Lot go first. He trusts that God will provide without him needing to control the situation. This story illustrates a simple solution to much of the strife in the world. It involves one of the interested parties giving up their right to control the situation. Imagine what a difference it would make if we all practiced this. If husbands and wives practiced this, if competitors and colleagues practiced this, if family members practiced this, if neighbors and even *nations* practiced this, why, the world would be a much more peaceful place. Our need to have first dibs, to be at the head of the line, to be in control of the spoils that might come our way, rarely give us the result we crave. How much better to live graciously and humbly with all those we encounter.

Prayer

Forgive us, Lord, for our grasping ways. So often we act as though there won't be enough for us, when the truth is, we already have an abundance. Give us faith to release our grip on all that concerns us and to trust that you will provide. In Christ's name we pray. AMEN.

Wednesday

Phil 3:4b–11

> If anyone else has reason to be confident in the flesh, I have
> more: [5] circumcised on the eighth day, a member of the people
> of Israel, of the tribe of Benjamin, a Hebrew born of Hebrews;
> as to the law, a Pharisee; [6] as to zeal, a persecutor of the church;
> as to righteousness under the law, blameless. [7] Yet whatever
> gains I had, these I have come to regard as loss because of
> Christ. [8] More than that, I regard everything as loss because of
> the surpassing value of knowing Christ Jesus my Lord. For his
> sake I have suffered the loss of all things, and I regard them as
> rubbish, in order that I may gain Christ [9] and be found in him,
> not having a righteousness of my own that comes from the law,
> but one that comes through faith in Christ, the righteousness
> from God based on faith. [10] I want to know Christ and the
> power of his resurrection and the sharing of his sufferings by
> becoming like him in his death, [11] if somehow I may attain the
> resurrection from the dead.

What St. Paul says here is really quite amazing. First, he names all his reasons for having confidence "in the flesh". By that he means confidence in his own status, in his own place in the world. Then he says that all these advantages and privileges are "rubbish" compared to knowing Christ. In other words, he puts them side by side—all his wealth and power, and his identity in Christ—and he says there is no comparison. It's like comparing a bag of gold and a bag of trash. What Paul sees clearly is the eternal nature of our relationship with Christ. Yes, fine things are nice for a time, but they fade. Christ never fades away. Yes, it's nice to be a person of prestige, a celebrity, somebody of note, but as we hear on Ash Wednesday, "You are dust and to dust you shall return." No matter how famous we become, we will still face death. Christ has already died and will never die again, and as we live in Him, we too have eternal life. Our treasure is Christ. It's that simple. If our life reflects this, what we gain is peace.

Prayer

Thank you, Gracious God, for all that you give us in Christ. Christ is the pearl of infinite price. He is the treasure beyond compare. He is the well that never runs dry. Grant us faith to trust in Him, and to live our lives in this abundance. We pray in Christ's marvelous name. AMEN.

Thursday

Exod 33:1–6

> The LORD said to Moses, "Go, leave this place, you and the
> people whom you have brought up out of the land of Egypt,
> and go to the land of which I swore to Abraham, Isaac, and
> Jacob, saying, 'To your descendants I will give it.' 2 I will send
> an angel before you, and I will drive out the Canaanites, the
> Amorites, the Hittites, the Perizzites, the Hivites, and the Je-
> busites. 3 Go up to a land flowing with milk and honey; but I
> will not go up among you, or I would consume you on the way,
> for you are a stiff-necked people." 4 When the people heard
> these harsh words, they mourned, and no one put on orna-
> ments. 5 For the LORD had said to Moses, "Say to the Israelites,
> 'You are a stiff-necked people; if for a single moment I should
> go up among you, I would consume you. So now take off your
> ornaments, and I will decide what to do to you.'" 6 Therefore
> the Israelites stripped themselves of their ornaments, from
> Mount Horeb onward.

What does it mean that the Israelites were "a stiff-necked people?" Perhaps because we Christians have for so long held a stereotype of Jews as those who rejected Jesus as Messiah out of sheer stubbornness, we have often understood this term to mean something like "proud" or "unyielding." While it is true that having such a characteristic can be a regrettable trait, some Jewish scholars have lifted up the fact that being stiff-necked is also an attribute that comes in handy when one is under duress. Indeed, they argue that it was *because* of their stiff necks that God chose the Jews in the first place. If you have ever had what we might call "a strong-willed child," you know what I mean. While that child may be hard to deal with because they have a mind of their own, it is also true that such a child will likely grow into an adult who can resist temptation others cannot. Because they are "stiff-necked," they will not go along with the crowd, they will not be drawn into foolish and thoughtless behavior, and they will not simply be blown along with the winds of the latest trends. So, if you find yourself frustrated with "stiff-necked" people, remember that it is both a gift and a burden to be so, as are all the attributes God gives us.

Prayer

Grant us ears to hear, and wills to obey you, dear Lord. We are, at times, stiff-necked, foolish, and wayward. Thank you also, Lord for the times when our willfulness is a gift, when we stand up to foolishness and evil, and when we refuse to bend to the whims of those who would lead us away from you. In your holy name we pray. AMEN.

Friday

1 Cor 10:1–5, 11–13

> [1] I do not want you to be unaware, brothers and sisters, that
> our ancestors were all under the cloud, and all passed through
> the sea, [2] and all were baptized into Moses in the cloud and in
> the sea, [3] and all ate the same spiritual food, [4] and all drank the
> same spiritual drink. For they drank from the spiritual rock
> that followed them, and the rock was Christ. [5] Nevertheless,
> God was not pleased with most of them, and they were struck
> down in the wilderness.

> [11] These things happened to them to serve as an example, and they were written down to instruct us, on whom the ends of the ages have come. [12] So if you think you are standing, watch out that you do not fall. [13] No testing has overtaken you that is not common to everyone. God is faithful, and he will not let you be tested beyond your strength, but with the testing he will also provide the way out so that you may be able to endure it.

Verse 13 in this passage has been misused over the years. Somehow, this verse has been used to say that God will never give you more than you can handle. That's a fine idea; the only trouble is, it's not true. Lots of times people are given more than they can handle. What about the citizens of Kjiv, Ukraine right now? What about the mothers who were in the Ukranian maternity hospital when it was bombed? What about the young mom diagnosed with cancer or the retired fellow who was just told he has ALS? To say to them that God will never give them more than they can handle is just about the cruelest thing you could say. The testing that this verse is talking about is not just any test; it is the test to despair or to fall into unbelief. The surrounding verses make it clear that what is being tested is one's faith in God, particularly one's faith in God's goodness and mercy. This is the thing St. Paul says will never be tested without having a way to endure it. The fact is, we have all been or will be in places where our faith is tested. At those times, we can be confident that God will provide a way for us to endure it.

Prayer

Gracious God, we praise you for your faithfulness and love. We thank you for your mercy and compassion. We remember your mighty works of love, shown most clearly in the giving of your Son, Jesus, for the sake of the world. Grant us faith in you, come what may. And give grace to any and all who struggle on this day. In the name of Jesus we pray. AMEN.

The Third Week in Lent

Monday

Ps 105:1–6

1 O give thanks to the Lord, call on his name,
make known his deeds among the peoples.
2 Sing to him, sing praises to him;
tell of all his wonderful works.
3 Glory in his holy name;
let the hearts of those who seek the Lord rejoice.
4 Seek the Lord and his strength;
seek his presence continually.
5 Remember the wonderful works he has done,
his miracles, and the judgments he has uttered,
6 O offspring of his servant Abraham,
children of Jacob, his chosen ones.

The Apostle Paul, in his letter to the Philippians, exhorted us to rejoice always, no matter the circumstance. This psalm tells us how we can do that—by remembering "the wonderful works God has done, his miracles, and the judgments he has uttered." These days, it is easy to forget to give thanks and praise to God. What with the war in Ukraine, pandemic fatigue, inflation, and all the other worries, just watching the news is enough to throw a person into depression. Perhaps we need to follow the psalmist's lead and spend some time remembering the wonderful works of God, the miracles of healing and hope we have seen, and the wise words that have encouraged us and kept us afloat these days. On my better days I do something that never ceases to put me in a good mood in the morning: as I am waking up, I lay in the bed for a bit and start naming the people, situations, events, and things I am most thankful for. Sometimes I lay there for quite a while thinking of my wife, my kids, my grandchildren, my church, my health, my colleagues, the opportunities before us, and on and on. I commend that practice to you.

Prayer

We praise and thank you, Gracious God, for all your goodness to us. We have seen your miracles of healing and hope. Thank you. We have been blessed by many people. Thank you. We have been encouraged, guided, and strengthened by your Word and by your Spirit. Thank you. Give us grace each day to live gratefully. In your holy name we pray. AMEN.

Tuesday

Num 14:11–18

> 11 And the LORD said to Moses, "How long will this people de-
> spise me? And how long will they refuse to believe in me, in
> spite of all the signs that I have done among them? 12 I will strike
> them with pestilence and disinherit them, and I will make of
> you a nation greater and mightier than they." 13 But Moses said
> to the LORD, "Then the Egyptians will hear of it, for in your
> might you brought up this people from among them, 14 and they
> will tell the inhabitants of this land. They have heard that you,
> O LORD, are in the midst of this people; for you, O LORD, are
> seen face to face, and your cloud stands over them and you go
> in front of them, in a pillar of cloud by day and in a pillar of
> fire by night. 15 Now if you kill this people all at one time, then
> the nations who have heard about you will say, 16 'It is because
> the LORD was not able to bring this people into the land he
> swore to give them that he has slaughtered them in the wilder-
> ness.' 17 And now, therefore, let the power of the LORD be great in
> the way that you promised when you spoke, saying,
>
> 18 'The LORD is slow to anger,
> and abounding in steadfast love,
> forgiving iniquity and transgression,
> but by no means clearing the guilty,

visiting the iniquity of the parents
upon the children
to the third and the fourth generation.'

This passage is one of the most interesting in all of Scripture. Here we have a picture of a God who is fit to be tied, so much so that God is ready to annihilate all of Israel. Moses is the one who talks God off the edge of the cliff. This is the kind of spirited dialogue with God that is common in the Hebrew tradition, but not so common amongst Christians. Perhaps it is long past time that we Christians follow the lead of our Hebrew siblings and allow ourselves the freedom to have some really frank conversations with God. It's pretty clear that God can take it. So, if you are really mad at God, or really frustrated or sad, or just confused, go ahead and tell God about it. It might just be the very thing that will draw you even nearer to the God who loves you.

Prayer

God of All Life, we know that you are well aware of all our ups and downs. You have said that nothing shall ever separate us from your love. Hear us when we cry out to you, and give us grace to trust you in all our days. In your name we pray. AMEN.

Wednesday

Luke 13:22–30

22 Jesus went through one town and village after another, teach-
ing as he made his way to Jerusalem. 23 Someone asked him,
"Lord, will only a few be saved?" He said to them, 24 "Strive to
enter through the narrow door; for many, I tell you, will try to
enter and will not be able. 25 When once the owner of the house
has got up and shut the door, and you begin to stand outside and
to knock at the door, saying, 'Lord, open to us,' then in reply he
will say to you, 'I do not know where you come from.' 26 Then
you will begin to say, 'We ate and drank with you, and you
taught in our streets.' 27 But he will say, 'I do not know where you
come from; go away from me, all you evildoers!' 28 There will
be weeping and gnashing of teeth when you see Abraham and
Isaac and Jacob and all the prophets in the kingdom of God, and

> you yourselves thrown out. 29 Then people will come from east
> and west, from north and south, and will eat in the kingdom of
> God. 30 Indeed, some are last who will be first, and some are first
> who will be last."

There has been endless speculation down through the ages as to who finally will enter the kingdom of heaven. Some say the group will be surprisingly small (an unsettling thought). Some say it will be vast, beyond imagination (better!). One thing Jesus makes clear here is that there will be some surprises, for "some are last who will be first, and some are first who will be last." In the Gospel of John, Jesus speaks about eternal life as something that starts right now, not just after we die. He says those who know him have life *right now*, and that to know him is to know life, now and into eternity. I like that. This view of things takes our eyes off "the sweet by and by" and puts our focus on the here and now and what we can do to make this world more like the kingdom of God. Recently I heard a rabbi say that the brokenness of the world is an indication that God wants us to be busy fixing it. In other words, we are called to do all we can to bring the kingdom of God to fruition right now. That's a lot better use of our time than worrying about who's in and who's out.

Prayer

Gracious Lord, forgive us for claiming to know your mind or judgement. Forgive us for our tendency to view others as somehow unfit for your kingdom while declaring ourselves undoubtedly fit. Give us humility and an authentic desire to be a blessing to others, this day and every day. In your precious name we pray. AMEN.

Thursday

Dan 3:13–18

> 13 Then Nebuchadnezzar in furious rage commanded that
> Shadrach, Meshach, and Abednego be brought in; so they
> brought those men before the king. 14 Nebuchadnezzar said to
> them, "Is it true, O Shadrach, Meshach, and Abednego, that you
> do not serve my gods and you do not worship the golden statue
> that I have set up? 15 Now if you are ready when you hear the
> sound of the horn, pipe, lyre, trigon, harp, drum, and entire

> musical ensemble to fall down and worship the statue that I have made, well and good. But if you do not worship, you shall immediately be thrown into a furnace of blazing fire, and who is the god that will deliver you out of my hands?"
>
> [16] Shadrach, Meshach, and Abednego answered the king, "O Nebuchadnezzar, we have no need to present a defense to you in this matter. [17] If our God whom we serve is able to deliver us from the furnace of blazing fire and out of your hand, O king, let him deliver us. [18] But if not, be it known to you, O king, that we will not serve your gods and we will not worship the golden statue that you have set up."

If you have never read the third chapter of the book of Daniel, you need to; it's a dramatic story. In the excerpt above, these three heroic Israelites refuse to bow down to the golden image that has been set up for veneration, even though they are faced with death if they do not. What is most remarkable is their testimony. They don't claim that their God will save them. They don't even ask God to save them. They simply say, "We will not serve other gods." Somehow that commandment to have no other gods is deep in their bones and they will not violate it, even if it means their life. This boldness is truly a remarkable thing. I can only understand it as a faith that the Spirit gives to those in such a situation. I don't think you can conjure up such a faith yourself. Could I do such a thing? Not without God's help. I have no illusion that somehow, come "hell or high water," I have a faith that will hold firm. But I do know that God can supply such a faith, should I need it. I am thankful for that.

Prayer

Give us an audacious faith, O God. Give us the ability to stay true to you and your Word even in the hour of tribulation. We are people of a feeble faith, sometimes wandering away from you at the slightest suggestion of difficulty. Come to us and strengthen us, Gracious God. In your precious name we pray. AMEN.

Friday

Rom 2:1–6

> Therefore you have no excuse, whoever you are, when you judge others; for in passing judgment on another you condemn yourself, because you, the judge, are doing the very same things. 2 You say, "We know that God's judgment on those who do such things is in accordance with truth." 3 Do you imagine, whoever you are, that when you judge those who do such things and yet do them yourself, you will escape the judgment of God? 4 Or do you despise the riches of his kindness and forbearance and patience? Do you not realize that God's kindness is meant to lead you to repentance? 5 But by your hard and impenitent heart you are storing up wrath for yourself on the day of wrath, when God's righteous judgment will be revealed. 6 For he will repay according to each one's deeds.

We store up lots of things these days. If you are like me, you have stuff in your garage that you haven't touched since you moved it there. Or you might have an attic or a cubby that has all kinds of treasures you just can't part with. I have an endless assortment of golf hats that I have never worn—I have no idea why I keep them. Someday, maybe I will part with them—or not! One of the things we are advised against storing up is God's wrath. St. Paul says that when we are judgmental of others, the judgment we inflict on others is not credited to those we despise, but it is credited to *our* account. In other words, our wrath comes back to us and is stored in our garage! Yikes! In view of this, it's undoubtedly best to avoid storing up *any* amount of God's wrath. How do we do that? Simply by being gracious, forgiving, and forbearing with others. That's the best way to keep from storing up God's wrath.

Prayer

Forgive us, Gracious Lord, when we judge others. We are so tempted to put others down so we can feel good about ourselves. What foolishness this is. Your mercy is endlessly available to all. Your love is immeasurable. There is no one who is outside your grace. Grant us humble and open hearts always, we pray. In Jesus' name. AMEN.

The Fourth Week in Lent

Monday

Rom 2:12–16

12 All who have sinned apart from the law will also perish apart
from the law, and all who have sinned under the law will be
judged by the law. 13 For it is not the hearers of the law who are
righteous in God's sight, but the doers of the law who will be jus-
tified. 14 When Gentiles, who do not possess the law, do instinc-
tively what the law requires, these, though not having the law,
are a law to themselves. 15 They show that what the law requires
is written on their hearts, to which their own conscience also
bears witness; and their conflicting thoughts will accuse or per-
haps excuse them 16 on the day when, according to my gospel,
God, through Jesus Christ, will judge the secret thoughts of all.

St. Paul, in this passage, is reminding his readers that the ancient people of God (i.e., the Jews) do not have any advantage in God's eyes over people who were not given God's law. As Paul says, everyone, by their actions, shows whether God's law is written on their hearts or not. Martin Luther, in his discussion of the behavior of Christians, famously argued that a person of faith simply cannot help but want to do good things. He said that good works follow faith naturally, like a well-rooted tree bears good fruit. Perhaps by taking the words of both St. Paul and Luther seriously, we are led to be watchful over what is "written on our hearts." What we spend our time reading, watching, and talking about are likely to find their way into our hearts. This in turn will bear fruit in our lives, either for good or for ill.

Prayer

Gracious God, give us attentive hearts and minds. Help us discern what will help us be more faithful, more compassionate, more generous, and more Christlike. Keep us from patterns of life that would lead us away from you, and grant us a generous portion of your spirit. We pray in the name of Christ. AMEN.

Tuesday

Luke 13:18–21

> 18 He said therefore, "What is the kingdom of God like? And
> to what should I compare it? 19 It is like a mustard seed that
> someone took and sowed in the garden; it grew and became a
> tree, and the birds of the air made nests in its branches."
>
> 20 And again he said, "To what should I compare the kingdom of
> God? 21 It is like yeast that a woman took and mixed in with three
> measures of flour until all of it was leavened."

Both of these parables speak of very small things that make a very big difference. They remind me of a saying that has stuck with me: "The moments add up." The person who said this wanted to make the point that life is made up of little encounters, a word here, a word there, a gesture, a look, a small act of kindness or meanness; they all add up and make us what we are. Often, we can remember a small word of affirmation or encouragement from someone we respect that made all the difference. Conversely, we may sometimes remember a word of discouragement or criticism that also influenced our life in a significant way. We have all dreamt of doing something grand or being someone whom people recognize. While such dreams are wonderful, the fact remains that life is still lived one breath, one minute, one hour, one day at a time, and what we do with the moments we have is what will finally matter most. Will we be a tree that bears much fruit? Will we be a glorious loaf of bread whose very aroma makes people smile? If we use the moments God gives us to bless others, the answer is yes!

Prayer

Thank you, Generous God, for using us to bless others. Thank you for giving us the gift of moments in which we can make a difference in someone's life. Help us to use our moments in the best ways possible, always seeking to bear the light of Christ in all we say and do. In your holy name we pray. AMEN.

Wednesday

Num 13:1–3, 25–28

> The LORD said to Moses, [2] "Send men to spy out the land of
> Canaan, which I am giving to the Israelites; from each of their
> ancestral tribes you shall send a man, every one a leader among
> them." [3] So Moses sent them from the wilderness of Paran, ac-
> cording to the command of the LORD, all of them leading men
> among the Israelites.
>
> [25] At the end of forty days they returned from spying out the
> land. [26] And they came to Moses and Aaron and to all the con-
> gregation of the Israelites in the wilderness of Paran, at Kadesh;
> they brought back word to them and to all the congregation,
> and showed them the fruit of the land. [27] And they told him,
> "We came to the land to which you sent us; it flows with milk
> and honey, and this is its fruit. [28] Yet the people who live in the
> land are strong, and the towns are fortified and very large; and
> besides, we saw the descendants of Anak there."

The Israelites had a dilemma. The land that God had promised to give them was very desirable, but, not surprisingly, it was already occupied. Taking it over was not going to be easy. Furthermore, the people of the land appeared to be very large, and the towns were well-fortified. What would they decide to do? One thing that is not highlighted in this account is that God had already promised to give them the land. Presumably, when God did this, God knew the land was already inhabited. Did the people of Israel remember this? This dilemma can be summed up by what St. Paul calls "faith versus sight." When we live by sight, our lives are controlled by fear. We see obstacles everywhere. We see risks in everything. We are frozen in place because the choices before us do not, and probably cannot, offer us any guarantees. When we live by faith, our lives are *not* controlled by fear. We still see obstacles and risks, and understand that success is not guaranteed, yet we hear God's call to action, and we step out, confident that, come what may, God will be with us. Life lived in this way often results in a few bumps and bruises along the way, but the richness of such a life makes all of that seem insignificant. "Sin boldly, but believe all the more boldly still," said Martin Luther. In other words, "Don't be afraid to make a mistake. God is with you."

Prayer

Generous God of All, thank you for calling us to bold living. Thank you for calling us out of our fears and into a life that truly is life. Keep us from being controlled by our fears; push us forward into daring acts of sacrifice and service, confident that wherever you lead us, you will support us all our days. In the Name of Christ we pray. AMEN.

Thursday

2 *Cor 4:16–5:5*

> [16] So we do not lose heart. Even though our outer nature is wast-
> ing away, our inner nature is being renewed day by day. [17] For
> this slight momentary affliction is preparing us for an eternal
> weight of glory beyond all measure, [18] because we look not at
> what can be seen but at what cannot be seen; for what can be
> seen is temporary, but what cannot be seen is eternal.
>
> 5 For we know that if the earthly tent we live in is destroyed,
> we have a building from God, a house not made with hands,
> eternal in the heavens. [2] For in this tent we groan, longing to be
> clothed with our heavenly dwelling— [3] if indeed, when we have
> taken it off we will not be found naked. [4] For while we are still in
> this tent, we groan under our burden, because we wish not to be
> unclothed but to be further clothed, so that what is mortal may
> be swallowed up by life. [5] He who has prepared us for this very
> thing is God, who has given us the Spirit as a guarantee.

I have a friend who has ALS, also known as Lou Gehrig's Disease. Nothing could be more true than to say that his "outer nature is wasting away." His "earthly tent" is being destroyed, and he groans, longing to be clothed in his "heavenly dwelling." What makes his suffering bearable for him and his family is knowing that heaven awaits him. Someday his suffering will end, and he will be embraced fully by Christ in a place where "death will be no more; mourning and crying and pain will be no more, for the first things have passed away" (Rev. 21:4). The fact is, *all* of us are dying. That's what it means to be mortal. And the older we get, the more we notice it. It usually doesn't happen in such dramatic fashion as it does when someone has a condition like ALS, but nonetheless, it is happening. For us mortals, the promise that we, as God's children, have been given the Spirit of God as a guarantee of our inheritance makes all the difference. As children of God, our mortality does not define us; instead, our relationship with God does. We are beloved. We are being remade in God's image through the work of Christ. In all our days, from our first to our last, we belong to God.

Prayer

Ruler of Life and Death, give us faith in you all our days. We know our days are numbered. Knowing that, help us live each day fully, gratefully, in your service. When our last day comes, give us peace, and embrace us in your love. We pray in the name of Jesus. AMEN.

Friday

Luke 15:1–7

> Now all the tax collectors and sinners were coming near to listen to him. [2] And the Pharisees and the scribes were grumbling and saying, "This fellow welcomes sinners and eats with them."
>
> [3] So he told them this parable: [4] "Which one of you, having a hundred sheep and losing one of them, does not leave the ninety-nine in the wilderness and go after the one that is lost until he finds it? [5] When he has found it, he lays it on his shoulders and rejoices. [6] And when he comes home, he calls together his friends and neighbors, saying to them, 'Rejoice with me, for I have found my sheep that was lost.' [7] Just so, I tell you, there will be more joy in heaven over one sinner who repents than over ninety-nine righteous persons who need no repentance.

Pope Francis once said this: "There are two ways of thinking and of having faith: we can fear to lose the saved and we can want to save the lost. We stand at the crossroads of these two ways of thinking." Another way of saying this is to say that we can either be controlled by fear or by love. Clearly, Jesus was advocating for love. In this parable, he was even lifting up God's *extravagant* love that was downright reckless. Leaving behind the ninety-nine to seek one lost sheep? That seems irresponsible. But that's what God did in Christ, and that's what love does. It does not count the cost; it simply responds in love and then rejoices when the lost are found. Maybe our churches should be a little more like hospital emergency rooms, existing mainly to help the ill and injured, and a little less like health clubs for the fit and active. In any case, seeking the lost is definitely the way of Jesus, and that is our call as well.

Prayer

All Compassionate God, give us hearts of compassion. Give us an authentic desire to care for those in need, and to minister to those for whom life is difficult. Forgive us when we turn in on ourselves, only worrying about our own well-being. We are your children; we never need to fear. In the name of Christ, we pray. AMEN.

The Fifth Week in Lent

Monday

Ps 53:1–5

[1] Fools say in their hearts, "There is no God."
They are corrupt, they commit abominable acts;
there is no one who does good.
[2] God looks down from heaven on humankind
to see if there are any who are wise,
who seek after God.
[3] They have all fallen away, they are all alike perverse;
there is no one who does good,
no, not one.
[4] Have they no knowledge, those evildoers,
who eat up my people as they eat bread,
and do not call upon God?
[5] There they shall be in great terror,
in terror such as has not been.
For God will scatter the bones of the ungodly;
they will be put to shame, for God has rejected them.

It is an irony of our present day that the Russian novelist Fyodor Dostoyevsky wrote these words: "If God does not exist, everything is permissible." It is ironic because this seems to be exactly what is going on in the case of Russian President Vladimir Putin, who, with his armies, continues to slaughter civilians and military alike in the war against Ukraine. In Ps 53, the psalmist makes the statement that when a person says, "There is no

God," or its corollary, "I am my own god," all sorts of perverse and horrific acts follow. Now, in the 21st century, we have unfortunately seen the truth of this many times over. The psalmist also calls such a person one "without knowledge," which is certainly a precarious way for a person to live. Finally, this writer predicts that those who inflict terror on others will themselves come to a place of great terror. Perhaps what the psalmist is saying is that finally they will see there *is* a God in the heavens and how we live and treat our fellow human beings matters to this God. May it be so.

Prayer

Come to the aid of your people, O God, and hear the cries of those who suffer from violence and war. Cause the plans of those who would inflict violence on the world to be thwarted at every turn. Bring wisdom and courage to those who negotiate peace, and to all give a strong sign that you are near. We pray this in the strong name of Christ Jesus, our Lord. AMEN.

Tuesday

2 Kgs 4:1–7

> Now the wife of a member of the company of prophets cried to Elisha, "Your servant my husband is dead; and you know that your servant feared the Lord, but a creditor has come to take my two children as slaves." 2 Elisha said to her, "What shall I do for you? Tell me, what do you have in the house?" She answered, "Your servant has nothing in the house, except a jar of oil." 3 He said, "Go outside, borrow vessels from all your neighbors, empty vessels and not just a few. 4 Then go in, and shut the door behind you and your children, and start pouring into all these vessels; when each is full, set it aside." 5 So she left him and shut the door behind her and her children; they kept bringing vessels to her, and she kept pouring. 6 When the vessels were full, she said to her son, "Bring me another vessel." But he said to her, "There are no more." Then the oil stopped flowing. 7 She came and told the man of God, and he said, "Go sell the oil and pay your debts, and you and your children can live on the rest."

There are a number of such miracle stories around the prophet Elisha recorded in the book of 2 Kings. Upon reading them, we are struck by their fantastic nature. They seem to suggest that some sort of magic or supernatural powers have been given to Elisha. We modern folk are likely very skeptical of the factual basis of such stories. But consider for a moment how much of life you truly understand? I would argue that there is little that we actually fully grasp, and that, in fact, mysteries abound even in everyday life. Why is one person born into a family with strength, health, and wisdom, while another is born into a family saddled with weaknesses of body and mind? Why is one nation blessed with abundant soil, water, and agreeable weather, while another knows only drought or flood or wasteland? Why do some come to faith in God and others do not? The questions are endless. I would submit that life is full of mystery, and our best posture is one of humble curiosity, even in the face of events we are certain couldn't have happened. It may just be that God is at work in ways that are well beyond our imagination.

Prayer

Give us humble hearts and minds, O God. Teach us to listen, watch, and ponder, rather than insisting that we have nothing to learn. Give us joy in the mysteries of life, and fill us every day with your Spirit, so that we might have true wisdom and goodness. In the name of Christ, we pray. AMEN.

Wednesday

Luke 9:12–17

12 The day was drawing to a close, and the twelve came to him
and said, "Send the crowd away, so that they may go into the sur-
rounding villages and countryside, to lodge and get provisions;
for we are here in a deserted place." 13 But he said to them, "You
give them something to eat." They said, "We have no more than
five loaves and two fish—unless we are to go and buy food for all
these people." 14 For there were about five thousand men. And
he said to his disciples, "Make them sit down in groups of about
fifty each." 15 They did so and made them all sit down. 16 And
taking the five loaves and the two fish, he looked up to heaven,
and blessed and broke them, and gave them to the disciples to
set before the crowd. 17 And all ate and were filled. What was left
over was gathered up, twelve baskets of broken pieces.

The story of the feeding of the five thousand is one of the few miracles stories of Jesus that is recorded in all four gospels. This makes it abundantly clear that the gospel writers were not shy about telling this story, but, in fact, wanted to be sure this story was remembered. We can decide to take it at face value, attributing the miracle to the divinity of Christ, or we can look beyond that and ask what more this story is teaching us. One of the clear teachings here is that God is an abundant provider. "Do not doubt God's abundant provision!" could well be a central teaching here. This miracle also seems dependent on the action of Christ, as he "blessed and broke" the loaves and fish. Many scholars have pointed out the similarity between these words and St. Paul's words describing Jesus' actions at the Last Supper. Are we being pointed to Christ as the Bread of Life? No matter how you understand it, this story is full of good news.

Prayer

We praise and thank you, God of All Life, for your abundant provision for this earth. Sun, soil, and seed all come together to bring food to all creatures. You are a God of abundance. Grant us faith in your provision all our days, and let us take joy in all that your hand provides. In your holy name we pray. AMEN.

Thursday

Phil 2:19–24

> 19 I hope in the Lord Jesus to send Timothy to you soon, so that
> I may be cheered by news of you. 20 I have no one like him who
> will be genuinely concerned for your welfare. 21 All of them are
> seeking their own interests, not those of Jesus Christ. 22 But
> Timothy's worth you know, how like a son with a father he has
> served with me in the work of the gospel. 23 I hope therefore to
> send him as soon as I see how things go with me; 24 and I trust
> in the Lord that I will also come soon.

Having a faithful friend is a great gift. The Apostle Paul knew this well. He experienced both loyalty and betrayal from those close to him, but it seems that Timothy was the one person who never wavered in his loyalty to Paul. As Paul says here, Timothy is like a son to him. His commendation is interesting: Paul describes him as one who is "genuinely concerned for your welfare" while others seek only "their own interests." One of the newspaper columnists I regularly enjoy reading is a businessman named Harvey Mackay. Mr. Mackay is clearly very successful in business, and he is also very clear that success in business does not come from simply pursuing your own interests. His columns are filled with stories of successful people whose success includes being genuinely concerned for the welfare of others, sometimes to the point of enduring tremendous self-sacrifice. Loyalty, integrity, faithfulness, and perseverance: these are the qualities, according to Mackay, that are consistently found in those who are successful. Perhaps what we have here is St. Paul lifting up his mentee, Timothy, as an example for others to follow, as they try to find good success.

Prayer

Thank you, Gracious God, for people of integrity and faithfulness. Thank you for business people whose aim it is to serve the broader community, even as they endeavor to provide for themselves and their families. Give your Church faithful pastors, leaders, and workers, that your gospel might go forth with vigor. Keep us from foolish and wasteful paths. Bless us with wisdom, we pray. In the name of Christ. AMEN.

Friday

Ps 126

1 When the LORD restored the fortunes of Zion,
we were like those who dream.
2 Then our mouth was filled with laughter,
and our tongue with shouts of joy;
then it was said among the nations,
"The LORD has done great things for them."
3 The LORD has done great things for us,
and we rejoiced.
4 Restore our fortunes, O LORD,
like the watercourses in the Negeb.
5 May those who sow in tears
reap with shouts of joy.

[6] Those who go out weeping,
bearing the seed for sowing,
shall come home with shouts of joy,
carrying their sheaves.

This psalm is both a song of praise and a prayer for deliverance. The psalmist is remembering a time when the hope of God's people had dried up like a watercourse in the time of drought. Perhaps a trickle of hope flowed amongst the people, but even that was certain to eventually disappear. But then, like a mighty thunderstorm, the deliverance of God came forth and the riverbanks were overflowing. The hope of God was restored and those who had sown in tears reaped with shouts of joy. It is a common experience for us all to have "dry times" in our spiritual life. We may feel no closeness with God. Our prayers seem unanswered. The words of Scripture and the beloved hymns that used to bring us joy now seem dull and dry. In those times we might even believe *our faith* has dried up. The psalmist would say otherwise. It might be that *joy* has dried up for a season, but faith has not, for even our complaints to God are evidence that our relationship with God is intact. Do not fear the dry times. The rains will come. God is faithful. Joy will return.

Prayer

Gracious God of All, you bless us with faith and joy. You give us the gift of your people to sustain us, even in times of weariness. Keep us from despair. Gather around us people who will remind us of your faithfulness. Bless us with your presence. In the Name of Jesus we pray. AMEN.

Holy Week Devotions

Monday

Ps 20:1–5

1 The Lord answer you in the day of trouble!
The name of the God of Jacob protect you!
2 May he send you help from the sanctuary,
and give you support from Zion.
3 May he remember all your offerings,
and regard with favor your burnt sacrifices.
4 May he grant you your heart's desire,
and fulfill all your plans.
5 May we shout for joy over your victory,
and in the name of our God set up our banners.
May the Lord fulfill all your petitions.

These verses, scholars tell us, were often spoken by a priest to a king in a worship service before going into battle. We can see here petitions for protection, for help and support, for favor, and finally, for victory. We can also hear in these petitions the hopes of those who would fight alongside the king, and ultimately all those whose lives and homes depended on the success of their king going into battle. One cannot help but think of this prayer as something we might pray for President Zelensky of Ukraine as he and his generals continue to the lead the fight against the Russian invasion that began over six weeks ago. We pray that God's favor would rest upon those who have been unjustly targeted in this war of aggression, and we pray that, ultimately, a just and lasting peace will come.

Prayer

God of the Nations, wars and rumors of war continue to plague our globe. In Ukraine, millions flee, and thousands lie dead because of a war of aggression. Bring aid, healing, and comfort to the refugees world-wide; give strength, resolve, and courage to those who fight; and give wisdom and a desire for peace to all those who negotiate an end to this horror. Help your Church to come to the aid of all in need, and give us courage to stand up to aggression wherever we encounter it. In your holy name, we pray. AMEN.

Tuesday

Heb 10:19–25

> [19] Therefore, my friends, since we have confidence to enter the
> sanctuary by the blood of Jesus, [20] by the new and living way
> that he opened for us through the curtain (that is, through
> his flesh), [21] and since we have a great priest over the house of
> God, [22] let us approach with a true heart in full assurance of
> faith, with our hearts sprinkled clean from an evil conscience
> and our bodies washed with pure water. [23] Let us hold fast to
> the confession of our hope without wavering, for he who has
> promised is faithful. [24] And let us consider how to provoke one
> another to love and good deeds, [25] not neglecting to meet to-
> gether, as is the habit of some, but encouraging one another, and
> all the more as you see the Day approaching.

Growing up, as I did, in a family of eight—three boys, three girls, Mom and Dad—there were more than a few times when I was accused of "provoking" my siblings. Usually this meant teasing them, or needling them, or just being generally annoying. Of course, I pleaded innocent of all charges, but I am sure of one thing: I was never *commended* for my actions. Without exception, provoking my siblings was looked upon as a no-no. In this passage we are actually *exhorted* to provoke our siblings in Christ—not to annoy them, but rather to encourage them to love and good deeds. The original Greek for this word comes from the root for "sharpening." What we are being asked to do here is to "sharpen" one another, to make us all more effective witnesses of the Gospel and more compassionate servants of Christ. Also, we are exhorted to encourage one another to gather regularly for worship, not neglecting this practice, since it is in gathering together that we gain our strength as God's people. It turns out, each one of us is important in "sharpening" one another for God's work through us.

Prayer

Gracious God, thank you for calling us into your community of faith. Thank you for making us your children in baptism. Help us to find our role in this family of God, and use each of us to stir up one another to love and good works, until that day when you call us all to our Heavenly Home. In Christ's name we pray. AMEN.

Wednesday

Judg 9:8–15

8 The trees once went out
to anoint a king over themselves.
So they said to the olive tree,
'Reign over us.'
9 The olive tree answered them,
'Shall I stop producing my rich oil
by which gods and mortals are honored,
and go to sway over the trees?'
10 Then the trees said to the fig tree,
'You come and reign over us.'
11 But the fig tree answered them,
'Shall I stop producing my sweetness
and my delicious fruit,
and go to sway over the trees?'
12 Then the trees said to the vine,
'You come and reign over us.'
13 But the vine said to them,
'Shall I stop producing my wine
that cheers gods and mortals,
and go to sway over the trees?'
14 So all the trees said to the bramble,

'You come and reign over us.'
[15] And the bramble said to the trees,
'If in good faith you are anointing me king over you,
then come and take refuge in my shade;
but if not, let fire come out of the bramble
and devour the cedars of Lebanon.

This simple parable was once told to a group of nobles who had chosen a tyrant as their leader. As the parable makes clear, when trees elect the bramble to be their king, no good will come of it. Indeed, "the cedars of Lebanon" (i.e., the nobles) did pay for their poor choice with their own lives. These days, we regularly hear of the awful price nations and peoples pay for choosing leaders whose only goal is to gather power and wealth to themselves. The most obvious example today is Vladimir Putin, but other autocrats reign elsewhere, and still others wait in the wings. This ancient parable would remind us that leadership that centers on the welfare of the common person is a treasure indeed, and as people of God, we are called to be part of the process for electing such leaders. It may even be the case that some of us are called to be those leaders.

Prayer

God of All, the history of the world is littered with the wreckage of failed leadership and the suffering that has come because of it. Come to the aid of this world you have made and raise up leaders who will steward its resources well and care for the people entrusted to them. Grant us wisdom in electing leaders and courage to walk in the ways of truth. We ask this through Christ our Lord. AMEN.

Maundy Thursday

1 Cor 11:23–26

[23] For I received from the Lord what I also handed on to you,
that the Lord Jesus on the night when he was betrayed took a
loaf of bread, [24] and when he had given thanks, he broke it and
said, "This is my body that is for you. Do this in remembrance
of me." [25] In the same way he took the cup also, after supper,
saying, "This cup is the new covenant in my blood. Do this, as

> often as you drink it, in remembrance of me." [26] For as often as you eat this bread and drink the cup, you proclaim the Lord's death until he comes.

These words are certainly familiar to anyone who takes Holy Communion regularly. They are often referred to as "the Words of Institution," for Jesus used these words, or something similar to them, to institute his Last Supper with his disciples. In giving First Communion instruction to 5th graders, I would often point to verse 26 in this passage and give them a scenario: Imagine that it was illegal to be a Christian, and you were in the middle of an illegal worship service that included Holy Communion, and the police came in during the communion service. Would your participation in that service be evidence of your faith? First Corinthians 11:26 says it would. When you eat this bread and drink this cup, you *proclaim*—that is to say, you tell the world—that you believe Jesus died for the sins of the world and for yours. Taking the bread and cup is not merely an act of individual piety; it is also an act of public witness. You are saying, "I am a Christian. Christ is my Savior. I am a believer." On Maundy Thursday we take the bread and cup and therein we proclaim our faith.

Prayer

Lord Jesus, Savior of the world, we praise and thank you for your great sacrifice for us all. We stand in awe of the love you showed for the world on the Cross, and the gifts you continue to give us in the bread and cup of Holy Communion. Draw us ever closer to you and make us bold proclaimers of your love. In your precious name we pray. AMEN.

Good Friday

Isa 53:10–12

> [10] Yet it was the will of the LORD to crush him with pain.
> When you make his life an offering for sin,
> he shall see his offspring, and shall prolong his days;
> through him the will of the LORD shall prosper.
> [11] Out of his anguish he shall see light;
> he shall find satisfaction through his knowledge.

The righteous one, my servant, shall make many righteous,
and he shall bear their iniquities.
12 Therefore I will allot him a portion with the great,
and he shall divide the spoil with the strong;
because he poured out himself to death,
and was numbered with the transgressors;
yet he bore the sin of many,
and made intercession for the transgressors.

These ancient words of the prophet Isaiah are often read at Good Friday services. Even though they were written to the Hebrew people centuries before Jesus came on the scene, Christians have, from early on, seen the sacrifice of Christ reflected in these words. What is clear is that the righteous person mentioned here is "pouring himself out" voluntarily. No one is forcing him to do this. This one called the Righteous Servant is willingly numbered with transgressors even though he, himself, is guiltless. He bears the sins "of many" and prays on their behalf. It is this marvelous sacrifice that leads Christians to see Christ here. As Jesus said in the Gospel of John, "For this reason the Father loves me, because I lay down my life in order to take it up again. No one takes it from me, but I lay it down of my own accord. I have power to lay it down, and I have power to take it up again. I have received this command from my Father" (John 10:17-18). We contemplate this great sacrifice at Good Friday worship. We sing of this great love of when we sing, "What Wondrous Love is This." We can only stand in awe of this great sacrifice.

Prayer

Loving Lord, Savior of the World, your great sacrifice and love stand before us and leave us speechless. The Cross on which you died stands as a witness to the sins of the world, and even our own sins. Forgive us, dearest Savior. Grant us true repentance and the will to live lives of faith and love. In your holy name we pray. AMEN.

The First Week of Easter

Monday

Acts 10:34–41

34 Then Peter began to speak to them: "I truly understand that
God shows no partiality, 35 but in every nation anyone who
fears him and does what is right is acceptable to him. 36 You
know the message he sent to the people of Israel, preaching
peace by Jesus Christ—he is Lord of all. 37 That message spread
throughout Judea, beginning in Galilee after the baptism that
John announced: 38 how God anointed Jesus of Nazareth with
the Holy Spirit and with power; how he went about doing good
and healing all who were oppressed by the devil, for God was
with him. 39 We are witnesses to all that he did both in Judea
and in Jerusalem. They put him to death by hanging him on a
tree; 40 but God raised him on the third day and allowed him
to appear, 41 not to all the people but to us who were chosen
by God as witnesses, and who ate and drank with him after he
rose from the dead.

It is striking how matter-of-fact the writer of this account is about Jesus' resurrection. The writer, Luke, seems to be saying that all that is true about Jesus is right before our eyes: he went about doing good, healing, and enjoying God's favor, and then, in a swift turn of events, was crucified, raised, and appeared to many. But when we look at that list of events in Jesus' life, one event—his resurrection—stands out because it's so unusual. We all can conceive of a person doing good, healing (at least in some way), and enjoying God's favor. We also know what dying looks like, even violent and unjust dying. But being raised from the dead? That is something out of the ordinary. St. Paul says that Jesus' resurrection is the first of many and is about *hope*. According to Paul, this is because our connection with Jesus assures us that we too are promised resurrection. Our connection with Adam, the first mortal, connects us with death. Our connection with Jesus connects us with life. And so, whether we live or die, we are connected with the Living Lord.

Prayer

Risen Lord, we praise you this day for the hope that the resurrection of Christ gives us. We praise you for the promise that we who are one with Christ now will be one with Christ always. We ask you to give us faith in this promise and joy in the hope that is ours. We ask this through Christ our Lord. AMEN.

Tuesday

John 20:11–16

> [11] But Mary stood weeping outside the tomb. As she wept, she
> bent over to look into the tomb; [12] and she saw two angels in
> white, sitting where the body of Jesus had been lying, one at the
> head and the other at the feet. [13] They said to her, "Woman, why
> are you weeping?" She said to them, "They have taken away my
> Lord, and I do not know where they have laid him." [14] When
> she had said this, she turned around and saw Jesus standing
> there, but she did not know that it was Jesus. [15] Jesus said to her,
> "Woman, why are you weeping? Whom are you looking for?"
> Supposing him to be the gardener, she said to him, "Sir, if you
> have carried him away, tell me where you have laid him, and I
> will take him away." [16] Jesus said to her, "Mary!" She turned and
> said to him in Hebrew, "Rabbouni!" (which means Teacher).

I can really identify with Mary. We never expect Jesus to show up when we are grieving. We think that because he is the Lord of Life, his place is with the living. And so, when we are awash in our grief, the last person we expect to stand with us is Jesus. And yet he does. And when we experience Jesus' presence in our grief, it makes all the difference. Sometimes that presence comes through the words, gestures, and kind support of members of the body of Christ—the Church. I remember so well the many, many cards I received from church members and friends during my recovery from a serious car accident. It meant the world to me. Sometimes Christ's presence comes to us as we worship or reflect on God's word, when we are struck by the words of a text or a hymn or a liturgy. Sometimes Christ's presence comes to us through the mystery of the Spirit of God that invades our psyche and quiets our spirit, giving us what St. Paul calls, "the peace that passes understanding." However he comes, Jesus *does* come to us in our grief. He calls us by name and assures us we are not alone.

Prayer

Lord Jesus Christ, we thank you for coming to us in our days of weakness, whether those days come to us through illness, injury, or death. Thank you for standing with us as we face our own death and come to terms with what that means for us. Thank you for your power over death. We are yours. Keep us always near you, we pray. In your holy name. AMEN.

Wednesday

Rev 1:12–18

> [12] Then I turned to see whose voice it was that spoke to me, and
> on turning I saw seven golden lampstands, [13] and in the midst
> of the lampstands I saw one like the Son of Man, clothed with
> a long robe and with a golden sash across his chest. [14] His head
> and his hair were white as white wool, white as snow; his eyes
> were like a flame of fire, [15] his feet were like burnished bronze,
> refined as in a furnace, and his voice was like the sound of many
> waters. [16] In his right hand he held seven stars, and from his
> mouth came a sharp, two-edged sword, and his face was like
> the sun shining with full force. [17] When I saw him, I fell at his
> feet as though dead. But he placed his right hand on me, saying,
> "Do not be afraid; I am the first and the last, [18] and the living
> one. I was dead, and see, I am alive forever and ever; and I have
> the keys of Death and of Hades."

This picture of the Christ from the Revelation of St. John is a spectacular one, with Jesus pictured in heavenly form and garb. What strikes me is what he says to John in the vision: "Do not be afraid . . . I have the keys of Death and of Hades." In the Apostles' Creed we confess that Jesus "was crucified, died, and was buried." Then we add, "He descended to the dead." This statement comes from several mysterious passages in the New Testament that indicate Jesus' entry, following his own death, into the place of the dead, where he defeated Death and the Devil for all time. In this passage in Revelation, we have a picture of the result of that trip to the place of the dead: when he left he took with him the keys of Death and Hades! It's almost as if we are to picture the ultimate reversal: Jesus breaking the bonds of prison, jailing the jailors, and taking the keys with him on his way out. If this all sounds a bit fantastical, it is. That's the way of the book of Revelation and its apocalyptic language. Suffice it to say, Christ is alive, and Death is defeated! Alleluia!

Prayer

Praise and glory to you, Lord Christ, on your resurrection and your victory over Death and the Devil. Because of your victory, we can indeed do as you command: we can live without fear. Death has no power over us. We are yours. Grant that each day we might live in the joy and hope of your resurrection. In your glorious name we pray. AMEN.

Thursday

1 Sam 17:41–50

41 The Philistine came on and drew near to David, with his
shield-bearer in front of him. 42 When the Philistine looked
and saw David, he disdained him, for he was only a youth,
ruddy and handsome in appearance. 43 The Philistine said to
David, "Am I a dog, that you come to me with sticks?" And the
Philistine cursed David by his gods. 44 The Philistine said to
David, "Come to me, and I will give your flesh to the birds of
the air and to the wild animals of the field." 45 But David said
to the Philistine, "You come to me with sword and spear and
javelin; but I come to you in the name of the LORD of hosts, the
God of the armies of Israel, whom you have defied. 46 This very
day the LORD will deliver you into my hand, and I will strike
you down and cut off your head; and I will give the dead bodies
of the Philistine army this very day to the birds of the air and
to the wild animals of the earth, so that all the earth may know
that there is a God in Israel, 47 and that all this assembly may
know that the LORD does not save by sword and spear; for the
battle is the LORD's and he will give you into our hand."

48 When the Philistine drew nearer to meet David, David ran
quickly toward the battle line to meet the Philistine. 49 David put
his hand in his bag, took out a stone, slung it, and struck the
Philistine on his forehead; the stone sank into his forehead, and

> he fell face down on the ground. [50] So David prevailed over the Philistine with a sling and a stone, striking down the Philistine and killing him; there was no sword in David's hand.

This well-known account of David's defeat of the Philistine giant, Goliath, has quite a bit of back story; if you haven't read it all, I highly recommend it. The back story highlights the fear this giant warrior caused in the Israelite camp, and the hopelessness that had set in prior to David's arrival. What's also often overlooked is the fact that David does not presume that *he* will defeat Goliath; no, it is *God* who will do this. David says, "This very day *the Lord* will deliver you into my hand . . . so that all the earth may know that there is a God in Israel." *David* did the deed, but *God* is the one who is given credit for the victory. When in our culture we say that a certain battle, like the war raging between Russia and Ukraine today, is a "David and Goliath" event, we usually mean it is the battle between two very unequal foes. This story reminds us that inequality can sometimes be the opposite of what we assume, for David is the one with the advantage, not Goliath. As Martin Luther's famous hymn tells us, "No strength of ours can match his might! We would be lost, rejected. But now a champion comes to fight, whom God himself elected. You ask who this may be? The Lord of hosts is he! Christ Jesus, mighty Lord, God's only Son, adored. *He* holds the field victorious."

Prayer

When we are afraid, Lord God, remind us of your power and love. When we are weak and frail, remind us of your strength. When we are feeling alone and lost, remind us that you are always near. You are our champion. You are the One who will prevail over all our adversaries. Grant us faith in you, dear Lord. In your name we pray. AMEN.

Friday

Ps 150

> [1] Praise the LORD!
> Praise God in his sanctuary;
>   praise him in his mighty firmament!
> [2] Praise him for his mighty deeds;
>   praise him according to his surpassing greatness!

3 Praise him with trumpet sound;
praise him with lute and harp!
4 Praise him with tambourine and dance;
praise him with strings and pipe!
5 Praise him with clanging cymbals;
praise him with loud clashing cymbals!
6 Let everything that breathes praise the LORD!
Praise the LORD!

There is a composer of grand orchestral music, long dead, whose music continues to inspire me. His name is Gustav Mahler. In the late 19th century and early 20th century, he composed some of the most magnificent music conceived of by the human mind. His grandest composition, Symphony No. 8, is known as "Symphony of a Thousand" because of the vast resources needed to perform it: a very large orchestra with strings, woodwinds, brass, percussion, and keyboard; an adult chorus; a children's chorus; and vocal soloists. If you ever hear it, you will, no doubt, be amazed. I think this is what the writer of Ps 150 was trying to convey: utter amazement. The psalmist was pulling out all the stops. He was calling on every instrument available, and every voice in all creation—"everything that breathes"—to join in praising God. Just imagine this: every person, every plant, every critter, every sea creature, every atom of every cell, all praising God together. Now there is a concert I want to hear!

Prayer

We praise you, Almighty and Triune God, for your majesty and power shown in the death and resurrection of Christ. We praise you for your wisdom in creating all that is, and for your Holy Spirit that sustains all life. We praise you chiefly for your Son, Jesus Christ our Lord, who has shown us the way to eternal life. Grant that by your grace we might be found ever praising you. In your victorious name we pray. AMEN.

The Second Week of Easter

Monday

Luke 24:36–43

> 36 While they were talking about this, Jesus himself stood among
> them and said to them, "Peace be with you." 37 They were startled
> and terrified, and thought that they were seeing a ghost. 38 He
> said to them, "Why are you frightened, and why do doubts arise
> in your hearts? 39 Look at my hands and my feet; see that it is I
> myself. Touch me and see; for a ghost does not have flesh and
> bones as you see that I have." 40 And when he had said this, he
> showed them his hands and his feet. 41 While in their joy they
> were disbelieving and still wondering, he said to them, "Have
> you anything here to eat?" 42 They gave him a piece of broiled
> fish, 43 and he took it and ate in their presence.

This post-resurrection appearance of Jesus is striking in two ways. First, Jesus wants to be clear that he, the Crucified One, is now the Resurrected One. These two are one and the same. Second, he wants his disciples to see that he has been *completely* raised, body and spirit, not simply his spirit, or as the Greeks might have said, his soul. This appearance of Jesus is an assurance to us regarding *our* resurrection. First of all, we are assured that the Crucified One has indeed defeated Death and the powers of evil, and has risen. Second, as St. Paul says in his first letter to the Corinthians, we are assured that, like Jesus, we will receive a new spirit and a new body at the resurrection. Paul says that the mortal puts on immortality. Or in some translations we read that the earthly puts on the heavenly. In any case, like Jesus in this story, we are told that all that is of this life is made new in the resurrection. Our resurrection is certain because the resurrection of Christ is certain. Alleluia!

Prayer

We praise you, Lord Christ, for your victory over Death and the Devil. We praise you that your power and love have come together in the resurrection, and because of that, we need no longer fear death. You have claimed us in our baptism. We are now part of the Body of the Resurrected One. We praise your name forever. AMEN.

Tuesday

Ps 122

1 I was glad when they said to me,
"Let us go to the house of the LORD!"
2 Our feet are standing
within your gates, O Jerusalem.
3 Jerusalem—built as a city
that is bound firmly together.
4 To it the tribes go up,
the tribes of the LORD,
as was decreed for Israel,
to give thanks to the name of the LORD.
5 For there the thrones for judgment were set up,
the thrones of the house of David.
6 Pray for the peace of Jerusalem:
"May they prosper who love you.
7 Peace be within your walls,
and security within your towers."
8 For the sake of my relatives and friends
I will say, "Peace be within you."
9 For the sake of the house of the LORD our God,
I will seek your good.

Scholars tell us that the opening verse of this psalm was recited by worshippers as they arrived at the temple in Jerusalem after their pilgrimage there. When, in verse 4, it says that "the tribes go up" it is referring to the tribes of Israel who are ascending the hills as they approach Jerusalem. I remember when I was a kid and we would go to visit my grandparents in Iowa. One of our favorite games was to see who could first spot the town water tower as we neared my grandparents' hometown. "I see it! I see it!" we'd cry as it would come into view. It was the assurance that we were nearing our destination. I imagine that the children who made pilgrimage to Jerusalem with their parents and grandparents had a similar experience as they approached Jerusalem and the Mount of Olives came into view. "I see it! I see it! There it is!" they would cry as they spotted the city coming into view in the distance. It was this same sort of joy that I sensed as people returned to in-person Easter worship this year after a two-year absence. I could just hear them saying in their singing and in their gathering, "I was glad when they said to me, 'Let us go to the house of the Lord!'"

Prayer

How blessed we are, Almighty God, to once again worship together as people of God. We thank you for the blessings of one another: the care and love, concern and support we feel. We thank you also for you eternal presence. You are ever with us, yet we thank you that we can once again gather in your house to hear your Word and sing your praises. All praise and blessing be yours, Almighty God, now and forever. AMEN.

Wednesday

Rev 2:1–8

> "To the angel of the church in Ephesus write: These are the words of him who holds the seven stars in his right hand, who walks among the seven golden lampstands:
>
> 2 "I know your works, your toil and your patient endurance. I
> know that you cannot tolerate evildoers; you have tested those
> who claim to be apostles but are not, and have found them to
> be false. 3 I also know that you are enduring patiently and bear-
> ing up for the sake of my name, and that you have not grown
> weary. 4 But I have this against you, that you have abandoned the
> love you had at first. 5 Remember then from what you have fallen;
> repent, and do the works you did at first. If not, I will come to you
> and remove your lampstand from its place, unless you repent.

In St. John's revelation he is commanded to write to the seven churches in ancient Asia that have been living under persecution. Ephesus is the first of the churches to whom he writes. Notice that he commends them for their patient endurance and their ability to discern true from false apostles. But then he also calls them to repentance for abandoning their first love. By this he seems to mean that they have forgotten that loving Christ and loving one another are finally the true tests of believers. It is not so much what we say or what we think that matters, but how it works itself out in our lives together. St. Paul, in his well-known letter to the Corinthians, said it this way, "If I give away all my possessions, and hand over my body [as a martyr] so that I may boast, but do not have love, I am nothing" (1 Cor 13:3). This word comes to us as well whenever we are tempted to believe that faith and knowledge and wisdom are all that is required of us as Christians. No, it is love that is most important in the end.

Prayer

Blessed and Holy God, forgive us when we act in unloving ways. Forgive us when we forget that following in the way of Jesus means living in the way of love. Grant us a new portion of your spirit so that every day we might go out into the world and love those we encounter, even those who are difficult to love. We ask this in your holy name. AMEN.

Thursday

Isa 5:11–16

11 Ah, you who rise early in the morning
in pursuit of strong drink,
who linger in the evening
to be inflamed by wine,
12 whose feasts consist of lyre and harp,
tambourine and flute and wine,
but who do not regard the deeds of the LORD,
or see the work of his hands!
13 Therefore my people go into exile without knowledge;
their nobles are dying of hunger,
and their multitude is parched with thirst.

14 Therefore Sheol has enlarged its appetite
and opened its mouth beyond measure;
the nobility of Jerusalem and her multitude go down,
her throng and all who exult in her.
15 People are bowed down, everyone is brought low,
and the eyes of the haughty are humbled.
16 But the LORD of hosts is exalted by justice,
and the Holy God shows himself holy by righteousness.

The picture we have here is of the nobility of the land feasting and partying while the regular folks are being hauled off into exile. It is a hideous scene akin to something I once encountered. Some friends and I were on a work trip in Atlantic City, New Jersey, and we decided to go to the casinos one night. As we walked along the sidewalks near the casinos we were struck by the brokenness and neglect that was evident. Right outside a glittering casino were empty lots with abandoned, burned out cars, piles of garbage, and broken glass. Sidewalks were heaving and broken, street lights were in disrepair, walls were filled with graffiti. But once inside the casino, all that disappeared. There, all was laughter and fun, with no notion that just yards away was a world of poverty and suffering. God's people must never allow themselves to be lulled into thinking that sitting in a comfortable pew on Sunday morning and never taking into account the brokenness of the world is fine with God. The prophet's last line says it all: "The Lord of hosts is exalted by justice, and the Holy God shows himself holy by righteousness."

Prayer

Grant us eyes to see the injustice in the world, Holy God, and the courage and resolve to be a force for justice. Forgive us when we have neglected or contributed to the poverty of others. Give us hearts that are sorrowful over those things that make you sorrowful. Use us to bring justice to your people. In your holy name we pray. AMEN.

Friday

Rev 3:14–19

14 “And to the angel of the church in Laodicea write: The words of the Amen, the faithful and true witness, the origin of God’s creation:

15 “I know your works; you are neither cold nor hot. I wish that you were either cold or hot. 16 So, because you are lukewarm, and neither cold nor hot, I am about to spit you out of my mouth. 17 For you say, ‘I am rich, I have prospered, and I need nothing.’ You do not realize that you are wretched, pitiable, poor, blind, and naked. 18 Therefore I counsel you to buy from me gold refined by fire so that you may be rich; and white robes to clothe you and to keep the shame of your nakedness from being seen; and salve to anoint your eyes so that you may see. 19 I reprove and discipline those whom I love. Be earnest, therefore, and repent.

This message from St. John to the congregation in Laodicea is a warning to any of us who are apt to grow “lukewarm” in faith. Lukewarm means complacent, satisfied, unconcerned about the needs of the world around us. It can be easy for us to become this way as we sit in our affluent congregations. St. John reminds us that we have been blessed to be a blessing. We have been given an abundance so that we might share abundantly. We have been given many gifts so that we might share much with others. Abundance need not lead us to feeling guilty; rather, abundance should lead us into a generosity of spirit that is contagious to all we encounter. As St. Paul wrote to Timothy, “As for those who in the present age are rich, command them not to be haughty, or to set their hopes on the uncertainty of riches, but rather on God who richly provides us with everything for our enjoyment. They are to do good, to be rich in good works, generous, ready to share, thus storing up for themselves the treasure of a good foundation for the future, so that they may take hold of the life that really is life.”

Prayer

Thank you, Generous God, for all your blessings. Thank you for showering us with abundance. Forgive us whenever we have failed to share generously with others. Give us open hearts and open hands to be always joyful in sharing what we have. We pray this in Christ’s name. AMEN.

The Third Week of Easter

Monday

Isa 6:1–5

> In the year that King Uzziah died, I saw the Lord sitting on a throne, high and lofty; and the hem of his robe filled the temple. [2] Seraphs were in attendance above him; each had six wings: with two they covered their faces, and with two they covered their feet, and with two they flew. [3] And one called to another and said:
>
> "Holy, holy, holy is the LORD of hosts;
> the whole earth is full of his glory."
>
> [4] The pivots on the thresholds shook at the voices of those who called, and the house filled with smoke. [5] And I said: "Woe is me! I am lost, for I am a man of unclean lips, and I live among a people of unclean lips; yet my eyes have seen the King, the LORD of hosts!"

The prophet Isaiah had it right. In his vision he saw himself in the literal presence of the Most High, and he was *terrified*. Why? Because he knew himself to be "a man of unclean lips" and living among "a people of unclean lips." In other words, he was an unholy person, sitting in the presence of a holy God. We don't often appreciate the difference between us and the Most High. We certainly are aware that God is Other, but when we use language like "children of God" or refer to God as Father or Divine Mother, we can easily be lulled into believing that God isn't so different from us. That's not true. God is holy. Holy means sacred, separate, apart. The Orthodox Church does a good job remembering this. If you have ever been to an Orthodox service, you probably noted how mystical it is, with incense and chanting and all sorts of postures that remind us of God's holiness. I was once asked why we confess our sins at the beginning of worship. In answer, I quoted one of my teachers: "We confess sin when we come into God's presence because God is holy, and we are not." A good reminder.

Prayer

We praise you, O God, for your holiness. We praise you that you are greater than us in every regard—in holiness, in wisdom, in love, and in power. We stand in awe of your glory. Grant us grace to live our lives in holy awe of you, even as we bask in your love, amazed that you call us children of God. In your holy name we pray. AMEN.

Tuesday

Gen 18:1–2, 9–15

> The LORD appeared to Abraham by the oaks of Mamre, as he
> sat at the entrance of his tent in the heat of the day. 2 He looked
> up and saw three men standing near him. When he saw them,
> he ran from the tent entrance to meet them, and bowed down
> to the ground.
>
> 9 They said to him, "Where is your wife Sarah?" And he said,
> "There, in the tent." 10 Then one said, "I will surely return to
> you in due season, and your wife Sarah shall have a son." And
> Sarah was listening at the tent entrance behind him. 11 Now
> Abraham and Sarah were old, advanced in age; it had ceased to
> be with Sarah after the manner of women. 12 So Sarah laughed
> to herself, saying, "After I have grown old, and my husband is
> old, shall I have pleasure?" 13 The LORD said to Abraham, "Why
> did Sarah laugh, and say, 'Shall I indeed bear a child, now that
> I am old?' 14 Is anything too wonderful for the LORD? At the set
> time I will return to you, in due season, and Sarah shall have a
> son." 15 But Sarah denied, saying, "I did not laugh"; for she was
> afraid. He said, "Oh yes, you did laugh."

This is one of the most delightful stories in Scripture. Abraham and Sarah have already been promised offspring and as a result have been re-named: Abram to Abraham, and Sarai to Sarah. This visit by the Lord confirms this promise: Sarah will conceive and bear a child. What is their response? We aren't told what Abraham's response is. I imagine a rolling of the eyes, a dropping of the jaw, a silent chuckle. Sarah's response is recorded: she laughs. She denies it, but we have the video, says the Lord. Laughing at the ridiculous notions of God is certainly something we are all capable of. I remember a couple who went childless for years, though they tried *everything*. Just when they had made all the arrangements for an adoption, and in fact, the baby was soon to be theirs, they found out they were pregnant. Surprise! Now they had two! I don't believe God is ever put off by our laughing at God's plans. After all, as St. Paul says, God "is able to accomplish abundantly far more than all we can ask or imagine." So, the next time you encounter one of God's promises or one of God's miracles, have a good laugh. God will laugh with you.

Prayer

God of All Life, we thank and praise you for your miraculous and mysterious ways. Sometimes you bless us in ways we couldn't have even imagined. Sometimes you provide for us with abundance that is extravagant. Sometimes you heal us from deadly diseases from which none thought we could recover. We praise you for your miracles. Give us faith to trust you ever. In the name of Christ, we pray. AMEN.

Wednesday

Luke 14:12–14

> [12] [Jesus]said also to the one who had invited him, "When you
> give a luncheon or a dinner, do not invite your friends or your
> brothers or your relatives or rich neighbors, in case they may
> invite you in return, and you would be repaid. [13] But when you
> give a banquet, invite the poor, the crippled, the lame, and the
> blind. [14] And you will be blessed, because they cannot repay you,
> for you will be repaid at the resurrection of the righteous."

Lest we misconstrue Jesus' words here, be assured that Jesus is not commanding us to quit partying with our friends and family. Far from it. What Jesus is reminding us of is our call to hospitality, especially for those who might never be invited to or sit down at a fine meal. I remember when my wife and I were brand new to the student housing at seminary. It was summer and the day we moved into our apartment was a hot one. My wife was 6 months pregnant. As we were schlepping the umpteenth box up the stairs to our apartment, a woman who lived on the first floor brought out an ice cold pitcher of fresh lemonade and some cookies. She offered these to us in all our sweatiness. It was an act of genuine welcome and hospitality that we remember to this day. She did not do it so that she could be repaid, or in order to gain some advantage; it was an act of true selflessness. This is what Jesus calls us to: simple words and acts of welcome and generosity to those who are in any need. The world needs this now more than ever.

Prayer

Gracious God, as you have been generous to us, grant that we might be generous with others. As you have looked on our poverty and blessed us, let us look upon the needs of others and be a blessing to them. Use us to bring joy and peace, mercy and compassion, to the world. We are your servants. We are blessed to be a blessing. In your holy name we pray. AMEN.

Thursday

Acts 9:26–31

> 26 When [Saul]had come to Jerusalem, he attempted to join the
> disciples; and they were all afraid of him, for they did not believe
> that he was a disciple. 27 But Barnabas took him, brought him
> to the apostles, and described for them how on the road he had
> seen the Lord, who had spoken to him, and how in Damascus
> he had spoken boldly in the name of Jesus. 28 So he went in and
> out among them in Jerusalem, speaking boldly in the name of
> the Lord. 29 He spoke and argued with the Hellenists; but they
> were attempting to kill him. 30 When the believers learned of it,
> they brought him down to Caesarea and sent him off to Tarsus.
> 31 Meanwhile the church throughout Judea, Galilee, and Samaria
> had peace and was built up. Living in the fear of the Lord and in
> the comfort of the Holy Spirit, it increased in numbers.

This story comes right on the heels of St. Paul's vision of Christ on the road to Damascus and his subsequent conversion and baptism. Prior to this, he was known as Saul. As a faithful Pharisee, Saul was determined to stomp out this new movement that had sprung up in the aftermath of Jesus' resurrection. In fact, he was so zealous to destroy the Jesus movement that he was even inspiring others to murder the followers of Christ. This explains why the disciples in Jerusalem were so reluctant to embrace him when he showed up at their door. They probably thought that this was merely a ploy to draw them out and identify them so he could haul them off to prison, or worse. But Barnabas comes to his aid, telling the believers in Jerusalem that Saul's conversion to the Jesus Way is authentic and they have nothing to fear. Have you ever had someone vouch for you in a tough situation? I have. It's a great gift. That person says, "Don't worry. He's with me. She's with me. I can vouch for them." That's actually what the name Barnabas means. *Bar* is the Hebrew word for son, and *nabas* means encouragement. So Barnabas means "a son of encouragement." And if we substitute the Hebrew word for daughter, *Bat*, we get Batnabas, "a daughter of encouragement." We can all be sons and daughters of encouragement, giving a defense to those who are under attack, and bringing peace to our divided world.

Prayer

Mold us into sons and daughters of encouragement, O God. Give us eyes to see those who need our support. Give us hearts that are open to the needs around us. Give us courage to follow in the way of Jesus, offering love and encouragement, strength and support, to all we encounter. In Jesus' name we pray. AMEN.

Friday

Ezek 1:15–21

15 As I looked at the living creatures, I saw a wheel on the earth
beside the living creatures, one for each of the four of them. 16 As
for the appearance of the wheels and their construction: their
appearance was like the gleaming of beryl; and the four had
the same form, their construction being something like a
wheel within a wheel. 17 When they moved, they moved in any
of the four directions without veering as they moved. 18 Their
rims were tall and awesome, for the rims of all four were full of
eyes all around. 19 When the living creatures moved, the wheels
moved beside them; and when the living creatures rose from
the earth, the wheels rose. 20 Wherever the spirit would go, they

> went, and the wheels rose along with them; for the spirit of the living creatures was in the wheels. [21] When they moved, the others moved; when they stopped, the others stopped; and when they rose from the earth, the wheels rose along with them; for the spirit of the living creatures was in the wheels.

When I was a kid I remember singing the African American spiritual, "Ezekiel saw the Wheel," a song about this mind-blowing vision of Ezekiel. The refrain goes like this: "Ezekiel saw the wheel, way up in the middle of the air. Ezekiel saw the wheel, way in the middle of the air. And the little wheel run by faith, and the big wheel run by the grace of God. A wheel in a wheel, way up in the middle of the air." The song warns against hypocrisy and a lack of attention to the coming Day of the Lord. In the final verse, the singer proclaims, "One of these days about twelve o'clock, way in the middle of the air, this old world's gonna reel and rock, way in the middle of the air." I think the song writers had it right: these fearsome images of God that include living creatures with eyes everywhere and spirits and wheels are given to us to remind us that a day is coming when this old earth will be gone and a new heaven and a new earth will be created by God. The new heaven and earth will be glorious, we are told, but they will be nothing we can imagine—way beyond our imagination, in fact. So, we do well to remember the words of the song writer and live our lives with a due sense of responsibility as we joyfully await the coming Day of the Lord.

Prayer

We are your people, Holy God. You have called us to lives of faith and love. You have also called us to lives of integrity and truth-seeking. Grant that each day we might live with a due sense of responsibility, being true to our calling, and spreading your compassion and love to all we encounter. In Jesus' name we pray. AMEN.

The Fourth Week of Easter

Monday

Luke 5:4–9

> [4] When [Jesus]had finished speaking, he said to Simon, "Put out into the deep water and let down your nets for a catch." [5] Simon answered, "Master, we have worked all night long but have caught nothing. Yet if you say so, I will let down the nets." [6] When they had done this, they caught so many fish that their nets were beginning to break. [7] So they signaled their partners in the other boat to come and help them. And they came and filled both boats, so that they began to sink. [8] But when Simon Peter saw it, he fell down at Jesus' knees, saying, "Go away from me, Lord, for I am a sinful man!" [9] For he and all who were with him were amazed at the catch of fish that they had taken.

The progression of faith in this story is remarkable. Jesus asks Simon to put into the deep water and let down the nets. First, he gives a pretty good reason why that would be pointless, but then, kind of like a child begrudgingly obeying a parent, he says, "If you say so . . . " You can almost see him rolling his eyes and getting ready to say later, "See, I told you there were no fish there." Of course, in spite of this less-than-enthusiastic obedience, the haul of fish is amazing. And what is Simon's response? A definite step up in his faith journey: "Go away from me, Lord, for I am a sinful man!" Notice that his address to Jesus changes from Master to Lord. A master is one who has a following of disciples. A lord is someone who rules, someone who is charge of others, perhaps even in charge of all things. In addition, Simon also recognizes his own unworthiness to be in the presence of this Lord. Perhaps Simon's journey resembles your own. Perhaps you, too, have known Christ as Master, and now you know him as Lord. Perhaps you, too, once described yourself as a disciple of Christ, but now your whole life is in his hands. Or perhaps you are on that journey right now. Blessings to you as you journey on.

Prayer

We thank you, Gracious God, for allowing us the privilege of growing in faith. Grant that each day we might know you more closely, love you more dearly, and walk in your ways more faithfully. In the name of Christ we pray. AMEN.

Tuesday

Rev 5:1–5

> Then I saw in the right hand of the one seated on the throne a
> scroll written on the inside and on the back, sealed with seven
> seals; 2 and I saw a mighty angel proclaiming with a loud voice,
> "Who is worthy to open the scroll and break its seals?" 3 And
> no one in heaven or on earth or under the earth was able to
> open the scroll or to look into it. 4 And I began to weep bitterly
> because no one was found worthy to open the scroll or to look
> into it. 5 Then one of the elders said to me, "Do not weep. See,
> the Lion of the tribe of Judah, the Root of David, has conquered,
> so that he can open the scroll and its seven seals."

In typical book of Revelation imagery, St. John is describing a vision he has had. In this vision he sees a scroll that contains the entire plan and purpose of God for the earth. But when the angel calls out for someone to come forward who can break the seals and make known God's will for all creation, there are none on earth, nor any above or below it, who are up to this task. John begins to weep. Just then, one of the elders who is present in John's vision calls out: "Look, the Lion of Judah. This One is the Conqueror of all our enemies. He can break the seals and open the scroll." The Lion of Judah is Christ, the one whom John calls earlier "The Lamb of God." Here, Christ is seen not as the Lamb of God in a sacrificial role, but as a Lion, a mighty beast whose strength exceeds any other creature's. This is the amazing Christ we have. Jesus is not only truly a man *and* truly divine, but also truly a lamb *and* truly a lion. His humility and majesty co-exist as in no other. Is this all beyond our comprehension? Yes. But we, like St. John, rejoice knowing that the One who breaks unbreakable seals is also the one who has died and been raised for us and our salvation. In him we live.

Prayer

God of Heaven and Earth, your majesty is beyond our understanding and your love deeper than anything we can imagine. Expand our hearts that we might gain a glimpse of your glory, and in so doing, live our lives in praise of you all our days. In your Holy name we pray. AMEN.

Wednesday

Ps 23

1 The LORD is my shepherd, I shall not want.
2 He makes me lie down in green pastures;
he leads me beside still waters;
3 he restores my soul.
He leads me in right paths
for his name's sake.
4 Even though I walk through the darkest valley,
I fear no evil;
for you are with me;
your rod and your staff—
they comfort me.
5 You prepare a table before me
in the presence of my enemies;
you anoint my head with oil;
my cup overflows.
6 Surely goodness and mercy shall follow me
all the days of my life,
and I shall dwell in the house of the LORD
my whole life long.

There are no more beloved verses in Scripture than Ps 23. These words speak to us in so many ways and in so many situations. One of the images

I particularly like is from verse 5, where we hear these words: "You prepare a table before me in the presence of my enemies." In this scene, our enemies watch as God lavishes abundance on us. This is how it has seemed to me sometimes at the funeral of a person of faith. The person has died. Mourning is definitely happening. People are weeping, and the sting of death is very present. Yet, in the midst of this grief come sounds of joy. Songs of faith are sung. Scriptures announcing Christ's victory over death are proclaimed. And through their tears, worshippers confess their faith. As this happens, I can just see the Devil raging, "But this can't be! I have destroyed you! Death has won! You can't possibly be joyful!" And yet it is so. A table of abundant grace has been laid out even in the presence of our Last Enemy, Death. We announce, "Christ is Alive, and our resurrection is sure as well!" What a great scene this is!

Prayer

In this season of resurrection, we praise and thank you, Victorious One, for your victory over death. It is true, we are mortal, and yet we are children of God as well. Through you we are children of the resurrection, assured that because you rose, we shall rise as well. Death is defeated, and we fear it no more. All thanks and praise to you, Lord Christ. AMEN.

Thursday

Ezek 37:1–6

> The hand of the LORD came upon me, and he brought me out by the spirit of the LORD and set me down in the middle of a valley; it was full of bones. 2 He led me all around them; there were very many lying in the valley, and they were very dry. 3 He said to me, "Mortal, can these bones live?" I answered, "O Lord God, you know." 4 Then he said to me, "Prophesy to these bones, and say to them: O dry bones, hear the word of the LORD. 5 Thus says the Lord God to these bones: I will cause breath to enter you, and you shall live. 6 I will lay sinews on you, and will cause flesh to come upon you, and cover you with skin, and put breath in you, and you shall live; and you shall know that I am the LORD."

If you have never read Ezek 37, I urge you to read the whole chapter. It is a wonderful description of God's work in places of desolation. This whole scene hearkens back to Gen 2, where we hear that "the Lord God formed the man from the dust of the ground, and breathed into his nostrils *the breath of life*; and the man became a living being." God's breath, or spirit, is what gives us life. It is what animates us. It is what takes us from being just a pile of skin, flesh, sinews, and bones, and makes us into God's image. I sometimes wish that we Lutherans had more regular spontaneous manifestations of the Spirit, like the Pentecostals do. I sometimes think it would be fun if, on a Sunday morning, people started calling out "Amen. Say it preacher!" I don't know what I'd do if people started speaking in tongues and rolling in the aisles, but I guess we would go with it. In any case, being spirit-filled, no matter how subtly we show it, is definitely one of the gifts of God. God's spirit is what gives us joy in sorrow, love in times of division, and faith in times of confusion. God's spirit gives us life.

Prayer

How we praise you, Lord God, for giving us your Spirit. Just as the Spirit descended upon Jesus at his baptism, so at our baptism, we were given that same spirit, and life was born anew in us. Renew us every day in our baptism, that we might be filled with your spirit and bear witness to the life you give. In Jesus' name we pray. AMEN.

Friday

John 10:31–39

31 The Jews took up stones again to stone him. 32 Jesus replied, "I
have shown you many good works from the Father. For which of
these are you going to stone me?" 33 The Jews answered, "It is not
for a good work that we are going to stone you, but for blasphemy,
because you, though only a human being, are making yourself
God." 34 Jesus answered, "Is it not written in your law, 'I said, you
are gods'? 35 If those to whom the word of God came were called
'gods'—and the scripture cannot be annulled— 36 can you say
that the one whom the Father has sanctified and sent into the
world is blaspheming because I said, 'I am God's Son'? 37 If I am
not doing the works of my Father, then do not believe me. 38 But
if I do them, even though you do not believe me, believe the
works, so that you may know and understand that the Father is

> in me and I am in the Father." [39] Then they tried to arrest him again, but he escaped from their hands.

Jesus made a simple statement: "I have shown you many good works from the Father. For which of these are you going to stone me?" It is really ironic, isn't it, that Jesus is targeted for doing good works. He heals, he exorcises demons, he blesses, he preaches, and for this, he is under attack. Of course his enemies claim they are attacking him for blasphemy, but the truth is, they cannot abide his good works. Jesus' works show their own failures too clearly. They are leaders of the religious community in Israel and have been tasked with doing good works for the people, but for many reasons they have fallen short. It is as Mark Twain once quipped, "There is no such thing so annoying as a good example!" This is a lesson for us as well whenever we do good works and suffer for it. If we stand up for the marginalized, claim justice for the oppressed, and give aid to the so-called undeserving, we might well find ourselves under attack. We should not be surprised. As Rabbi Kushner once said, "Expecting the world to treat you fairly because you are a good person is like expecting the bull not to charge you because you are a vegetarian." So it is.

Prayer

Give us courage, Lord, to do the works we are called to do. Give us resilience in the face of opposition. Give us strength when we falter. Give us faith that you stand with us in our call to bring justice to all. We are your people. Keep us near. In your strong name, we pray. AMEN.

The Fifth Week of Easter

Monday

Ps 148:1–6

1 Praise the LORD!
Praise the LORD from the heavens;
praise him in the heights!
2 Praise him, all his angels;
praise him, all his host!
3 Praise him, sun and moon;
praise him, all you shining stars!
4 Praise him, you highest heavens
and you waters above the heavens!
5 Let them praise the name of the LORD,
for he commanded and they were created.
6 He established them forever and ever;
he fixed their bounds, which cannot be passed

When it comes to praising God, the psalmist has an imagination like no other. Not only does the psalmist call all sentient beings, both on earth and in heaven, to praise God, but the call goes out to the planets, the sun, and the moon and stars as well! What would it look like if the whole cosmos started praising God? Would there be a grand light show, like the Fourth of July, only infinitely better? Would the moons chase each other around and fly out of orbit in ecstasy? Would the sun of our solar system compete with vast suns in other solar systems to see which one could shine brightest? This summer, on a particularly sunny day, maybe it would be good to look up into the sky and feel the sun on your face and think, "This sun is praising God right now. This sun is giving God the glory." Who knows, perhaps that is exactly right.

Prayer

We praise you, Creator of All Things. Your majesty is beyond all understanding, your wisdom is unfathomable, and your beauty is without bounds. Grant us glad and grateful hearts that we, along with all things, might join in declaring your praise, this day and in the all the days you give us. In your holy name we pray. AMEN.

Tuesday

Dan 7:13–14

13 As I watched in the night visions,
I saw one like a human being
coming with the clouds of heaven.
And he came to the Ancient One
and was presented before him.
14 To him was given dominion
and glory and kingship,
that all peoples, nations, and languages
should serve him.
His dominion is an everlasting dominion
that shall not pass away,
and his kingship is one
that shall never be destroyed.

This vision of the prophet Daniel comes right at the end of a series of visions that are noted in Chapter 7. They are typically fantastic, nightmarish visions that disturb Daniel very much. What is clear, however, in this final vision, is that this One who looks like a human being is being given particular honors by God. To this one is given "dominion and glory and kingship," and this dominion shall be eternal. We Christians have for centuries understood this vision to be a vision of Christ. Jesus himself declares his identity as a king, saying to Pilate, "My kingdom is not from this world" (John 18:36). As people of God, this eternal dominion of Christ should give us hope. Since Christ has claimed us as his own in our baptism, and his dominion has no end, we can confidently believe that our future is secure. Even death cannot end Christ's dominion; Christ's resurrection showed that. And as members of the Body of Christ, we too will know resurrection. Christ reigns!

Prayer

Lord Christ, we praise you for your eternal dominion. We praise you for your victory over death and the devil. We praise you for your infinite love that has claimed us and will never let us go. Put your Spirit deep within us, that all our days might be lived in praise of you. In your strong name we pray. AMEN.

Wednesday

1 Sam 20:18–23

> 18 Jonathan said to him, "Tomorrow is the new moon; you will
> be missed because your place will be empty. 19 On the day after
> tomorrow, you shall go a long way down; go to the place where
> you hid yourself earlier, and remain beside the stone there. 20 I
> will shoot three arrows to the side of it, as though I shot at a
> mark. 21 Then I will send the boy, saying, 'Go, find the arrows.' If
> I say to the boy, 'Look, the arrows are on this side of you; collect
> them,' then you are to come, for, as the LORD lives, it is safe for
> you and there is no danger. 22 But if I say to the young man,
> 'Look, the arrows are beyond you,' then go, for the LORD has
> sent you away. 23 As for the matter about which you and I have
> spoken, the LORD be between you and me forever."

The title given to the 20th chapter of 1 Sam is "The Friendship of David and Jonathan." If you have never read this, it is well worth the read. Jonathan is the son of King Saul, the very king who has grown increasingly jealous and obsessed with the upstart, David. King Saul is clearly threatened by David's popularity and sure that David's only aim is to dethrone him and make himself king of Israel. Nothing David can say or do will convince Saul otherwise. Nevertheless, Jonathan and David remain friends, and as you hear in this passage, make a pact that will warn David if his life is in danger. Faithful friendship like this is such a gift. If you have experienced it, you know this to be true. We may have had our differences with these friends, but we have stuck it out. We are going to be lifelong friends, and we know it. Friendship is how Jesus sometimes describes his relationship with us. In John's gospel, Jesus says: "I do not call you servants any longer, because the servant does not know what the master is doing; but I have called you friends, because I have made known to you everything that I have heard from my Father" (John 15:15). What a gift to know that Jesus calls us friends.

Prayer

We are so thankful, Lord Jesus, for your faithful friendship with us. Though we certainly disappoint you and even betray you time and time again, you stand with us. Though we are unsteady and wavering in our friendship with you, you are steadfast in your friendship with us. How can we ever thank you? Strengthen us each day, Lord, that we might be your faithful friend. In your precious name we pray. AMEN.

Thursday

Acts 11:19–26

> Now those who were scattered because of the persecution that
> took place over Stephen traveled as far as Phoenicia, Cyprus, and
> Antioch, and they spoke the word to no one except Jews. [20] But
> among them were some men of Cyprus and Cyrene who, on
> coming to Antioch, spoke to the Hellenists also, proclaiming
> the Lord Jesus. [21] The hand of the Lord was with them, and a
> great number became believers and turned to the Lord. [22] News
> of this came to the ears of the church in Jerusalem, and they
> sent Barnabas to Antioch. [23] When he came and saw the grace
> of God, he rejoiced, and he exhorted them all to remain faithful
> to the Lord with steadfast devotion, [24] for he was a good man,
> full of the Holy Spirit and of faith. And a great many people
> were brought to the Lord. [25] Then Barnabas went to Tarsus to
> look for Saul, [26] and when he had found him he brought him
> to Antioch. So it was that for an entire year they met with the
> church and taught a great many people, and it was in Antioch
> that the disciples were first called "Christians."

It's curious to think that there was a time when Christians were not called Christians. We know from the book of Acts that one of the early titles given to Jesus' followers was "followers of the Way." It seems probable that many names could have arisen, like "disciples of Christ" or "Jesus followers." I remember a friend of mine who did ministry in the jails around Chicago, specifically Cook County Jail, who told me that he never called himself a Christian when he entered the jail. When I asked why, he told me that for many of the inmates the title "Christian" brought with it all sorts of baggage, because many people of ill will had "played the Jesus card" (as he said) and, after gaining the trust of the people, had shown themselves to be abusive and untrustworthy. "What do you call yourself then?" I asked. He said, "A Jesus guy." There continue to be those who use the title "Christian" to manipulate people and gain power. Martin Luther was known to say that the ones who most often broke the Second Commandment were clergy and politicians who invoked the Lord's name in vain, only for their own gain. We are wise to consider how closely our words and actions mirror those of Jesus whenever we claim the title "Christian."

Prayer

Forgive us, Lord, whenever we have called ourselves Christians and not lived up to that name. Forgive us for not bearing the name of Christ in truth and integrity. Give us a deep resolve to follow you faithfully, to live compassionately, and to believe fervently, that all we do and say might be to your glory. In your holy name we pray. AMEN.

Friday

Luke 10:25–28

> An expert in the law stood up to test Jesus. "Teacher," he said, "what must I do to inherit eternal life?" [26] He said to him, "What is written in the law? What do you read there?" [27] He answered, "You shall love the Lord your God with all your heart and with all your soul and with all your strength and with all your mind and your neighbor as yourself." [28] And he said to him, "You have given the right answer; do this, and you will live."

I love the way the Hebrew people understood the human psyche. They thought of it like concentric circles, starting with the heart, then the soul, then the strength, and then the mind. If you picture an archery target with the heart as the bullseye, and then the soul, strength, and mind as outer circles, you will have the right idea. The Hebrews thought that God called us to love God from the very center of our being to its outermost parts. We might say from our head to our feet, or the top of our head to the tips of our toes, but however you say it, we are called to love God with everything we are. Notice, also, that Jesus doesn't stop there in calling us to love God. He says that we should love God with everything we are *and* love our neighbor as ourselves. This suggests that those around us are really just an additional concentric circle. They are part of God's plan for us. So, we are called to love God from the innermost parts of ourselves all the way to those around us and even beyond that. What a grand call we have from God!

Prayer

You have given us a grand call, O God. You have called us to love you with everything we are and even beyond. We praise and thank you for this grand call. Fill us with your Spirit so that we might be great lovers, filled with your love as we live our lives in you. In your name we pray. AMEN.

The Sixth Week of Easter

Monday

Ps 67

[1] May God be gracious to us and bless us
  and make his face to shine upon us,
[2] that your way may be known upon earth,
  your saving power among all nations
[3] Let the peoples praise you, O God;
  let all the peoples praise you.
[4] Let the nations be glad and sing for joy,
  for you judge the peoples with equity
  and guide the nations upon earth.
[5] Let the peoples praise you, O God;
  let all the peoples praise you.
[6] The earth has yielded its increase;
  God, our God, has blessed us.
[7] May God continue to bless us;
  let all the ends of the earth revere him.

Psalm 67 begins in a familiar way; the opening verse sounds very much like a blessing that is often spoken at the end of worship services. It is an ancient blessing, found in its most familiar form in Num 6:24–26. But verse 2 here is something new; it is a purpose statement. It says in effect, "May God bless us *so that* God's way might be known on the earth and God's saving power among all nations." I wonder how often we think of things this way. We might regularly ask God to bless us, but do we make that request so that God's ways might be known more widely? Just think of the effect this could have on the world. We might ask God to bless us so that we might make God's compassion known to the world through greater generosity. We might ask God to bless us with good health so that God's way of humble service might be more evident in our lives. We might ask God to bless our relationships so that God's ways of reconciliation would spread to all people. There is no end to the blessings that could come to people if God's ways were known more widely.

Prayer

Gracious God, grant us your blessing, not only so that we might prosper, but so that your saving ways might be known to all. Grant us health and wisdom so that we might serve and guide others according to your gracious will. Grant us prosperity and peace so that your ways of reconciliation and abundance might be spread to all. In all things, grant us your blessing so that others might be blessed. In your gracious name we pray. AMEN.

Tuesday

Prov 2:1–5

My child, if you accept my words
    and treasure up my commandments within you,
2 making your ear attentive to wisdom
    and inclining your heart to understanding,
3 if you indeed cry out for insight
    and raise your voice for understanding,
4 if you seek it like silver
    and search for it as for hidden treasures—
5 then you will understand the fear of the LORD
    and find the knowledge of God.

Notice the words that are used in this proverb as we are urged to seek wisdom: *treasure* my commandments, be *attentive* to wisdom, *incline* to understanding, *cry out* for insight, *raise your voice* for understanding, *seek* and *search* for it as for a hidden treasure. All of these urge us to be very diligent and determined when it comes to seeking wisdom. Perhaps this hints at the obstacles to gaining wisdom. Or perhaps it is meant as encouragement when we are tired and likely to give up. Maybe the writer just means to emphasize how important it is to seek. In any case, we are exhorted here to do everything in our power to obtain wisdom. Why? So that we will "understand the fear of the Lord and find the knowledge of God." To understand the *fear* of the Lord means to discern God's "otherness" and appreciate how appropriate holy awe is in the presence of God. It means to come to terms with the fact that God is holy, and we are not. To find the *knowledge* of God is simply to understand that obedience to God is the way of life. May we all find such wisdom.

Prayer

God of all Wisdom, come to our aid so that we might truly know you as you are. Keep us from false notions of you that would lead us into foolishness and destruction. Grant us a heart for wisdom, so that we grow in all ways into the image of your Son, our Lord Jesus Christ, in whose name we pray. AMEN.

Wednesday

Acts 16:1–5

> Paul went on also to Derbe and to Lystra, where there was a
> disciple named Timothy, the son of a Jewish woman who was a
> believer, but his father was a Greek. 2 He was well spoken of by
> the brothers and sisters in Lystra and Iconium. 3 Paul wanted
> Timothy to accompany him, and he took him and had him
> circumcised because of the Jews who were in those places, for
> they all knew that his father was a Greek. 4 As they went from
> town to town, they delivered to them for observance the decisions that had been reached by the apostles and elders who
> were in Jerusalem. 5 So the churches were strengthened in the
> faith and increased in numbers daily.

The final verse of this passage indicates that the church was strengthened and growing because of "the decisions reached by the apostles and elders." Here we learn that conflicts must be resolved before we can grow and prosper together. Sometimes we are tempted to believe that if we just push it under the rug, ignore it, or stomp out any discussion of an issue, a conflict will magically go away and we will prosper in spite of it. Nothing could be further from the truth. When families do this, family life suffers. When couples do this, marriages suffer. When churches or other organizations do this, the mission of the organization is hampered or even stalled completely. But when we courageously confront our problems, come to some resolution, and reconcile, we are assured that new life is ahead for us.

Prayer

God of all Wisdom, grant us the courage to face our conflicts and difficulties. Grant us wisdom and patience, compassion and understanding, as we work through those difficult yet human problems we often encounter. Help us to be people of peace, seeking always the greatest good for the greatest number. Guide us, we pray. In the name of Christ. AMEN.

Thursday

Luke 19:1–10

> He entered Jericho and was passing through it. [2] A man was
> there named Zacchaeus; he was a chief tax collector and was
> rich. [3] He was trying to see who Jesus was, but on account of
> the crowd he could not, because he was short in stature. [4] So
> he ran ahead and climbed a sycamore tree to see him, because
> he was going to pass that way. [5] When Jesus came to the place,
> he looked up and said to him, "Zacchaeus, hurry and come
> down, for I must stay at your house today." [6] So he hurried
> down and was happy to welcome him. [7] All who saw it began
> to grumble and said, "He has gone to be the guest of one who is
> a sinner." [8] Zacchaeus stood there and said to the Lord, "Look,
> half of my possessions, Lord, I will give to the poor, and if I
> have defrauded anyone of anything, I will pay back four times
> as much." [9] Then Jesus said to him, "Today salvation has come
> to this house, because he, too, is a son of Abraham. [10] For the
> Son of Man came to seek out and to save the lost."

It is amazing how little Jesus says to Zacchaeus in this passage. All he says is, "I must stay at your house today." Why is this so powerful? There are several reasons. First, it indicates Jesus' refusal to judge Zacchaeus for his actions in the past. Second, it indicates Jesus' acceptance of him. Third, it indicates Jesus' willingness to accept his hospitality and to be found in Zacchaeus' company. In a word, Jesus' words *honor* Zacchaeus, something with which Zacchaeus was likely unfamiliar. We might take a lesson from Jesus here by remembering that small acts of acceptance, forgiveness, and welcome go a long way toward honoring others. Maybe something as simple as remembering our neighbor's name or complimenting them on their gardens can honor them. Maybe thanking a person for some small act of kindness or responsible service, like good waitstaff at a restaurant, can honor them. What if, every day, we made it our aim to honor those we encounter? How would that change us and them?

Prayer

You have honored us in so many ways, O God. As the psalmist has said, "You have made us little lower than the angels and crowned us with glory and honor." You have forgiven, welcomed, and rescued us, despite our unworthiness and ingratitude. We thank you for your constant gifts. Help us so to receive these gifts that we might pass them on to others as well. In the name of Christ we pray. AMEN.

Friday

2 Chr 15:1–7

> The spirit of God came upon Azariah son of Oded. [2] He went out
> to meet Asa and said to him, "Hear me, Asa, and all Judah and
> Benjamin: The LORD is with you while you are with him. If you
> seek him, he will be found by you, but if you abandon him, he
> will abandon you. [3] For a long time Israel was without the true
> God and without a teaching priest and without law, [4] but when
> in their distress they turned to the LORD, the God of Israel, and
> sought him, he was found by them. [5] In those times it was not
> safe for anyone to go or come, for great disturbances afflicted all
> the inhabitants of the lands. [6] They were broken in pieces, nation
> against nation and city against city, for God troubled them with
> every sort of distress. [7] But you, take courage! Do not let your
> hands be weak, for your work shall be rewarded."

The prophet Azariah is not a prophet we know because there is no prophetic book named for him. Nevertheless, you can hear in his words many of the themes spoken by other prophets like Jeremiah or Zephaniah. Like those prophets, Azariah links conflict and lack of security to the abandonment of God by the inhabitants of the land. This is certainly a theme that has been lifted up in our modern day as well, even though it has been politicized beyond recognition. The fact remains, when people of faith and good will have authority, and when people of compassion and generosity lead, the inhabitants of the land are blessed. Conversely, when people who are their own god and have no concern for others are given power, and when people who lack compassion and live only to satisfy their own lusts are in charge, all suffer. As people of God, we are exhorted to both *be* people of faith and *elect* people of faith who will lead and serve with integrity and compassion.

Prayer

We pray for our country these days, O God. We pray that we would be drawn to elect leaders who are people of faith, compassion, and love. We pray that those who wish to gain power only to serve themselves would be thwarted in their pursuit of power, and that those who follow in your ways would emerge. Grant us courage these days, O God. We pray in your holy name. AMEN.

The Seventh Week of Easter

Monday

Ps 97:1–9

1 The LORD is king! Let the earth rejoice;
let the many coastlands be glad!
2 Clouds and thick darkness are all around him;
righteousness and justice are the foundation of his throne.
3 Fire goes before him
and consumes his adversaries on every side.
4 His lightnings light up the world;
the earth sees and trembles.
5 The mountains melt like wax before the LORD,
before the Lord of all the earth.
6 The heavens proclaim his righteousness,
and all the peoples behold his glory.
7 All servants of images are put to shame,
those who make their boast in worthless idols;
all gods bow down before him.
8 Zion hears and is glad,
and the towns of Judah rejoice
because of your judgments, O God.
9 For you, O LORD, are most high over all the earth;
you are exalted far above all gods.

This psalm reminds us of one of the most fundamental claims we make as people of faith: The Lord is king, and there is no other. Or, as Martin Luther wrote in his Large Catechism: "You shall worship me *alone* as your God." This is important to remember as we celebrate Memorial Day, because sometimes it is easy to confuse allegiance to our country with obedience to God. We pledge allegiance to our country, yes. This means that we are loyal and devoted citizens, striving to uphold the highest ideals of our country. But to God we do more than pledge allegiance; we worship, we adore, we praise God for life. Our deepest desires and hopes are bound up in God. Our bond with Christ is beyond any bond we have with our nation, our neighbor, or even our own flesh and blood. Our very soul— that is to say, the core of our being— is claimed by God. As St. Paul said, "We are not our own, but we have been bought with a price." As you celebrate Memorial Day and give thanks for our country, remember the God who is the Giver of all good things.

Prayer

We thank you, Giver of Life, for our nation. We thank you for the blessings that come our way as citizens of this country. Grant us humble gratitude for all we have received and a willingness to share eagerly our blessings with others. We ask this in Christ's name. AMEN.

Tuesday

John 1:14–18

> [14] And the Word became flesh and lived among us, and we
> have seen his glory, the glory as of a father's only son, full of
> grace and truth. [15] (John testified to him and cried out, "This
> was he of whom I said, 'He who comes after me ranks ahead of
> me because he was before me.'") [16] From his fullness we have all
> received, grace upon grace. [17] The law indeed was given through
> Moses; grace and truth came through Jesus Christ. [18] No one has
> ever seen God. It is the only Son, himself God, who is close to
> the Father's heart, who has made him known.

I remember one particular time in my life when I was really discouraged. I was tired. I was broke. I felt like my life was going nowhere. It was during this period that I read this passage from John's gospel, and I was stopped dead in my tracks. "From his fullness we have all received, grace upon grace." As I read that sentence I realized how true it was. My entire life had been one of receiving grace. My growing up days had been everything a boy could desire—good friends, a supportive family, a lake to swim and fish in right down the hill from the house, and on and on. My college days had also been filled with grace—wonderful teachers, new and life-long friends, a start to a life-long career, and many wonderful experiences. Grace upon grace, gift upon gift, all received without my deserving—that was my life story. How could I be discouraged? Counting blessings is an age-old cure for discouragement. After all, as the old song says, "Since Christ is Lord of heaven and earth, how can I keep from singing?"

Prayer

Thank you, Generous God, for blessing us with so much. We are recipients of grace upon grace. Your forgiveness is unending. Your provision for our lives is abundant. Your people are a continual source of encouragement and support. Thank you for all your gifts. In your holy name we pray. AMEN.

Wednesday

Ps 130:1–8

1 Out of the depths I cry to you, O LORD.
2 Lord, hear my voice!
Let your ears be attentive
to the voice of my supplications!
3 If you, O LORD, should mark iniquities,
Lord, who could stand?
4 But there is forgiveness with you,
so that you may be revered.
5 I wait for the LORD; my soul waits,
and in his word I hope;
6 my soul waits for the Lord
more than those who watch for the morning,
more than those who watch for the morning.

[7] O Israel, hope in the LORD!
For with the LORD there is steadfast love,
and with him is great power to redeem.
[8] It is he who will redeem Israel
from all its iniquities.

As I view the grief surrounding the shootings that took place in an elementary school in Uvalde, Texas last week, the opening verses of Ps 130 ring in my ears: "Out of the depths I cry to you, O Lord. Lord, hear my voice!" The depths of grief, anger, and despair are certainly where this community lies right now. Parents and grandparents, brothers and sisters, teachers and fellow citizens all grieve together over the deaths of these little ones and the two adults who were also killed. "Hear our voices, Lord!" we cry. "Hear our cries, Lord, that something be done to end this madness that plagues our nation." The collective power of people of faith is strong. Perhaps the "great power to redeem" that the psalmist speaks of here is ours to claim. Perhaps God's steadfast love for the world is the rock on which we stand as we cry out for an end to the powers of this world that perpetuate this violence.

Prayer

Lord God, come to our aid. Give us courage to confront the evil before us. Keep us from despair or indifference. Give strength to us all as we resolve to put an end to the systems that perpetuate violence in our land. We ask this in the strong name of Christ Jesus, our Lord. AMEN.

Thursday

Ezek 3:16–19

[16] At the end of seven days, the word of the LORD came to
me: [17] Mortal, I have made you a sentinel for the house of Is-
rael; whenever you hear a word from my mouth, you shall give
them warning from me. [18] When I say to the wicked, "You shall
surely die," and you give them no warning and do not speak
to warn the wicked from their wicked way in order to save
their lives, those wicked persons shall die for their iniquity, but
their blood I will require at your hand. [19] But if you warn the
wicked and they do not turn from their wickedness or from

their wicked way, they shall die for their iniquity, but you will have saved your life.

This passage is a tough one. The prophet Ezekiel is being given an order here to bring a word of warning to the wicked. Do you know how tough that is? We don't usually want to warn the wicked about their impending doom; we would just as soon see them get what's coming to them. But the Lord says here, "Warn the wicked about the consequences of wickedness." In other words, "Care about them. Love them as I do. Do not wish them ill." I remember, as a kid, taking wicked pleasure in seeing my siblings punished for their misdeeds. I thought, "It's about time they got what they have long had coming!" I had little compassion for them, but instead gloated in the fact that someone else was getting what I thought they deserved. God asks us to be better than that. God asks us to love as we have been loved.

Prayer

Forgive us, Lord, for our hard hearts. Forgive us for our unforgiving spirits. Forgive us for wishing ill to people we don't like. Fill us with your spirit that we might find our way to the grace and mercy you have shown us in Christ, in whose name we pray. AMEN.

Friday

Luke 9:18–24

[18] Once when Jesus was praying alone, with only the disciples near
him, he asked them, "Who do the crowds say that I am?" [19] They
answered, "John the Baptist; but others, Elijah; and still others,
that one of the ancient prophets has arisen." [20] Then he said to
them, "But who do you say that I am?" Peter answered, "The
Messiah of God." [21] He sternly ordered and commanded them
not to tell anyone, [22] saying, "The Son of Man must undergo
great suffering and be rejected by the elders, chief priests, and
scribes and be killed and on the third day be raised."

[23] Then he said to them all, "If any wish to come after me, let
them deny themselves and take up their cross daily and follow
me. [24] For those who want to save their life will lose it, and those
who lose their life for my sake will save it.

This classic passage is a reminder that following Christ is not designed to bring fame and fortune to us. Yes, there are those who follow Christ who have become famous and wealthy, but the two are not related. Following Christ always has to do with "losing our life". Following Christ is about listening for what Christ is calling us to and heeding that call, no matter the cost. The first disciples were sure that following Christ would mean being given places of honor and glory in his new kingdom on earth. They envisioned all sorts of power coming their way. They soon found out this would not be the case. What they were guaranteed, instead, was a way of life that brought blessing to others and all sorts of ups and downs to them. It is the same with us. Christ says, "Follow me, for in that is life, even life to the full."

Prayer

We are your disciples, Lord. We are those who have decided to follow you. Help us to be faithful in this following. Help us to decide each day to give up our life. We know that the abundant life comes in following you. Grant us such life. In your precious name we pray. AMEN.

The Week of Pentecost

Monday

Ps 104:24–30

24 O LORD, how manifold are your works!
In wisdom you have made them all;
the earth is full of your creatures.
25 There is the sea, great and wide;
creeping things innumerable are there,
living things both small and great.
26 There go the ships
and Leviathan that you formed to sport in it.
27 These all look to you
to give them their food in due season;
28 when you give to them, they gather it up;
when you open your hand, they are filled with good things.
29 When you hide your face, they are dismayed;
when you take away their breath, they die
and return to their dust.
30 When you send forth your spirit, they are created,
and you renew the face of the ground.

A number of years ago, some friends invited my wife and me to spend time with them at their condominium in Hawaii. As part of that trip, we went whale watching. What fun it was! The humpback whales were plentiful that year. They would rise up out of the water without warning and make the biggest splash, apparently just for the sport of it, as the psalmist says. It is delightful to think that God the Creator made some creatures just so they could play in the water and we could delight in their splashing. Perhaps God has done that with many creatures: rabbits hopping about, mosquitoes buzzing in our ear, crows cawing to one another. Maybe they are all just saying, "Look at me. Look at what I can do. Am I not marvelously made?" We might take some instruction from the creatures all about us and be sure to indulge in play ourselves on a regular basis. Perhaps that is what Sabbath entails as well.

Prayer

Thank you, Creator God, for the world you have made, complete with creatures of every kind. You have given us great delight in watching everything from the wren to the great blue whale. Grant us joy in all you have made and a determination to steward and protect all with which you have entrusted us. In your holy name we pray. AMEN.

Tuesday

Gal 5:16–25

> 16 Live by the Spirit, I say, and do not gratify the desires of the flesh. 17 For what the flesh desires is opposed to the Spirit, and what the Spirit desires is opposed to the flesh, for these are opposed to each other, to prevent you from doing what you want. 18 But if you are led by the Spirit, you are not subject to the law. 19 Now the works of the flesh are obvious: sexual immorality, impurity, debauchery, 20 idolatry, sorcery, enmities, strife, jealousy, anger, quarrels, dissensions, factions, 21 envy drunkenness, carousing, and things like these. I am warning you, as I warned you before: those who do such things will not inherit the kingdom of God.22 By contrast, the fruit of the Spirit is love, joy, peace, patience, kindness, generosity, faithfulness, 23 gentleness, and self-control. There is no law against such things. 24 And those who belong to Christ have crucified the flesh with its passions and desires. 25 If we live by the Spirit, let us also be guided by the Spirit.

Verse 24 is the key verse in this passage. It gives us the only strategy that can result in a life that resembles the way of the Spirit. It says that "those who belong to Christ have crucified the flesh with its passions and desires." This means that daily dying—the daily process of giving our lives over to God—is the *only* way to combat our passions and desires. Our will alone is not enough. As St. Paul says elsewhere, "I can will what is good, but I cannot do it." No, the way to live a Christlike life is to give up the "self" life every day, and say to Christ, "It is not I who live, but you who live in me. Let it be so." The amazing thing is that, when we *do* give our lives over to Christ, we do not even notice the transformation. Our eyes are on our neighbor, as we work to help them, and we are no longer consumed with our own failures or successes. That is the way of joy.

Prayer

Put us to death every day, Lord Christ. Put us to death and come and live within us so that our lives might resemble yours. Take away from us every habit or thought that would lead us away from you, and fill us with the joy of your salvation. We ask this in your precious name. AMEN.

Wednesday

Isa 44:1–5

But now hear, O Jacob my servant,
    Israel whom I have chosen!
2 Thus says the LORD who made you,
    who formed you in the womb and will help you:
Do not fear, O Jacob my servant,
    Jeshurun whom I have chosen.
3 For I will pour water on the thirsty land
    and streams on the dry ground;
I will pour my spirit upon your descendants
    and my blessing on your offspring.
4 They shall spring up like a green tamarisk,
    like willows by flowing streams.
5 This one will say, "I am the LORD's";
    another will be called by the name of Jacob;
yet another will write on the hand, "The LORD's,"
    and adopt the name of Israel.

The vegetable garden is now planted and, after only a few weeks, little leaves are poking through the soil, promising radishes, beans, lettuce, and all sorts of other things to come. My wife faithfully waters and weeds this little garden, and through this simple process, a miracle that changes a minute seed into a bountiful harvest takes form. This is what God promises to the ancient people of God: "I will pour my spirit upon your descendants and my blessing on your offspring. They shall spring up like a green tamarisk, like willows by flowing streams." God promises to water us with the Spirit. We might feel like we are little seeds in a thirsty ground, with little hope of bearing fruit, but God sends the Spirit to encourage, empower, and guide us. Through this watering, we become a blessing to the world. Fruit is borne in us through this gracious Spirit, and in response we joyfully declare, "I am the Lord's."

Prayer

We thank and praise you, Almighty God, for your gentle Spirit that is poured out oh so carefully on us, your people. We often wonder if any fruit will be borne in our life, and yet you say, "Trust me. You will bear fruit." Grant us grace to believe your promises and trust that we will bear fruit in the lives of those around us, and be a blessing to all. We ask this in your holy name. AMEN.

Thursday

1 Cor 2:10–16

> [10] God has revealed to us through the Spirit, for the Spirit
> searches everything, even the depths of God. [11] For what hu-
> man knows what is truly human except the human spirit that is
> within? So also no one comprehends what is truly God's except
> the Spirit of God. [12] Now we have received not the spirit of the
> world but the Spirit that is from God, so that we may under-
> stand the gifts bestowed on us by God. [13] And we speak of these
> things in words not taught by human wisdom but taught by the
> Spirit, interpreting spiritual things to those who are spiritual.
>
> [14] Those who are unspiritual do not receive the gifts of God's
> Spirit, for they are foolishness to them, and they are unable to
> understand them because they are spiritually discerned. [15] Those

who are spiritual discern all things, and they are themselves subject to no one else's scrutiny.

16 "For who has known the mind of the Lord
so as to instruct him?"
But we have the mind of Christ.

Jean Vanier, the founder of L'Arche, an international organization of communities for people with developmental disabilities, once wrote this: "To love someone is not first of all to do things for them, but to reveal to them their beauty and value . . . To love someone is to reveal to them their capacity for life, the light that is shining in them." I love that saying. It defines love in a way that is rarely thought of: as a means to show someone their gifts. St. Paul says that the Spirit does this for us. He says that one of the reasons we have received the Spirit from God is so that "we may understand the gifts bestowed on us by God." We all have gifts, yet sometimes they are hidden to us. Do you love to open your home to others? That is the gift of hospitality. Do you love to provide generously for those in need? That is the gift of giving. Do you love to study and preach? That is the gift of proclamation. And there are many more gifts. The Spirit shows us these things. This is one more way God shows us divine love.

Prayer

Gracious God, you are all generosity and love. You constantly bestow on us gifts galore, many of which we are not even aware. Make us attentive to your Spirit, and let us take joy in all you reveal to us through your Spirit, so that we might be used by you every day to bring glory to your name and blessing to the world. We ask this in Christ's name. AMEN.

Friday

John 14:8–14

8 Philip said to him, "Lord, show us the Father, and we will be
satisfied." 9 Jesus said to him, "Have I been with you all this time,
Philip, and you still do not know me? Whoever has seen me has
seen the Father. How can you say, 'Show us the Father'? 10 Do
you not believe that I am in the Father and the Father is in me?
The words that I say to you I do not speak on my own, but the

> Father who dwells in me does his works. [11] Believe me that I am in the Father and the Father is in me, but if you do not, then believe because of the works themselves. [12] Very truly, I tell you, the one who believes in me will also do the works that I do and, in fact, will do greater works than these, because I am going to the Father. [13] I will do whatever you ask in my name, so that the Father may be glorified in the Son. [14] If in my name you ask me for anything, I will do it.

I understand how Philip is thinking in this story. He knows who God is and he knows who Jesus is; he just never put the two together. Who could fault him? God is seemingly far off and Jesus is right there in front of him. Yet, Jesus rebukes him for not realizing that whoever has seen Jesus has seen God the Father. It is a good thing Philip is so confused because Jesus' answer to him is helpful to us. If you ever wonder what God is like, look at Jesus and you will know. Do you see Jesus healing? That's what God does. Do you see Jesus refusing to condemn sinners? That's what God does. Do you see Jesus railing against those who abuse their authority? That's what God does. There is much that we do not know about God, but of this we can be sure: God's characteristics are those we see in our Lord.

Prayer

You are a great mystery to us, Almighty God. We struggle to understand your ways and to fathom your wisdom. Yet you have revealed yourself to us in Christ. You are loving. You are merciful. You are long-suffering. Help us always to trust in you, and to live our lives in thankfulness and joy all our days. In the name of Christ we pray. AMEN.

The Week of the Holy Trinity

Monday

Prov 3:13–18

13 Happy are those who find wisdom
and those who get understanding,
14 for her income is better than silver
and her revenue better than gold.
15 She is more precious than jewels,
and nothing you desire can compare with her.
16 Long life is in her right hand;
in her left hand are riches and honor.
17 Her ways are ways of pleasantness,
and all her paths are peace.
18 She is a tree of life to those who lay hold of her;
those who hold her fast are called happy.

In the *Lutheran Study Bible*, these verses from Prov 3 are entitled "The True Wealth." In this passage, wisdom is held up as the source of life as well as the source of abundance. There are many who would agree with this. Newspaper columnist Harvey MacKay often peppers his columns with words of wisdom about business as well as general advice on how to get along with others. MacKay, it seems to me, has completely adopted the notion that true wealth is the result of wisdom, whether one finds oneself wealthy by worldly standards or not. Some of the titles of his books could be right out of the book of Proverbs: *Dig Your Well Before You're Thirsty*, and *Beware the Naked*

Man Who Offers You His Shirt. It's no surprise that contemporary writers and ancient writers agree: happy are those who find wisdom.

Prayer

God of All Wisdom, we thank and praise you for the guidance of your Holy Spirit through Scripture, through ancient wisdom, and through your people, the Church. Give us open minds and hearts to receive your wisdom with joy, and help us to live it out. In your holy name we pray. AMEN.

Tuesday

Eph 1:15–19

> 15 I have heard of your faith in the Lord Jesus and your love to-
> ward all the saints, and for this reason 16 I do not cease to give
> thanks for you as I remember you in my prayers, 17 that the God
> of our Lord Jesus Christ, the Father of glory, may give you a
> spirit of wisdom and revelation as you come to know him, 18 so
> that, with the eyes of your heart enlightened, you may perceive
> what is the hope to which he has called you, what are the riches
> of his glorious inheritance among the saints, 19 and what is the
> immeasurable greatness of his power for us who believe, accord-
> ing to the working of his great power.

This is part of a prayer that St. Paul prayed for his beloved Ephesians. Notice how thankful he is for their faith and love. But then notice what his prayer is for *them*: he prays that they may be given "a spirit of wisdom and revelation." Why does he pray this? So that they might perceive the hope to which they are called, know the riches of their inheritance, and appreciate the "immeasurable greatness of God's power in all who believe." It's almost as if Paul is saying that yes, your heart and soul are engaged, now engage your *mind* as well. Sometimes we may think that faith and love are exclusive of wisdom. Perhaps we have the notion that either a person is intellectually gifted *or* a person has a deep faith or a compassionate heart. Paul says otherwise. He says that all of these traits are needed, and all are equally celebrated. We need to cultivate a deep faith and a profound love for all people, *and* we need to dig deep into the mysteries of life and faith. Why? So that our joy might be complete.

Prayer

Gracious and All-Wise God, thank you for our minds. Thank you for wise scholars, persistent scientists, thoughtful theologians, and master teachers who show us the mysteries of life. Grant us always a deep faith, a broad love, and a hunger for godly wisdom, so that we might be all that you have designed us to be. In your Son's name we pray. AMEN.

Wednesday

Luke 2:41–50

> [41] Now every year his parents went to Jerusalem for the festival
> of the Passover. [42] And when he was twelve years old, they went
> up as usual for the festival. [43] When the festival was ended and
> they started to return, the boy Jesus stayed behind in Jerusalem,
> but his parents were unaware of this. [44] Assuming that he was in
> the group of travelers, they went a day's journey. Then they start-
> ed to look for him among their relatives and friends. [45] When
> they did not find him, they returned to Jerusalem to search for
> him. [46] After three days they found him in the temple, sitting
> among the teachers, listening to them and asking them ques-
> tions. [47] And all who heard him were amazed at his understand-
> ing and his answers. [48] When his parents saw him they were
> astonished, and his mother said to him, "Child, why have you
> treated us like this? Your father and I have been anxiously look-
> ing for you." [49] He said to them, "Why were you searching for me?
> Did you not know that I must be in my Father's house?"[k][50] But
> they did not understand what he said to them.

I love this story about the boy Jesus. The part I find most fascinating is the description of his action in the temple. He is "listening to [the teachers] and asking them questions." This is a pattern that will continue throughout Jesus' entire ministry. A number of years ago, a pastor named Martin Copenhaver wrote a book entitled *Jesus is the Question*. In his book *Jesus is the Question,* pastor Martin Copenhaver notes that, in the New Testament, Jesus asks 307 questions and only answers 3! Copenhaver says we often think of Jesus as the Answer Man, but in reality he is quite the opposite. Jesus is the one who, by asking us challenging questions, invites us to discover for ourselves what it means to follow him, to live the crucified life, and to know real wisdom. Jesus doesn't tell us the answers to these questions, but continually asks so that we might discover them for ourselves. If you feel like you just don't know much when it comes to faith, take heart; questioning is at the heart of the life of a disciple.

Prayer

Thank you for modeling humility and curiosity, Dear Lord. You are both the great Learner and the great Teacher. Encourage us in our quest to learn what it means to follow you. Guide us through faithful colleagues and wise mentors. Bring us closer to you each day as we seek your ways. We ask this in your precious name. AMEN.

Thursday

Ps 124

1 If it had not been the LORD who was on our side
—let Israel now say—
2 if it had not been the LORD who was on our side,
when our enemies attacked us,
3 then they would have swallowed us up alive,
when their anger was kindled against us;
4 then the flood would have swept us away;
the torrent would have gone over us;
5 then over us would have gone
the raging waters.
6 Blessed be the LORD,
who has not given us
as prey to their teeth.
7 We have escaped like a bird
from the snare of the hunters;
the snare is broken,
and we have escaped.
8 Our help is in the name of the LORD,
who made heaven and earth.

This is the central confession of God's people throughout the ages: our help is in the name of the Lord. There have been many times through the ages that it seemed unlikely God's people would endure. Certainly, while in Egypt and much later in exile, the people of Israel wondered if they would survive as a people. The followers of Jesus also must have felt very vulnerable in their modest beginnings. Only a few followers in cities scattered around the Mediterranean basin formed the basis of the earliest Christian community. What were the chances they would survive? Then down through the ages, God's people across the globe have endured all sorts of attempts to snuff out the faith. Yet here we are today, still proclaiming the Good News and following in the way of Jesus. What accounts for this? It is that "our help is in the name of the Lord." Even today, we might be tempted to despair and say, "The Church is in decline. Will it survive? Will God's people finally disappear from the earth?" And the answer once again is, "The Church will live, for our help is in the name of the Lord."

Prayer

Thank you, Almighty One, for sustaining your people down through the ages. From slavery in Egypt to the present war in Ukraine, your people have been threatened with extinction, yet you sustain us. You give us strength. You give us hope. You give us courage. Bless all those who feel attacked by enemies within and without these days. Protect, bless, and strengthen your people, we pray. In Jesus' name. AMEN.

Friday

Eph 4:7, 11–16

7 But each of us was given grace according to the measure of Christ's gift.

11 He himself granted that some are apostles, prophets, evan-
gelists, pastors and teachers 12 to equip the saints for the work
of ministry, for building up the body of Christ, 13 until all of
us come to the unity of the faith and of the knowledge of the Son of God, to maturity, to the measure of the full stature of
Christ. 14 We must no longer be children, tossed to and fro and blown about by every wind of doctrine by people's trickery, by
their craftiness in deceitful scheming; 15 but speaking the truth

> in love, we must grow up in every way into him who is the head, into Christ, [16] from whom the whole body, joined and knit together by every ligament with which it is equipped, as each part is working properly, promotes the body's growth in building itself up in love.

These verses tell us clearly why the people of God are a gifted people. We are gifted so that we might "equip the saints for the work of ministry, for building up the body of Christ, until all of us come [. . .]to maturity, to the measure of the full stature of Christ." That's it. We are given gifts, not for ourselves, but for the building up of the people of God. Do you love to care for children? Use that gift to build up the body of Christ. Do you have a gift for hospitality? Use that gift to build up Christ's body. Do you love to teach or to pray or to work with your hands or do work of administration or work of compassion? Then do what you do to build up the body of Christ. Notice what Paul also says about the effect of this building up. The final goal is not that God's people will be superhuman, but that the whole body of Christ might be working properly. This will manifest itself in love. In short, we are built up so that we might be a conduit of God's love to the world. As God said to Abraham, "You are blessed to be a blessing."

Prayer

Gracious and Almighty God, we give you thanks for the gifts you have given your people. Thank you for workers of compassion, faithful teachers, skilled preachers, and passionate evangelists. Help all your people to know their gifts and grant that each of us would use all we have to bless others and bring glory to you. In the name of Christ we pray. AMEN.

The Second Week After Pentecost

Monday

Luke 1:46–55

46 And Mary said,
"My soul magnifies the Lord,
47 and my spirit rejoices in God my Savior,
48 for he has looked with favor on the lowly state of his servant.
Surely from now on all generations will call me blessed,
49 for the Mighty One has done great things for me,
and holy is his name;
50 indeed, his mercy is for those who fear him
from generation to generation.
51 He has shown strength with his arm;
he has scattered the proud in the imagination of their hearts.
52 He has brought down the powerful from their thrones
and lifted up the lowly;
53 he has filled the hungry with good things
and sent the rich away empty.
54 He has come to the aid of his child Israel,
in remembrance of his mercy,
55 according to the promise he made to our ancestors,
to Abraham and to his descendants forever."

In typical medieval Roman Catholic fashion, as a young monk, Martin Luther regarded Mary, the mother of Christ, as a saint and a mediator between God and human beings. As he grew in his understanding, Luther rejected that earlier teaching and saw Mary simply as a wonderful example of faith and humility. You can hear in this famous song, often known by its Latin name, *Magnificat*, some of those characteristics. She calls herself a lowly servant and yet one who is blessed by the Mighty One who has done great things for her. She gives praise to God for the divine pattern of lifting up the lowly and scattering the proud and haughty. She testifies to God's ability to fill the hungry with good things and to come to the aid of God's people. All this God does, she says, "in remembrance of his mercy." That is to say, God does these things not because of something *we* do, but because it is the nature of God to do them. Are you feeling low, hungry, weak, or poor? Take heart, says Mary, it is God's good pleasure to fill you and give you strength and life.

Prayer

Thank you, Gracious God, that you have heard our cries and filled our hungry souls with good food. You have sent your Holy Spirit to bear witness to your goodness in the world, and brought hope and faith to us once again. Be near all who struggle, who hunger, or who suffer in any way. Fill them and grant them your peace. We pray in Christ's name. AMEN.

Tuesday

Dan 2:20–23

20 Daniel said:
"Blessed be the name of God from age to age,
for wisdom and power are his.
21 He changes times and seasons,
deposes kings and sets up kings;
he gives wisdom to the wise
and knowledge to those who have understanding.
22 He reveals deep and hidden things;
he knows what is in the darkness,
and light dwells with him.
23 To you, O God of my ancestors,

I give thanks and praise,
for you have given me wisdom and power
and have now revealed to me what we asked of you,
for you have revealed to us what the king ordered."

Daniel, the Hebrew sage who served in the court of Nebuchadnezzar, king of Babylon, is, like Mary the mother of Christ, an example for us. He too shows us what praise looks like, as well as faith and humility. When he and all the wise ones of Babylon could not tell the king the meaning of his dream it was decreed that they should all die if no one was found to interpret the dream. Daniel prayed to God and was given the meaning. You can hear in his song of praise how he responded. He blessed God as the source of all wisdom and power. He testified to God's control over times and seasons, kingships and sagely wisdom. He acknowledged God as the source of all knowledge and understanding. Daniel is an example for us in this. Have you known confusion? Pray and ask God for clarity. Have you been uncertain about the right path forward? Pray and ask God for guidance. Have you been at a loss to know what to say or do in a certain situation? Pray and ask God to give you the words to say and the courage to do what needs to be done. As Jesus said, "Ask and it will be given to you. Seek and you will find. Knock and the door will be opened to you."

Prayer

We praise you, Almighty God for your wisdom and strength. We praise and thank you for the wisdom of Scripture, for the wise guidance of faithful friends, and for the mysterious leading of your Spirit. Help us to listen closely for your guidance and give us the courage to follow. In Christ's name we pray. AMEN.

Wednesday

Ps 92:12–15

12 The righteous flourish like the palm tree
and grow like a cedar in Lebanon.
13 They are planted in the house of the LORD;
they flourish in the courts of our God.

14 In old age they still produce fruit;
they are always green and full of sap,
15 showing that the LORD is upright;
he is my rock, and there is no unrighteousness in him.

I have always loved these verses, particularly the ones that testify to the elders amongst God's people who continue to bear fruit and "are always green and full of sap." I remember one man, Paul who, I think it is fair to say, was full of sap. Well into his nineties, he could be found helping out at church by painting, fixing things, raking the lawn, or doing whatever was needed. He was distinguished by his constant whistling while he worked. Paul found reasons to bear fruit wherever he went. He encouraged others. He supported those in need. He was a constant source of joy to those around him. One day during a summer fishing trip to Canada, Paul and his grandson came in with a mess of walleyes. "Why don't you go lay down and take a nap while I clean these fish, grandpa," said his grandson. So that is what Paul did; he laid down and, even before the fish were fried, he died. Right there. I have often thought about Paul, the way he lived, and the way he died. He was one who, even in old age, still produced fruit. What a blessing.

Prayer

Thank you for our elders, Dearest Lord. Thank you for those aged amongst us who show us how to bear fruit in the twilight of life. Bless them in their serving. Bless them in their living and in their dying. In every way, embrace them, we pray. In the name of Christ. AMEN.

Thursday

1 Thess 4:13–18

13 But we do not want you to be uninformed, brothers and sisters,
about those who have died, so that you may not grieve as others
do who have no hope. 14 For since we believe that Jesus died
and rose again, even so, through Jesus, God will bring with him
those who have died. 15 For this we declare to you by the word of
the Lord, that we who are alive, who are left until the coming of
the Lord, will by no means precede those who have died. 16 For
the Lord himself, with a cry of command, with the archangel's

> call and with the sound of God's trumpet, will descend from heaven, and the dead in Christ will rise first. [17] Then we who are alive, who are left, will be caught up in the clouds together with them to meet the Lord in the air, and so we will be with the Lord forever. [18] Therefore encourage one another with these words.

An unforgettable woman in one of the churches I served was named Freida. Well into her golden years she was a leader in the congregation, especially in the area of teaching Bible studies. She also regularly attended my Bible studies and was a life-long learner. Not too many years before Freida died, she invited the pastors at the church where I served to her house for lunch. To our surprise, when we arrived we found out that it was not simply a social call, but she had invited us three pastors so that she could give us our "marching orders" regarding her funeral. One of us was to preach, one was to sing, and I was assigned the task of playing my trombone on "When the Saints Go Marching In" as we exited the church following the service. In all of this planning, Freida was completely joyful, without dread, in fact, quite matter-of-fact about her death and passing. She seemed, rather to look forward to it, as the day when she would celebrate her reunion with her Lord. This is the picture we have in Paul's letter to the Thessalonians: "Do not fear death; it is merely the gate to a wonderful reunion with Christ and those who have died before you."

Prayer

Lord of All Life, we praise and thank you for your victory over death. On the Cross you put to death all that is Death. You declared victory over the grave, over all sin, and over the Evil One. There is nothing left that can keep us from you. Grant us faith each day to remember your promises and live in the joy they provide. In Christ's name, we pray. AMEN.

Friday

Jer 29:10–14

> [10] For thus says the LORD: Only when Babylon's seventy years are completed will I visit you, and I will fulfill to you my promise and bring you back to this place. [11] For surely I know the plans I have for you, says the LORD, plans for your welfare and not

> for harm, to give you a future with hope. [12] Then when you call upon me and come and pray to me, I will hear you. [13] When you search for me, you will find me; if you seek me with all your heart, [14] I will let you find me, says the LORD, and I will restore your fortunes and gather you from all the nations and all the places where I have driven you, says the LORD, and I will bring you back to the place from which I sent you into exile.

Verse 11 of today's passage is one often quoted on religious graduation cards. In an affirmation of God's good plans for a graduate, the giver assures the graduate that God is going before them. What is often missed in this verse is that the word translated "welfare" is a much richer word in Hebrew; it is the word *shalom*. *Shalom* means prosperity and peace in the deepest sense. It means having a life that is characterized by abundance and strength. There is no greater blessing than to be blessed with *shalom*. Also easily missed in this verse is the fact that the word translated "plans" is better thought of as "purposes." "Plans" suggest that God has written out a roadmap for our lives that cannot be altered. But this passage is better understood as describing a God who has *purposes* in mind for each of us. God wills for us to lead lives of abundance and strength, primarily so that we can fulfill the purpose God has for us, which is to bear fruit in our lives. We are not granted shalom only for our own benefit, but for the benefit of all we encounter. Abraham's mantra, "blessed to be a blessing," is ours too. What a blessing it is to be granted shalom.

Prayer

In every season you bless us, Holy One. You grant us peace and strength, faith and hope. You give us a future with a purpose. Show us your purposes for our life every day, and give us the will to live them out. In Christ's name we pray. AMEN.

The Third Week After Pentecost

Monday

Ps 1

1 Happy are those
    who do not follow the advice of the wicked
or take the path that sinners tread
    or sit in the seat of scoffers,
2 but their delight is in the law of the LORD,
    and on his law they meditate day and night.
3 They are like trees
    planted by streams of water,
which yield their fruit in its season,
    and their leaves do not wither.
In all that they do, they prosper.
4 The wicked are not so
    but are like chaff that the wind drives away.
5 Therefore the wicked will not stand in the judgment
    nor sinners in the congregation of the righteous,
6 for the LORD watches over the way of the righteous,
    but the way of the wicked will perish.

What is a scoffer? According to Webster's Dictionary, it is a person who treats others with disrespect or contempt using derisive language. In short, a scoffer is a person who puts down others regularly, treating them as though they aren't worthy of respect. It is a sad commentary on our culture that the breaking of this commandment seems almost continuous in our present age. Comedians are noteworthy in this regard; so are talk show hosts on radio and TV. Social media sites are regularly cesspools of scorn as are many blog sites and podcasts. Given all this, it is no wonder that we are, as the psalmist promises, withering as a culture. We need so badly for 'rain' to fall on us: kind words, respectful dialogue, civil discourse. Paul Tournier, a 20th century Swiss psychologist, once said that what we all need most is to be listened to, to be understood, and to be taken seriously. That has never been more true than today. As God's people, we can do this. We can offer some 'rain' to others. We call it grace.

Prayer

Loving God, we have received much grace from you. We have also received much instruction in how to live graciously. Fill us with your gracious Spirit so that we might be people who rain grace upon others, each and every day. In your Son's name we pray. AMEN.

Tuesday

1 Cor 16:5–12

> [5] I will visit you after passing through Macedonia—for I intend
> to pass through Macedonia— [6] and perhaps I will stay with you
> or even spend the winter, so that you may send me on my way,
> wherever I go. [7] I do not want to see you now just in passing, for
> I hope to spend some time with you, if the Lord permits. [8] But
> I will stay in Ephesus until Pentecost, [9] for a wide door for ef-
> fective work has opened to me, and there are many adversaries.
>
> [10] If Timothy comes, see that he has nothing to fear among you,
> for he is doing the work of the Lord just as I am; [11] therefore
> let no one despise him. Send him on his way in peace, so that
> he may come to me, for I am expecting him with the brothers
> and sisters.
>
> [12] Now concerning our brother Apollos, I strongly urged him to
> visit you with the other brothers and sisters, but he was not at all
> willing to come now. He will come when he has the opportunity.

This last chapter of 1 Corinthians reminds me that this really was *a letter* that the Apostle Paul was writing. He was including the things we might write in a letter: his hopes for a visit, his plans for the ministry, his advice concerning others they knew and loved, etc. What becomes obvious when we read this is something we often overlook: the Church is really just people. It's just people worshipping God, serving one another, and caring for the world. The Church is certainly unique in its reception of God's Spirit, and in its responsibility to share the Gospel, but still it remains, finally, a community: a group of people with a common concern and belief. William Temple, who served as the Archbishop of Canterbury in the early 20th century, once said, "It is a grave mistake to think that God is chiefly interested in religion." So it is. God is interested in life. God is interested in people. God is interested in how we live together. That must be our concern as well.

Prayer

We thank and praise you, Almighty God, for the gift of the community of faith and for people who bless us every day by their faith, humor, patience, and wisdom. Help us to treasure one another, knowing that we are all children of God, called to share the abundant life given to us in Jesus Christ. We ask this through Christ our Lord. AMEN.

Wednesday

Prov 5:7–14

7 And now, my child, listen to me,
  and do not depart from the words of my mouth.
8 Keep your way far from her,
  and do not go near the door of her house,
9 lest you give your honor to others
  and your years to the merciless,
10 and strangers take their fill of your wealth,
  and your labors go to the house of an alien,
11 and at the end of your life you groan,
  when your flesh and body are consumed,
12 and you say, "Oh, how I hated discipline,
  and my heart despised reproof!
13 I did not listen to the voice of my teachers

or incline my ear to my instructors.
[14] Now I am at the point of utter ruin
in the public assembly."

It is interesting that in the book of Proverbs, both wisdom and foolishness are personified as women. In this passage we are advised to steer clear of foolishness. In the earlier verses in this chapter, the writer points out how seductive foolishness is. He says that foolishness has the taste of honey, but its end is bitterness. In this passage, the results of following foolish ways are laid out: we lose our honor, our wealth, our health, and at our end, even flesh and body are consumed. We need to pray for ourselves and one another that we are not seduced by foolishness these days. As Lutherans, we believe that the powers that lead us away from God's ways are (a) our own lusts and desires, (b) the world's lies and deceptions, and (c) The destroyer, Satan. We pray against all these things. The wisdom writer is clear: God's wisdom is the way of life. Worldly foolishness only leads to sorrow and regret.

Prayer

Send your angels to guard us these days, O God. Surround us with faithful voices who will speak with truth and integrity. Protect your Church from being drawn into the ways of destruction. Thwart the plans of liars and despots. Bring sanity and wholeness to our common life, and by your Spirit, grant us peace. We pray all this in the strong name of Christ our Lord. AMEN.

Thursday

Luke 4:31–37

[31] [Jesus]went down to Capernaum, a city in Galilee, and was
teaching them on the Sabbath. [32] They were astounded at his
teaching because he spoke with authority. [33] In the synagogue
there was a man who had the spirit of an unclean demon, and
he cried out with a loud voice, [34] "Leave us alone! What have
you to do with us, Jesus of Nazareth? Have you come to destroy
us? I know who you are, the Holy One of God." [35] But Jesus
rebuked him, saying, "Be quiet and come out of him!" Then
the demon, throwing the man down before them, came out of
him without doing him any harm. [36] They were all astounded

> and kept saying to one another, "What kind of word is this, that with authority and power he commands the unclean spirits and they come out?" [37] And news about him began to reach every place in the region.

This story about Jesus and his dialogue with an unclean demon illustrates how authority works. The demon knows Jesus has authority, and because of this he fears him. He knows a person who truly has authority has the capability of doing anything they please, even to the point of destroying another. And so, the demon cries out on behalf of his demonic community: "Leave us alone!" This story illustrates how important it is that people in authority are trustworthy. Whether they be law enforcement personnel, judges, attorneys, doctors, teachers, pastors, or any others in authority, being able to trust them is paramount, for their authority gives them the power to do things they otherwise would not be entitled to do. As people of God, when we are given authority, God calls us to use it wisely and justly. As people of God, we are also called to hold others accountable when they misuse their authority. Nothing less than the well-being of our world is at stake.

Prayer

Almighty God, you have given each of us a certain degree of authority, whether as parents or leaders or supervisors of others. Forgive us whenever we misuse this authority. Grant us faithfulness and wisdom in our decision-making. Grant that we who have authority might be found to be using it always to your glory and for the blessing of all. In Christ's name we pray. AMEN.

Friday

Ps 96:1–9

[1] O sing to the LORD a new song;
    sing to the LORD, all the earth.
[2] Sing to the LORD; bless his name;
    tell of his salvation from day to day.
[3] Declare his glory among the nations,
    his marvelous works among all the peoples.

4 For great is the LORD and greatly to be praised;
he is to be revered above all gods.
5 For all the gods of the peoples are idols,
but the LORD made the heavens.
6 Honor and majesty are before him;
strength and beauty are in his sanctuary.
7 Ascribe to the LORD, O families of the peoples,
ascribe to the LORD glory and strength.
8 Ascribe to the LORD the glory due his name;
bring an offering, and come into his courts.
9 Worship the LORD in holy splendor;
tremble before him, all the earth.

We, as 21st-century Lutherans, do not often talk about idols. Perhaps we know or know of others for whom worship includes small objects of veneration, but idols are not a part of traditional Lutheran worship. In the days of the psalmist, however, idols were common and an accepted part of the culture. Notice how clear the psalmist is in delineating between the Lord and idols: "All the gods of the peoples are idols, *but the Lord made the heavens*." It's as if the psalmist is saying, "Yes, you have idols that you may attribute some power to, but here's the difference, *the Lord God made all things*!" In other words, our God and anything else you may be tempted to worship are not even to be compared; they are worlds apart in power and authority. This reminds me of St. Paul's succinct statement regarding idols. He said, "Indeed, even though there may be so-called gods in heaven or on earth—as in fact there are many gods and many lords—yet for us there is one God, the Father, from whom are all things and for whom we exist, and one Lord, Jesus Christ, through whom are all things and through whom we exist" (1 Cor 8:5–6). There it is: there are idols and there is the Living God. We need never confuse the two.

Prayer

Almighty God, Gracious Creator of all, we praise you for your power and wisdom. You have created all things, and you are worthy of all praise. Keep us from following false gods that have neither power nor goodness. Keep us close to you, listening to your wisdom, following in your ways, and walking in the way of your Son, Jesus Christ our Lord, in whose name we pray. AMEN.

The Fourth Week After Pentecost

Monday

Ps 5:1–5, 11–12

1 Listen to my words, O Lord;
attend to my sighing.
2 Listen to the sound of my cry,
my King and my God,
for to you I pray.
3 O Lord, in the morning you hear my voice;
in the morning I plead my case to you and watch.
4 For you are not a God who delights in wickedness;
evil will not sojourn with you.
5 The boastful will not stand before your eyes;
you hate all evildoers.
11 But let all who take refuge in you rejoice;
let them ever sing for joy.
Spread your protection over them,
so that those who love your name may exult in you.
12 For you bless the righteous, O Lord;
you cover them with favor as with a shield.

Whenever my wife hears me sigh, she says, "What's wrong?" She knows that sighing is a sign of weariness or worry or consternation. Here, the psalmist is sighing. Clearly this writer is weary of the wickedness that seems to have the upper hand or the evil that will not go away. We all know what this is like. We, too, grow weary of wickedness and evildoers that seem to have their way in the world. We sigh when we see dictators prevail and despots gain power. We groan when liars and grifters continue to gain influence. Yet, we stand with the psalmist who declares God's truth: God does not delight in wickedness but in righteousness. God blesses the righteous, those who walk in the ways of integrity and compassion, those who live uprightly and seek out the common good. God will not abandon those who walk in God's ways, but promises blessings evermore.

Prayer

Gracious and Merciful God, be near us in our sighing. When we are downhearted, lift us up. When we are weak, strengthen us. When we are feeling as though we are all alone, remind us of your presence. You are our God. You stand with us. Give us faith. In the name of Christ, we pray. AMEN.

Tuesday

Jon 3:10–4:5

> [10] When God saw what [the Ninevites]did, how they turned from their evil ways, God changed his mind about the calamity that he had said he would bring upon them, and he did not do it.
>
> 4 But this was very displeasing to Jonah, and he became an-
> gry. [2] He prayed to the Lord and said, "O Lord! Is not this what
> I said while I was still in my own country? That is why I fled to Tarshish at the beginning, for I knew that you are a gracious and merciful God, slow to anger, abounding in steadfast love,
> and relenting from punishment. [3] And now, O Lord, please take
> my life from me, for it is better for me to die than to live." [4] And
> the Lord said, "Is it right for you to be angry?" [5] Then Jonah
> went out of the city and sat down east of the city and made a booth for himself there. He sat under it in the shade, waiting to see what would become of the city.

The book of Jonah is a very clever parable about repentance. Repentance is understood as turning away from a certain practice or way of thinking and turning anew toward something life-giving. Jonah was commanded by God to go to the hated city of Nineveh and preach repentance to the people. Jonah refused and famously ended up in the belly of a large fish because of it. Eventually *he* repented and did what God had commanded. Much to his dismay, when he *did* preach to the Ninevites, they repented, and Jonah knew what that meant: they would not be destroyed. He was not pleased. Notice Jonah's response, "I knew that you are a gracious God, slow to anger, abounding in steadfast love, and relenting from punishment. And now, O Lord, please take my life from me, for it is better for me to die than to live." God's mercy was a scandal to Jonah. He would rather die than have God spare the Ninevites. He didn't want the Ninevites to repent; he wanted them judged! Jonah's attitude is one we may well recognize. Are there people that we would rather have God judge than forgive?

Prayer

Gracious God, forgive us for not wanting mercy for all. Forgive us for our failure to love our enemies as Christ commands. Grant us your generous Holy Spirit so that we might gain a spirit of compassion and love for all. And grant us your mercy, we pray. In Jesus' name. AMEN.

Wednesday

Acts 8:26–31, 35–38

> [26] Then an angel of the Lord said to Philip, "Get up and go to-
> ward the south to the road that goes down from Jerusalem to
> Gaza." (This is a wilderness road.) [27] So he got up and went.
> Now there was an Ethiopian eunuch, a court official of the
> Candace, the queen of the Ethiopians, in charge of her entire
> treasury. He had come to Jerusalem to worship [28] and was re-
> turning home; seated in his chariot, he was reading the prophet
> Isaiah. [29] Then the Spirit said to Philip, "Go over to this chariot
> and join it." [30] So Philip ran up to it and heard him reading
> the prophet Isaiah. He asked, "Do you understand what you
> are reading?" [31] He replied, "How can I, unless someone guides
> me?" And he invited Philip to get in and sit beside him.
>
> [35] Then Philip began to speak, and starting with this scripture
> he proclaimed to him the good news about Jesus. [36] As they
> were going along the road, they came to some water, and the
> eunuch said, "Look, here is water! What is to prevent me from
> being baptized?" [38] He commanded the chariot to stop, and

> both of them, Philip and the eunuch, went down into the water, and Philip baptized him.

The story of Philip the evangelist and the Ethiopian official is one of the most unlikely evangelism stories you will ever encounter. First of all, the evangelist is commanded to go to a place where he is likely to encounter no one—the wilderness. Second, when he does encounter a person, this person is the most unlikely of persons, indeed a person whom most Hebrews would have understood as outside of God's grace: (a) a foreigner, (b) a eunuch (a castrated male) and (c) a court official, who happens, at that very moment, to be reading the Hebrew bible. Finally, to top it off, though they are in the wilderness, water suddenly comes into view and the official is baptized. It seems clear that God's Spirit was very active in causing these events to take place, no matter how unlikely. This story remains to this day a formative story for Ethiopian Christians. If you ask them, they will tell you that this is where the Ethiopian Christian Church began, rather than with European colonial missionaries who brought the gospel to their shores. Indeed, Ethiopia remains one of the only countries in Africa that never lived under colonial rule. Perhaps this story serves as a reminder to us to never underestimate God's ability to make the unlikely a part of history.

Prayer

God of all times and places, increase our faith in your eternal activity in the world. Grow our ability to see you at work in all circumstances, despite appearances to the contrary. Give us eyes to see you at work and faith to believe that you are growing your Church so that people everywhere might come to know the life that is truly life. In your Son's name we pray. AMEN.

Thursday

Mark 7:24–30

> 24 From there [Jesus]set out and went away to the region of
> Tyre. He entered a house and did not want anyone to know he
> was there. Yet he could not escape notice, 25 but a woman whose
> little daughter had an unclean spirit immediately heard about
> him, and she came and bowed down at his feet. 26 Now the
> woman was a gentile, of Syrophoenician origin. She begged him

> to cast the demon out of her daughter. [27] He said to her, "Let the children be fed first, for it is not fair to take the children's food and throw it to the dogs." [28] But she answered him, "Sir, even the dogs under the table eat the children's crumbs." [29] Then he said to her, "For saying that, you may go—the demon has left your daughter." [30] And when she went home, she found the child lying on the bed and the demon gone.

This story has long been a source of consternation to preachers. How could Jesus say these things? How could he be so cruel? Actually, the truth is, he was doing what the people of his day would have assumed he'd do; he was paying no attention to a foreign woman. She had no right to even address him, a Hebrew rabbi, much less ask him for a favor. Yet, Jesus *did* hear her, and hearing her, he rethought his position. We aren't told that Jesus paused at the woman's response to him, but it's not hard to imagine that there was some silence between the woman's response and Jesus' next words, for he says to her, "For saying *that,* you may go—the demon has left your daughter." He might have said, "For believing in God's mercy with such fervor, for not being willing to let go of God's love for you and your daughter, yes, your request is granted." What a surprise that must have been to those who observed this. Mercy for this woman? Mercy for a foreigner? Mercy for one who has no claim on you? How *could* you Jesus? Yet, that's how God's love is: expansive beyond anything we can imagine.

Prayer

We praise you, Gracious God, for your vast storehouse of mercy. From your abundance we are forgiven again and again. From your abundance we are healed of our diseases, given strength in our weakness, offered light in our darkness. Grant us grace every day to receive your gifts and live in gratitude. In your holy name we pray. AMEN.

Friday

Neh 2:1–6

> [1] In the month of Nisan, in the twentieth year of King Artaxerxes, when wine was served him, I carried the wine and gave it to the king. Now, I had never been sad in his presence before. [2] So the king said to me, "Why is your face sad, since

> you are not sick? This can only be sadness of the heart." Then I was very much afraid. [3] I said to the king, "May the king live forever! Why should my face not be sad, when the city, the place of my ancestors' graves, lies waste and its gates have been destroyed by fire?" [4] Then the king said to me, "What do you request?" So I prayed to the God of heaven. [5] Then I said to the king, "If it pleases the king, and if your servant has found favor with you, I ask that you send me to Judah, to the city of my ancestors' graves, so that I may rebuild it." [6] The king said to me (the queen also was sitting beside him), "How long will you be gone, and when will you return?" So it pleased the king to send me, and I set him a date.

The book of Nehemiah is unusual in that Nehemiah was neither a priest nor a prophet; he was the cupbearer of a Babylonian king. In the first chapter of this book, he receives a report from his brother Hanani that Judah was in shambles. As he reports to the king, "The city, the place of my ancestors' graves, lies waste and its gates have been destroyed by fire." This gives him great sorrow. The king then says to him, "What do you request?" And he replies, "Let me return home to rebuild the city." His request is granted, but only on the condition that he will return to Babylon, which we assume he does. Nehemiah is an example for those of us who will never be pastors or teachers in the Church. God is at work through *all* of us. We might be only "cupbearers of the king" (e.g., engineers, nurses, data analysts, teachers, day care workers) and yet God can use us for important tasks. What is required? Only a compassionate heart, a willing spirit, and a faith in God's call. God's people have never *all* been called to be professional church workers. No, God's work is done in many times and places by people of faith, heeding God's call.

Prayer

We are your servants, Holy One. We are those who live under your gentle rule, who know you as Lord and Savior, who honor you as Creator and Sustainer of all life. Help us see ourselves as agents in your work to bring life to the world. Use us again and again to bring your saving gospel to a world in disrepair. In the name of Jesus we pray. AMEN.

The Fifth Week After Pentecost

Monday

Acts 22:6–11

> [6] "While I was on my way and approaching Damascus, about
> noon a great light from heaven suddenly shone about me. [7] I fell
> to the ground and heard a voice saying to me, 'Saul, Saul, why
> are you persecuting me?' [8] I answered, 'Who are you, Lord?'
> Then he said to me, 'I am Jesus of Nazareth whom you are
> persecuting.' [9] Now those who were with me saw the light but
> did not hear the voice of the one who was speaking to me. [10] I
> asked, 'What am I to do, Lord?' The Lord said to me, 'Get up
> and go to Damascus; there you will be told everything that has
> been assigned to you to do.' [11] Since I could not see because of
> the brightness of that light, those who were with me took my
> hand and led me to Damascus.

I recently read an article in the newspaper about a couple of kids who spent a lot of time in detention and in the principal's office during their school days. They were apparently "free spirits," but that was often interpreted as less than helpful to their teachers and administrators. In any case, at the end of the article, it was pointed out that they now were the joint-CEOs of a major construction firm, building the very schools that they had formerly terrorized. St. Paul, then called Saul, was exhibit A in this regard. He was a genuine terrorist to the early followers of Christ. We read in the book of Acts that he not only routinely rounded up Christians and sent them to prison, but even inspired others to do the same. Yet, God saw fit to appoint Paul to be one of the most important Church leaders the world has ever known. How amazing our God is, using the most unlikely amongst us to further the work of Christ.

Prayer

Thank you, Lord Jesus, for St. Paul and other unlikely saints whom you have chosen to bring the gospel to the world. Grant us faith in your ability to use all people to bring your good news to the world. Help us to be open to your call. In Christ's name we pray. AMEN.

Tuesday

Matt 9:2–8

> 2 And some people were carrying to him a paralyzed man lying
> on a stretcher. When Jesus saw their faith, he said to the para-
> lytic, "Take heart, child; your sins are forgiven." 3 Then some of
> the scribes said to themselves, "This man is blaspheming." 4 But
> Jesus, perceiving their thoughts, said, "Why do you think evil in
> your hearts? 5 For which is easier: to say, 'Your sins are forgiven,'
> or to say, 'Stand up and walk'? 6 But so that you may know that
> the Son of Man has authority on earth to forgive sins"—he then
> said to the paralytic—"Stand up, take your bed, and go to your
> home." 7 And he stood up and went to his home. 8 When the
> crowds saw it, they were filled with awe, and they glorified God,
> who had given such authority to human beings.

There is much to ponder in this healing story, but one line sticks out for me: "When Jesus saw *their faith,* he said to the paralytic, 'Take heart, child; your sins are forgiven.'" This whole miracle story apparently begins by Jesus recognizing the faith of the people bringing the paralyzed man to him, without any attention paid to the faith of the man himself, as we might expect. We tend to assume that what is essential in a healing is *the patient's* faith, rather than the faith of others. Yet, here, it is clearly the faith of those who care for the man that sets things in motion. Non-Western cultures would not find this story curious at all; they know the importance of community. Indeed, many cultures hold up the community as much more important than the individual. This is precisely what St. Paul means when he writes about the Body of Christ. He says, "When one suffers, all suffer, and when one rejoices, all rejoice." We might add, "When one has faith, *all* have faith."

In other words, the faith of the *community* is what is crucial, not simply the faith of the individual. How freeing this is, to know that even when *our* faith falters, the faith of God's people is there to hold us up.

Prayer

Thank you for your people, the Church, Lord Jesus. Thank you for the faith and love you give to your people. Thank you for the gifts you bestow on us. Thank you for the gifts that your people share with all of us and the world. Grant us faith so that all may be healed. In your holy name we pray. AMEN.

Wednesday

Ps 68:32–35

32 Sing to God, O kingdoms of the earth;
 sing praises to the Lord,
33 O rider in the heavens, the ancient heavens;
 listen, he sends out his voice, his mighty voice.
34 Ascribe power to God,
 whose majesty is over Israel
 and whose power is in the skies.
35 Awesome is God in his sanctuary,
 the God of Israel;
 he gives power and strength to his people.
Blessed be God!

Psalm 68 is one of the oldest psalms in the Bible. This psalm pictures God riding on a chariot of storm clouds, bringing deliverance to the oppressed and hope to God's people. I wonder if Marvel Comics ever referred to this psalm. You know how the superheroes in those comics are always riding around on thunderbolts and such. Who knows, maybe the makers of Marvel Comics got their inspiration from the Psalms! The point is, *God is powerful.* The psalmist wants to make that point. "Ascribe power to God," the writer says. But beyond that, notice what God does with that power: God "gives power and strength to his people." This is something that no comic book character ever did. Yes, God has all power and strength, but God also bestows that incredible power upon people, so that God's people can overcome their own enemies: unbelief, fear, despair, and doubt. In response to this gift, we shout with the psalmist, "Blessed be God!"

Prayer

We praise you, Almighty God, for your strength and power. We praise you that our enemies are no match for you. We praise you that your love and concern for us includes fighting our enemies alongside us. Assure us always of your love and power, O God, and help us to have courage whenever we are called to fight the good fight. In your holy name we pray. AMEN.

Thursday

Gen 22:1–3, 7–8

> After these things God tested Abraham. He said to him, "Abra-
> ham!" And he said, "Here I am." [2] He said, "Take your son, your
> only son Isaac, whom you love, and go to the land of Moriah and
> offer him there as a burnt offering on one of the mountains that I
> shall show you." [3] So Abraham rose early in the morning, saddled
> his donkey, and took two of his young men with him and his son
> Isaac; he cut the wood for the burnt offering and set out and went
> to the place in the distance that God had shown him.
>
> [7] Isaac said to his father Abraham, "Father!" And he said, "Here I
> am, my son." He said, "The fire and the wood are here, but where
> is the lamb for a burnt offering?" [8] Abraham said, "God himself
> will provide the lamb for a burnt offering, my son." And the two
> of them walked on together.

This well-known Old Testament story is one of the most troubling stories in all of Scripture. From our point of view, God's request seems utterly unthinkable. How could a good and gracious God ask this of a loving parent? What kind of a God would test a person in this way? What is at least as startling is the fact that Abraham, apparently without hesitation, obeys. At least, if he did put up a fuss, it is not recorded. The writer to the Hebrews has an explanation for Abraham's obedience: "By faith, Abraham, when put to the test, offered up Isaac . . . He considered the fact that God is able even to raise someone from the dead—and figuratively speaking, he did receive him back" (Heb. 11:17–19). Another explanation is that Abraham, who lived in a culture where child sacrifice was not unknown, may have wrongly assumed that God was like the cruel gods of the culture surrounding him. Perhaps he, unlike us, actually thought God might make this demand on him. Imagine his delight when, at the end of this story, God is shown to be utterly *unlike* those false gods, ever merciful, ever loving, ever just.

Prayer

Ever Gracious and Loving God, how we praise you for your never-changing love. How we praise you for continuing to be the Merciful One, the God of Steadfast Love, the Lover of All Life. Keep us from ever seeing you as cruel, merciless, or without regard for creation. Give us faith in you and in your Son Jesus, who is the face of all mercy, in whose name we pray. AMEN.

Friday

Luke 8:42b–48

> As he went, the crowds pressed in on him. [43] Now there was
> a woman who had been suffering from a flow of blood for
> twelve years, and though she had spent all she had on physi-
> cians, no one could cure her. [44] She came up behind [Jesus]and
> touched the fringe of his cloak, and immediately her flow of
> blood stopped. [45] Then Jesus asked, "Who touched me?" When
> they all denied it, Peter said, "Master, the crowds are hemming
> you in and pressing against you." [46] But Jesus said, "Some-
> one touched me, for I noticed that power had gone out from
> me." [47] When the woman realized that she could not remain
> hidden, she came trembling, and falling down before him, she
> declared in the presence of all the people why she had touched
> him and how she had been immediately healed. [48] He said to
> her, "Daughter, your faith has made you well; go in peace."

There is an interesting image in this miracle story. Jesus says that he noticed that power had gone out from him. It's almost as if Jesus is pictured as a well or a storehouse of power from which others might receive what they need. It's equally interesting that access to Jesus' power warehouse appears to be on the honor system. Anyone can access it at any time; at least that's what seems to have happened here. This woman, who had been suffering for 12 years, reached out and touched the cloak of Jesus and his healing power flowed into her. It wasn't until later that we learn of her faith. Jesus' power came into her despite Jesus not even knowing who she was. This is a hopeful story for us because it assures us that God's healing power is available to us as well. We certainly don't know why some prayers for healing seem to be answered and others are not, but we pray believing it is God's will to heal. We pray understanding that God's unlimited storehouse of power and love is available to us whenever we need it. Thanks be to God for God's abundant mercy!

Prayer

We are ever in need of your healing power, O God. Illnesses of every kind beset us: mental and physical illness, emotional instability, addictions, and injuries galore. Grant us healing from your great storehouse of power. Grant our loved ones your protection and healing as well. In all things, provide your people wholeness that leads to joy. We ask this through Christ our Lord. AMEN.

The Sixth Week After Pentecost

Monday

2 Sam 13:23–29, 37–39

23 After two full years Absalom had sheepshearers at Baal-
hazor, which is near Ephraim, and Absalom invited all the
king's sons. 24 Absalom came to the king and said, "Your servant
has sheepshearers; will the king and his servants please go with
your servant?" 25 But the king said to Absalom, "No, my son, let
us not all go, or else we will be burdensome to you." He pressed
him, but he would not go but gave him his blessing. 26 Then Ab-
salom said, "If not, please let my brother Amnon go with us."
The king said to him, "Why should he go with you?" 27 But Ab-
salom pressed him until he let Amnon and all the king's sons go
with him. Absalom made a feast like a king's feast. 28 Then Ab-
salom commanded his servants, "Watch when Amnon's heart is
merry with wine, and when I say to you, 'Strike Amnon,' then
kill him. Do not be afraid; have I not myself commanded you?
Be courageous and valiant." 29 So the servants of Absalom did to
Amnon as Absalom had commanded. Then all the king's sons
rose, and each mounted his mule and fled.

37 But Absalom fled and went to Talmai son of Ammihud, king
of Geshur. David mourned for his son day after day. 38 Absalom,
having fled to Geshur, stayed there three years. 39 And the heart
of the king went out, yearning for Absalom, for he was now con-
soled over the death of Amnon.

This tale of a murder between brothers is part of a larger, more tragic narrative that happens between the children of King David. Absalom, David's son, has planned this murder in response to the rape of his sister, Tamar, by his brother Amnon. It is an act of revenge. Absalom feels justified in his actions partly because his father has failed to address the issue of his sister's rape. Needless to say, this family is a mess. We sometimes assume that families of godly men and women don't have any problems. We might think that if Mom and Dad go to church, are good to each other, and raise their children in a loving, supportive, and God-fearing home, all will be well. Tragically, this is not always the case. In fact, in faithful families, just like in all families, problems inevitably arise: sibling rivalries, jealousy, envy, resentment, and yes, even hatred. Like King David, parents grieve over such scenarios but often feel helpless to make peace. In times like these, we return again to our Lord's command to forgive not just seven times, but seventy times seven. In other words, forgiveness is *always* the place to begin.

Prayer

Help us, Merciful God, whenever we are tempted to live in resentment or long-held contempt of another. Free us from believing that somehow such behavior is life-giving. Release us from our resentments and grant us the grace to forgive as we have been forgiven. In the name of Christ, we pray. AMEN.

Tuesday

Rom 11:1–6

> I ask, then, has God rejected his people? By no means! I myself am an Israelite, a descendant of Abraham, a member of the tribe of Benjamin. [2] God has not rejected his people whom he foreknew. Do you not know what the scripture says of Elijah, how he pleads with God against Israel? [3] "Lord, they have killed your prophets, they have demolished your altars; I alone am left, and they are seeking my life." [4] But what is the divine reply to him? "I have kept for myself seven thousand who have not bowed the knee to Baal." [5] So, too, at the present time there is a remnant chosen by grace. [6] But if it is by grace, it is no longer on the basis of works, otherwise grace would no longer be grace.

St. Paul is speaking here about something very personal to him. He, a Jew, is wondering if God's new covenant through Jesus Christ has nullified the covenant God made with Israel. His conclusion? By no means! When God makes a covenant, it is *forever*. God's covenant people are and always will be God's covenant people. It's just that now that covenant is expanded. And beyond that, when we are tempted to despair that God's people will someday be wiped out, Paul reminds us of the Lord's word to the prophet Elijah: "I have kept for myself seven thousand who have not bowed the knee to Baal." Baal was the name of one of the chief gods of the culture in which Israel was embedded. God was saying, "Do not fear; faithful people will always be present." This passage assures us of two things: God's covenant is everlasting, and God's ability to raise up faithful people is equally everlasting. In short, in all times and places, God is at work, creating life and faith, hope and peace. We can count on that.

Prayer

We thank you, Gracious God, for your everlasting faithfulness, your boundless power, and your immeasurable love. We live by your gracious hand. Grant us faith to live in your promises every day, to take joy in your work within and around us, and to find strength to answer your call. In your holy name we pray. AMEN.

Wednesday

Jas 4:1–6

Those conflicts and disputes among you, where do they come
from? Do they not come from your cravings that are at war
within you? 2 You want something and do not have it, so you
commit murder. And you covet something and cannot obtain
it, so you engage in disputes and conflicts. You do not have
because you do not ask. 3 You ask and do not receive because
you ask wrongly, in order to spend what you get on your plea-
sures. 4 Adulterers! Do you not know that friendship with the
world is enmity with God? Therefore whoever wishes to be a
friend of the world becomes an enemy of God. 5 Or do you sup-
pose that the scripture speaks to no purpose? Does the spirit
that God caused to dwell in us desire envy? 6 But God gives all
the more grace; therefore it says,

"God opposes the proud
but gives grace to the humble."

Adultery is the metaphor the Bible has long used for idolatry. In the Old Testament, particularly, whenever God's people wander off to worship other gods, the prophets call them adulterers: they are wandering away from their First Love and seeking pleasure with another. Here, in the book of James, the writer compares friendship with the world to adultery. He says, in effect, that if you "get into bed" with the ways of this world, you will inevitably be breaking your marriage covenant with God. This follows other verses in the New Testament that remind us that the ways of the Spirit and the ways of the flesh are opposed to one another. The metaphor of adultery is all the more powerful because it speaks of betrayal. God is our first love. God is the one who has cared for us and supported us and stood with us all our days. When we wander off to other suitors, we are betraying the very One who has loved us all the way to the Cross.

Prayer

Forgive us, Lord, for our wanderings. Forgive us for our penchant to leave behind all that is life-giving for that which promises only momentary satisfaction. Forgive us for betraying you in thought, word, and deed, and, at times, giving no second thought to it. We stand in need of your mercy. Have mercy on us, and draw us again close to you, that we may dwell in your embrace forevermore. In the name of Christ, we pray. AMEN.

Thursday

Gal 3:1–5

> You foolish Galatians! Who has bewitched you? It was before
> your eyes that Jesus Christ was publicly exhibited as cruci-
> fied! 2 The only thing I want to learn from you is this: Did you
> receive the Spirit by doing the works of the law or by believing
> what you heard? 3 Are you so foolish? Having started with the
> Spirit, are you now ending with the flesh? 4 Did you experience
> so much for nothing?—if it really was for nothing. 5 Well then,
> does God supply you with the Spirit and work miracles among
> you by your doing the works of the law or by your believing
> what you heard?

We hear in this passage the central question of the Apostle Paul's theology: Does salvation come by works or by faith? He is chastising the Galatians because they have apparently been duped into believing that it is because they have been so faithful in observing God's laws that they are loved by God. God has, to be crass, *paid them* for their service. To have this transactional view of God is a common temptation for us all. In our language about heaven, we often talk about rewards. This is perhaps best shown in the many jokes we tell about St. Peter's gate. Here's one: A preacher and a lawyer ended up together at the pearly gates where St. Peter greeted them with the words, "Welcome. Let me show you to your heavenly home." Walking down the lane, St. Peter noted a small cottage in the woods and said to the preacher, "Here you go, Rev. This will be your home for eternity." "Very nice," said the preacher, "but what about him?" "Oh, don't worry about him," said St. Peter, "We have a mansion for him on the other side of town." "How's that fair?" said the preacher. "Well, it's like this," said St. Peter. "Guys like you are a dime a dozen around here, but we've *never* had a lawyer." This funny story is soaked through and through with a transactional view of God, where we are rewarded in heaven based on our activities on earth. St. Paul reminds us that this is *not* God's way. God's way is the way of love, not the way of the marketplace. We receive far more from God than we could ever hope to earn. That's called grace.

Prayer

Thank you, God of all Life, that your grace is endless and your love inexhaustible. Help us to live, believing in your love and grace, knowing that it all depends on you, not us. In your holy name, we pray. AMEN.

Friday

Ps 22:25–31

25 From you comes my praise in the great congregation;
my vows I will pay before those who fear him.
26 The poor shall eat and be satisfied;
those who seek him shall praise the LORD.
May your hearts live forever!
27 All the ends of the earth shall remember
and turn to the LORD,
and all the families of the nations

shall worship before him.
28 For dominion belongs to the LORD,
and he rules over the nations.
29 To him, indeed, shall all who sleep in the earth bow down;
before him shall bow all who go down to the dust,
and I shall live for him.
30 Posterity will serve him;
future generations will be told about the Lord
31 and proclaim his deliverance to a people yet unborn,
saying that he has done it.

Psalm 22 is a lament psalm, a cry for deliverance. It is striking, therefore, that it ends with praise. Why is that? Because in the course of the psalm, the cries for deliverance are heard and answered, and the one in distress is given help. What is also striking is the extent to which this praise is spoken. First, the writer says that "the great congregation" (i.e., the worshipping community) will praise God. Then it is the poor who will praise God, and then "all the families of the nations" join in. But the writer doesn't stop there: even "all who sleep in the earth" shall bow down. This means that those already dead will rise and praise God. And finally, future generations and even "people yet unborn" will rise and praise God. Why? Because God is faithful today, tomorrow, and even beyond time. God's faithfulness never ends. As St. Paul reminds us elsewhere, "Whether we live or whether we die, we are the Lord's." And we might add, "And whether we live or whether we die, we will praise the Lord," for God's faithfulness endures forever. Alleluia!

Prayer

We praise you for your faithfulness, Almighty and Gracious God. We praise you for your power and love. We praise you for your wisdom and compassion. Give us faith every day to live in trust of you. As we near our final days, remind us that even in death, we will praise you. In Christ's name we pray. AMEN.

The Seventh Week After Pentecost

Monday

Isa 56:3–7

3 Do not let the foreigner joined to the LORD say,
"The LORD will surely separate me from his people,"
and do not let the eunuch say,
"I am just a dry tree."
4 For thus says the LORD:
To the eunuchs who keep my Sabbaths,
who choose the things that please me
and hold fast my covenant,
5 I will give, in my house and within my walls,
a monument and a name
better than sons and daughters;
I will give them an everlasting name
that shall not be cut off.
6 And the foreigners who join themselves to the LORD,
to minister to him, to love the name of the LORD,
and to be his servants,
all who keep the Sabbath and do not profane it
and hold fast my covenant—
7 these I will bring to my holy mountain
and make them joyful in my house of prayer;
their burnt offerings and their sacrifices
will be accepted on my altar,

for my house shall be called a house of prayer
for all peoples.

These verses from the last section of Isaiah speak of God's radical welcome. For most of Israel's history it was understood that eunuchs (males whose sexual organs had been removed) and foreigners were not welcome in God's house or amongst God's people. Indeed, the local synagogue was set up with very clear boundaries as to who could be present and how close they could be to the holy vessels and Scriptures. Isaiah's new vision breaks down all those distinctions. Importance is no longer given to bloodlines and heritage or origin and clan, but instead faithfulness to God is prioritized. Those who hold fast to the covenant and do the things that please God now give one "a name better than sons and daughters." This is a radical statement. No more do those who were born outside of Israel have to fear that God will not embrace them. "For my house shall be called a house of prayer for *all people*," says the Lord.

Prayer

How we thank and praise you, Almighty God, for your generous welcome of us all. Forgive us for ever believing there are limits to your grace. As we have been welcomed, let us welcome others. In the name of Christ we pray. AMEN.

Tuesday

Matt 9:27–34

[27] As Jesus went on from there, two blind men followed him,
crying loudly, "Have mercy on us, Son of David!" [28] When he
entered the house, the blind men came to him, and Jesus said to
them, "Do you have faith that I can do this?" They said to him,
"Yes, Lord." [29] Then he touched their eyes and said, "According to
your faith, let it be done to you." [30] And their eyes were opened.
Then Jesus sternly ordered them, "See that no one knows of
this." [31] But they went away and spread the news about him
through all of that district. [32] After they had gone away, a demon-
possessed man who was mute was brought to him. [33] And when
the demon had been cast out, the one who had been mute spoke,
and the crowds were amazed and said, "Never has anything like

this been seen in Israel." [34] But the Pharisees were saying, "By the ruler of the demons he casts out the demons."

This passage reminds me of our present-day media. A couple of amazing events happen—Jesus opens the eyes of a blind man and casts out a demon from a man who had been mute—and immediately the spin doctors go into action. Some who witnessed the events are amazed, rejoice, apparently believe this Jesus is a man of God, and declare it to be so. Others, the opponents of Jesus who are eager to discredit him, interpret these spectacular events as the work of Satan. "Sure, he has power; there's no denying that. But where does it come from?" Their aim is to sow doubt in the hearts of those who might be ready to believe. The obvious fact that the Pharisees fail to see, however, is that what Jesus has done is *life-giving*. He gave sight to a blind man and speech to a mute. Satan has no interest in giving people life. These life-giving acts are clearly of God because that's what God does. Whenever we are confronted with people who claim to know or do the will of God, the simple question we need to ask is, "Is what they are saying or doing life-giving?" As Jesus said, "By their fruits you shall know them."

Prayer

Give us discernment, Gracious Lord, whenever we encounter spectacular events. Grant us faith to see and believe your gracious work and wisdom to know when the works before us are not of you. Thwart the efforts of Satan and other evil powers, and keep us all faithful to you. In your Son's name we pray. AMEN.

Wednesday

Ps 64:1–8

[1] Hear my voice, O God, in my complaint;
preserve my life from the dread enemy.
[2] Hide me from the secret plots of the wicked,
from the scheming of evildoers,
[3] who whet their tongues like swords,
who aim bitter words like arrows,
[4] shooting from ambush at the blameless;

they shoot suddenly and without fear.
5 They hold fast to their evil purpose;
they talk of laying snares secretly,
thinking, "Who can see us?
Who can search out our crimes?
We have thought out a cunningly conceived plot."
For the human heart and mind are deep.
7 But God will shoot his arrow at them;
they will be wounded suddenly.
8 Because of their tongue he will bring them to ruin;
all who see them will shake with horror.

This psalm is remarkable in that it compares bitter words to arrows. It lays out a scene where an enemy speaks ill of us secretly, without fear, and thinks "Who can see us? Who can search out our crimes?" This scene is one we seem to encounter regularly in the news these days. From the January 6 hearings in Congress, for example, we have heard over and over of high government officials who have done this very thing: slandering, lying, conspiring, and doing it all with impunity, saying, "No one will ever know." Of course, as the psalmist points out, those who act in such ways forget that whatever they have been up to has not gone unnoticed by God. God sees all things, and, as Jesus said, the day will come when all will be disclosed. This should give us pause if we are ever foolish enough to believe that dishonesty can be hidden from God. As the old saying goes, "Honesty is the best policy." It is also what God calls us to.

Prayer

Forgive us for our dishonesty, Lord. Forgive us, especially, whenever we have been foolish enough to believe that we can hide anything from you. Give us courage and faith to live lives of integrity and honesty, and to honor those who do the same. We pray this in the strong name of Christ our Lord. AMEN.

Thursday

1 Cor 1:18–24

> [18] For the message about the cross is foolishness to those who are perishing, but to us who are being saved it is the power of God. [19] For it is written,
>
> "I will destroy the wisdom of the wise,
> and the discernment of the discerning I will thwart."
>
> [20] Where is the one who is wise? Where is the scholar? Where is the debater of this age? Has not God made foolish the wisdom of the world? [21] For since, in the wisdom of God, the world did not know God through wisdom, God decided, through the foolishness of the proclamation, to save those who believe. [22] For Jews ask for signs and Greeks desire wisdom, [23] but we proclaim Christ crucified, a stumbling block to Jews and foolishness to gentiles, [24] but to those who are the called, both Jews and Greeks, Christ the power of God and the wisdom of God.

The opening verse of this passage has always fascinated me. It suggests that "perishing" and "being saved" is not a static identity for any of us. In other words, both are ongoing. Perhaps it is even likely that all of us are at one point drawn to the life that is perishing, but then at another point drawn to the life that leads to salvation. This reminds me of a great scene in C. S. Lewis' book, *The Great Divorce*. The scene depicts a meeting between a ghost (Lewis' term for those who are "perishing" on earth after death) and a "Bright Spirit" (Lewis' term for people who are saved and taken to heaven). The two are discussing their lives on earth: "'Oh, of course. I'm wrong,' said the ghost. 'Everything I say and do is wrong, according to you.' 'But of course!' said the Spirit, shining with love and mirth [...]'That's what we all find when we reach [heaven]. We've all been wrong! That's the great joke. There's no need to go on pretending one was right! After that we begin living'" (p. 93). This is what St. Paul means when he says God makes foolish the wisdom of the world. Someday we will find out we've all been wrong about lots of things. And then we will be free.

Prayer

Your wisdom is beyond our comprehension, O God. Our wisdom is so small. Give us humility to hold all our wisdom lightly and to trust in your amazing grace. In Christ's name we pray. AMEN.

Friday

Job 19:1–7, 21–22

Then Job answered:
2 "How long will you torment me
  and break me in pieces with words?
3 These ten times you have cast reproach upon me;
  are you not ashamed to wrong me?
4 And even if it is true that I have erred,
  my error remains with me.
5 If indeed you magnify yourselves against me
  and make my humiliation an argument against me,
6 know then that God has put me in the wrong
  and closed his net around me.
7 Even when I cry out, 'Violence!' I am not answered;
  I call aloud, but there is no justice.
21 Have pity on me, have pity on me, O you my friends,
  for the hand of God has touched me!
22 Why do you, like God, pursue me,
  never satisfied with my flesh?

The book of Job is an argument about the justice of God. The friends of Job insist that Job is suffering because he is wicked. Job insists this is not the case. Still, his friends continue to beat this drum, unwilling to consider that suffering comes to the righteous as well as the wicked. In this passage, Job cries out to his friends and asks them why they torment him. "Have pity on me, O you my friends," he cries. He simply wants them to be supportive of him in his suffering instead of making everything worse. This reminds me of a children's book by Cori Doerrfeld titled, *The Rabbit Listened*. In the book, little Taylor builds a wonderful tower of blocks that comes tumbling down when some pesky birds fly into it. Taylor is devastated. One by one,

Taylor's friends, the chicken, the bear, the elephant, and the kangaroo, come by and give their advice. Finally, the rabbit comes by, but rather than advising Taylor, the rabbit sits quietly while she grieves her loss. That's all Taylor needs. We do well to remember stories like these whenever we are tempted to try to explain the cause of someone else's suffering. Listening to them and being present with them might be all they really need.

Prayer

Gracious God, you have mourned with us and rejoiced with us. You have been near us in good times and in bad. Help us to be this way with others. Keep us from needing to explain all things, and show us the quiet way of love. In your Son's name we pray. AMEN.

The Eighth Week After Pentecost

Monday

Eph 2:17–22

> [17] So [Christ]came and proclaimed peace to you who were far
> off and peace to those who were near, [18] for through him both
> of us have access in one Spirit to the Father. [19] So then, you are
> no longer strangers and aliens, but you are fellow citizens with
> the saints and also members of the household of God, [20] built
> upon the foundation of the apostles and prophets, with Christ
> Jesus himself as the cornerstone; [21] in him the whole struc-
> ture is joined together and grows into a holy temple in the
> Lord, [22] in whom you also are built together spiritually into a
> dwelling place for God.

In this letter to the Ephesians, we hear the announcement that Christ has proclaimed peace to those "far off" and peace to those "near." The writer is talking here about Jews and Gentiles. He says that Christ's death on the cross has put to death the hostility between the two groups and now all believers are "fellow citizens with the saints and also members of the household of God." This is important to remember. Sometimes we forget that those who don't worship as we do or don't believe precisely as we do are members of the household of God too. They are not "fraudulent Christians" simply because they baptize by immersion instead of sprinkling, or because they only have Holy Communion twice a year. We sometimes squabble and make a fuss about all sorts of things that, finally, may not matter a great deal at all. With all the divisions in our society *outside* of the Church, perhaps it behooves us to keep to a minimum the divisions *within* the Church. Maybe if we modeled the peace that Christ brought to the world, we might help be the healing presence that is so badly needed.

Prayer

God of All Wisdom, forgive us for our petty infighting. Forgive us for failing to see all your children as members of the household of God. Grant us a new spirit, a spirit of peace, so that when we are confronted with difference, we might strive for the unity found in you. In your holy name we pray. AMEN.

Tuesday

Ps 16:5–11

5 The LORD is my chosen portion and my cup;
    you hold my lot.
6 The boundary lines have fallen for me in pleasant places;
    I have a goodly heritage.
7 I bless the LORD, who gives me counsel;
    in the night also my heart instructs me.
8 I keep the LORD always before me;
    because he is at my right hand, I shall not be moved.
9 Therefore my heart is glad, and my soul rejoices;
    my body also rests secure.
10 For you do not give me up to Sheol
    or let your faithful one see the Pit.
11 You show me the path of life.
    In your presence there is fullness of joy;
    in your right hand are pleasures forevermore.

This is a psalm for those of us who live comfortably, for we who have been blessed to have "the boundary lines fall in pleasant places." This can rightly be said about many of us who have been raised in this country. We live in a land where war, famine, and government collapse are unknown. We live in a land where a vast infrastructure of education, transportation, medicine, commerce, and industry is in place. We live in a land where fine crops and abundant harvests are taken for granted, along with so many other things.

Many around the globe lack these things, and can only dream of taking them for granted as we do. And so, as those who have a "good heritage," it befits us to do as the psalmist does and "keep the Lord always before us." This means paying close attention to where God is leading us and doing all we can to follow. This means taking our cues from Jesus when it comes to our words and actions toward others. This means living in gratitude for all we have in Christ. This means being generous in sharing our abundance. It is true, as the psalmist says, that God shows us "the path of life." In Christ's presence there *is* fullness of joy, and in Christ's right hand there *are* pleasures forevermore.

Prayer

God of All Life, thank you for your countless blessings to us, your people. We do not know why we have been so blessed, but we thank you for the abundance we enjoy. Help us to be good stewards of your abundance, and to keep our eyes ever turned toward you, so that we might walk in the ways of peace and love all our days. We ask this in Christ's name. AMEN.

Wednesday

2 Cor 13:5–10

> [5] Examine yourselves to see whether you are living in the faith.
> Test yourselves. Do you not realize that Jesus Christ is in you?—
> unless, indeed, you fail to meet the test! [6] I hope you will find
> out that we have not failed. [7] But we pray to God that you may
> not do anything wrong—not that we may appear to have met
> the test but that you may do what is right, though we may seem
> to have failed. [8] For we cannot do anything against the truth but
> only for the truth. [9] For we rejoice when we are weak but you are
> strong. This is what we pray for, that you may be restored. [10] So
> I write these things while I am away from you, so that when I
> come I may not have to be severe in using the authority that the
> Lord has given me for building up and not for tearing down.

This is the very end of St. Paul's last letter to the Corinthians. Some scholars have called it the "severe letter." It has the tone of a parent who has heard that the teenagers, left to their own devices while Mom and Dad are away, are *not* fulfilling their promises. "Do you not realize that Jesus Christ is in you?" says the apostle. St. Paul is reminding the Corinthians who they are. They bear the name of Christ. Their behavior is a witness to the world. Their words and actions will announce to the world that this is what followers of Christ look like. This reminds me of a time when a Vietnamese family was moving into our community and our church was helping them get settled. When I arrived with a pickup full of furniture for their new apartment, they were baffled. Since they did not speak English, I drew a picture of a church with a cross on it and pointed to all the stuff I had brought. The man's face lit up and he said, "Ah, Christian!" He understood; these gifts were from Christians. Every day we have the opportunity to bear witness to Christ. Our witness can be one that brings honor to Jesus and blesses others, or one that scandalizes his name and causes hurt. We need no reminder which witness we must choose.

Prayer

Almighty and Gracious God, we thank you for the opportunity we have each day to bear witness to the name of Christ. Help us to be faithful in this calling. We are your people. In your holy name we pray. AMEN.

Thursday

Luke 9:21–27

> 21 [Following Peter's declaration, Jesus]sternly ordered and com-
> manded [his disciples]not to tell anyone, 22 saying, "The Son of
> Man must undergo great suffering and be rejected by the elders,
> chief priests, and scribes and be killed and on the third day be
> raised." 23 Then he said to them all, "If any wish to come after
> me, let them deny themselves and take up their cross daily and
> follow me. 24 For those who want to save their life will lose it,
> and those who lose their life for my sake will save it. 25 For what
> does it profit them if they gain the whole world but lose or forfeit
> themselves? 26 Those who are ashamed of me and of my words,
> of them the Son of Man will be ashamed when he comes in his
> glory and the glory of the Father and of the holy angels. 27 In-
> deed, truly I tell you, there are some standing here who will not
> taste death before they see the kingdom of God."

Losing one's life in order to save it—this one of the hardest things to understand, and yet it is the crux of the Jesus way. We so much want to believe that it's the other way around, that if we only do lots of spiritual weightlifting so that we are spiritual superheroes, will we ensure that our spiritual life is safe. We want to believe that if we only study enough and pray enough and serve enough, our salvation is ensured. But Jesus says no. Jesus says, you must let go of the need to build yourself up and, in fact, *die*, if you want to live. That is to say, we must let go of our own life so that the life of Jesus can live within us. It is as St. Paul said in the letter to the Galatians: "It is no longer I who live, but Christ who lives in me, and the life I now live in the flesh I live by faith in the Son of God who loved me and gave himself for me." This is how we lose our life in order to save it.

Prayer

Lord Christ, release us from our continual quest for salvation. Help us to release our life into your safekeeping and to trust that the more we are yours, the more we are truly alive. Give us faith to live each day in your grace. We pray this in your holy name. AMEN.

Friday

Gen 24:42–48

2 "I came today to the spring and said, 'O LORD, God of my mas-
ter Abraham, if now you will only make successful the way I am
going! 43 I am standing here by the spring of water; let the young
woman who comes out to draw, to whom I shall say, "Please
give me a little water from your jar to drink," 44 and who will say
to me, "Drink, and I will draw for your camels also"—let her be
the woman whom the LORD has appointed for my master's son.'

45 "Before I had finished speaking in my heart, there was Re-
bekah coming out with her water jar on her shoulder, and she
went down to the spring and drew. I said to her, 'Please let me
drink.' 46 She quickly let down her jar from her shoulder and
said, 'Drink, and I will also water your camels.' So I drank, and
she also watered the camels. 47 Then I asked her, 'Whose daugh-
ter are you?' She said, 'The daughter of Bethuel, Nahor's son,
whom Milcah bore to him.' So I put the ring on her nose and the
bracelets on her arms. 48 Then I bowed my head and worshiped

> the LORD and blessed the LORD, the God of my master Abraham, who had led me by the right way to obtain the daughter of my master's kinsman for his son.

If you haven't read the story of how Abraham sent a trusted servant to his kinsman seeking a wife for his son, Isaac, it is worth reading the whole of Gen 24. It is a love story, even though, of course, it tells of an arranged marriage, which was how things were done in the days of Abraham. What is worth noting in this story is how the servant simply trusts that God will lead him to the woman that is right for his master's son. He asks for a specific sign, and when it is fulfilled, he is certain God has led him to this point. I wonder if our modern skepticism of such methods doesn't often keep us from looking for God's hand in our everyday lives. Unlike Abraham's servant, we don't ask God for guidance, and we don't expect any; we simply assume that we are to live by the wits God has given us. What if, instead, we began to be attentive to, or even expectant of God's guidance in our lives? What if, instead of simply living by our wits, or as St. Paul said, "by sight," we decided to walk by faith? What then? Would we perhaps notice that God *is* active, leading and guiding us each day? Might that not be quite an adventure?

Prayer

Give us faith, Gracious God, to believe in your guiding. Give us faith to live each day expectant that you are watching over us and leading us. Help us to see you at work, and give us joy in our seeing. We pray this in the name of Jesus. AMEN.

The Ninth Week After Pentecost

Monday

1 John 2:7–11

7 Beloved, I am writing you no new commandment but an old
commandment that you have had from the beginning; the old
commandment is the word that you have heard. 8 Yet I am writ-
ing you a new commandment that is true in him and in you,
because the darkness is passing away and the true light is al-
ready shining. 9 Whoever says, "I am in the light," while hating
a brother or sister, is still in the darkness. 10 Whoever loves a
brother or sister abides in the light, and in such a person there is
no cause for stumbling. 11 But whoever hates a brother or sister
is in the darkness, walks in the darkness, and does not know the
way to go, because the darkness has brought on blindness.

Considerable harm is done whenever the name of Christ is used to promote hate: that is the message of this passage. John was familiar with people who mistakenly thought being a follower of Christ only entailed *intellectual* assent to certain tenets, but had nothing to do with how one treated one's fellow believers. John reminds his readers that this notion is false. Hating others and claiming to "walk in the light" do *not* go hand-in-hand. When Jesus was asked by his followers how one would know who was a true follower and who was not, he famously said, "By their fruits you shall know them." In other words, whenever the fruits of the Spirit—love, joy, peace, patience, kindness, and so forth—are present in a person, we can be confident they are people of authentic faith. When those things are *not* present, beware.

Prayer

Give us wisdom and humility, Gracious Lord, to know the truth and to live in it. Keep us from deceptive practices and from being misled by deceivers. Grant that all your people would be faithful to live in Christlike ways each day, to live in ways that bless others and bring glory to you. We pray this in your precious name. AMEN.

Tuesday

Ps 141:1–5

1 I call upon you, O LORD; come quickly to me;
give ear to my voice when I call to you.
2 Let my prayer be counted as incense before you
and the lifting up of my hands as an evening sacrifice.
3 Set a guard over my mouth, O LORD;
keep watch over the door of my lips.
4 Do not turn my heart to any evil,
to busy myself with wicked deeds
in company with those who work iniquity;
do not let me eat of their delicacies.
5 Let the righteous strike me;
let the faithful correct me.
Never let the oil of the wicked anoint my head,
for my prayer is continually against their wicked deeds.

The first two verses of this psalm will sound familiar to anyone who has sung the Evening Prayer service. In one of my favorite settings of this service, Holden Evening Prayer by Marty Haugen, these verses are set to a beautiful song that we sing in canon. What is most striking about the prayer is found in verse 5. The writer prays that God would raise up faithful people *to correct him* lest he go astray. He asks God to keep him from busying himself "with wicked deeds" and asks that "the oil of the wicked" never anoint his head. In other words, he asks that he never be found in the favor of the wicked. I wonder how often we pray for correction. I wonder how often we pray that God would raise up other believers who will let us know when we are going astray. Maybe that's exactly what we should be praying for these days. After all, what did St. Peter remind us of? "Discipline yourself, keep alert. Like a roaring lion your adversary the devil, prowls around, looking for someone to devour" (1 Pet 5:8).

Prayer

Give us faithful saints who will tell us the truth about ourselves, Gracious God. Give us courageous friends who love us enough to let us know when we are going astray. Keep us from the devil's lair, and guide us always into the way of peace and joy. We ask this through Christ our Lord. AMEN.

Wednesday

Jer 3:15–18

> 15 I will give you shepherds after my own heart who will feed
> you with knowledge and understanding. 16 And when you
> have multiplied and increased in the land, in those days, says
> the LORD, they shall no longer say, "The ark of the covenant
> of the LORD." It shall not come to mind or be remembered or
> missed, nor shall another one be made. 17 At that time Jeru-
> salem shall be called the throne of the LORD, and all nations
> shall gather to it, to the presence of the LORD in Jerusalem, and
> they shall no longer stubbornly follow their own evil will. 18 In
> those days the house of Judah shall join the house of Israel, and
> together they shall come from the land of the north to the land
> that I gave your ancestors for a heritage.

Jeremiah's vision in this passage is a glorious one: a united nation of Israel, all worshipping together in Jerusalem. No longer will the land of Judah and the land of Israel be separate, but they will once again be one great people of God. This could be a vision for Christians too. Just think: Lutherans, Presbyterians, Methodists, Roman Catholics, Episcopalians, and all other Christian denominations, all worshipping together in one great Body of Christ! Just imagine the great works of compassion and healing, encouragement and evangelism, that could be done if we worked together regularly. We see hints of this even now as groups like Church World Service and the Red Cross do wonderful interdenominational work. We see wonderful signs of this vision whenever we join with other churches and faith communities to advocate for the poor. We even see signs of this vision when we join with our neighbors in taking care of one another, no matter what their faith. Unity is a blessing.

Prayer

God of all life, give us hearts that long for unity. Keep us from being tools of divisiveness in a world where people are so divided already. Bring us together around works of compassion and care for the world and all who dwell in it. We pray this in Jesus' name. AMEN.

Thursday

Matt 10:16–22

> [16] "I am sending you out like sheep into the midst of wolves, so
> be wise as serpents and innocent as doves. [17] Beware of them, for
> they will hand you over to councils and flog you in their syna-
> gogues, [18] and you will be dragged before governors and kings
> because of me, as a testimony to them and the gentiles. [19] When
> they hand you over, do not worry about how you are to speak or
> what you are to say, for what you are to say will be given to you at
> that time, [20] for it is not you who speak, but the Spirit of your Fa-
> ther speaking through you. [21] Sibling will betray sibling to death
> and a father his child, and children will rise against parents and
> have them put to death, [22] and you will be hated by all because
> of my name. But the one who endures to the end will be saved.

We are sometimes surprised when people of faith are given a hard time. It is as though we expect that when we act in good faith others will recognize this and treat us with respect and dignity. Jesus reminds us in this passage from Matthew that persecution is part of the life of faith. People who are threatened by us when we live and speak in the ways of Jesus will not always be quiet. They may even, at times, become hostile toward us. Jesus said we should expect this. Naturally, we don't seek such a reaction, nor do we glory in it, as though martyrdom is some kind of badge of courage. No, we do as St. Peter admonishes us: "Always be ready to make your defense to anyone who demands from you an accounting for the hope that is in you; yet do it with gentleness and reverence. Keep your conscience clear, so that, when you are maligned, those who abuse you for your good conduct in Christ may be put to shame" (1 Pet 3:15–16).

Prayer

Give us courage these days, Loving Lord. Give us courage to follow in the way of Christ, despite any opposition we might face. Grant that we might be well-spoken, self-controlled, and gracious in all our words and ways. And bless your Church that a world-wide witness of peace and love might prevail. In your holy name we pray. AMEN.

Friday

Eph 5:6–14

> [6] Let no one deceive you with empty words, for because of
> these things the wrath of God comes on those who are disobe-
> dient. [7] Therefore do not be associated with them, [8] for once
> you were darkness, but now in the Lord you are light. Walk as
> children of light, [9] for the fruit of the light is found in all that is
> good and right and true. [10] Try to find out what is pleasing to
> the Lord. [11] Take no part in the unfruitful works of darkness;
> rather, expose them. [12] For it is shameful even to mention what
> such people do secretly, [13] but everything exposed by the light
> becomes visible, [14] for everything that becomes visible is light.
> Therefore it says,
>
> "Sleeper, awake!
> Rise from the dead,
> and Christ will shine on you."

Here, St. Paul is reminding his readers that, because of their new-found faith in Christ, their whole identity has changed: "Once you were darkness, but now in the Lord you are light." Notice the words that St. Paul uses. He doesn't say that you were walking in darkness and now you are walking in the light; he says that you *were* darkness, and now you *are* light. St. John says it another way. He says that in Christ *we are reborn*, we become completely new, we are given a new life. St. Paul says elsewhere that our old self is crucified with Christ and now it is no longer we who live, but Christ who lives in us. All of these statements point to the radical change that comes over us as we live in Christ. Christ's life becomes our life, and our life becomes a thing of the past. This is all God's doing. It is the miracle of new birth in Christ.

Prayer

We praise you, Loving God, for making us new in Christ. We praise you for the light of Christ that can shine through us. We praise you for the light of Christ that gives us faith and joy. Help us to live each day in its glow. We pray this in the name of Christ our Lord. AMEN.

The Tenth Week After Pentecost

Monday

Ps 66:5–12

5 Come and see what God has done:
he is awesome in his deeds among mortals.
6 He turned the sea into dry land;
they passed through the river on foot.
There we rejoiced in him,
7 who rules by his might forever,
whose eyes keep watch on the nations—
let the rebellious not exalt themselves.
8 Bless our God, O peoples;
let the sound of his praise be heard,
9 who has kept us among the living
and has not let our feet slip.
10 For you, O God, have tested us;
you have tried us as silver is tried.
11 You brought us into the net;
you laid burdens on our backs;
12 you let people ride over our heads;
we went through fire and through water;
yet you have brought us out to a spacious place.

Psalm 66 is certainly a communal song of praise, but notice that the writer includes not only praise for God's mighty act of deliverance at the Red Sea (vs. 6) and God's rescue from slavery (vs. 12c), but also the times of testing and the burdens that God's people have borne. In other words, these words of praise do not come from the mouths of those unaccustomed to suffering and trials. Quite the opposite, in fact: These words come from those who have been tested greatly. This is important to remember lest we think that words of praise can only be spoken by those whose lives have been easy. No, God's people have always experienced times of trial, and always will, even as we also have experienced God's deliverance and healing. So, let the ancient people of God be our teachers this day as we look back at those times of deliverance and, even amidst suffering, give praise to God, knowing that God's faithfulness is sure.

Prayer

We praise you amidst our suffering, Lord Christ. We know that you also knew suffering in your lifetime and especially as you died. Keep us near you in difficult times, and strengthen our faith that in all times we might praise you. In your loving name we pray. AMEN.

Tuesday

Rom 7:14–25a

> 14 For we know that the law is spiritual, but I am of the flesh,
> sold into slavery under sin. 15 I do not understand my own ac-
> tions. For I do not do what I want, but I do the very thing I
> hate. 16 Now if I do what I do not want, I agree that the law is
> good. 17 But in fact it is no longer I who do it but sin that dwells
> within me. 18 For I know that the good does not dwell within
> me, that is, in my flesh. For the desire to do the good lies close
> at hand, but not the ability. 19 For I do not do the good I want,
> but the evil I do not want is what I do. 20 Now if I do what I do
> not want, it is no longer I who do it but sin that dwells within
> me. 21 So I find it to be a law that, when I want to do what is
> good, evil lies close at hand. 22 For I delight in the law of God
> in my inmost self, 23 but I see in my members another law at
> war with the law of my mind, making me captive to the law of
> sin that dwells in my members. 24 Wretched person that I am!
> Who will rescue me from this body of death? 25 Thanks be to
> God through Jesus Christ our Lord!

This passage from St. Paul's letter to the Romans is perhaps the greatest piece ever written on what Luther called "bondage to sin." Luther understood that the human condition includes brokenness, a brokenness which we are powerless to fix ourselves. We are simply held by a power too great for our humanity. We might desire to be righteous, but the actual accomplishment of that eludes us. We need a power greater than ourselves to break out of this bondage, and that power belongs to Christ. Christ then is the One who comes and breaks the power of sin and gives us the freedom to live in love. Needless to say, even in this freedom we do not always choose love, but we now *have* a choice. And, lest we forget, whenever we choose the ways of sin, God stands ready to forgive. Such is the way of the Christian life.

Prayer

Thank you, Jesus, for coming to us in our brokenness and saving us from the ways of sin that bind us. We wish to do good, but so often we do not do it. Forgive us, Lord. Fill us with your Spirit, so that day by day we might grow in our desire and ability to follow in your ways. In your precious name we pray. AMEN.

Wednesday

2 Cor 8:1–7

> We want you to know, brothers and sisters, about the grace of
> God that has been granted to the churches of Macedonia, [2] for
> during a severe ordeal of affliction their abundant joy and their
> extreme poverty have overflowed in a wealth of generosity on
> their part. [3] For, as I can testify, they voluntarily gave accord-
> ing to their means and even beyond their means, [4] begging
> us earnestly for the favor of partnering in this ministry to the
> saints, [5] and not as we expected. Instead, they gave themselves
> first to the Lord and, by the will of God, to us, [6] so that we might
> urge Titus that, as he had already made a beginning, so he should
> also complete this generous undertaking among you. [7] Now as
> you excel in everything—in faith, in speech, in knowledge, in
> utmost eagerness, and in your love for us—so we want you to
> excel also in this generous undertaking.

This passage is one of the first examples we have in the New Testament of benevolence being commanded. St. Paul is writing to the believers in Corinth but is lifting up the churches of Macedonia, who, though very poor, gave generously for the needs of the Church in Jerusalem. It turns out there was a famine in Jerusalem and so on one of Paul's trips abroad he passed the plate for the starving saints there. Notice what Paul especially notes: "They gave themselves *first* to the Lord and, by the will of God, to us." He is reminding the Corinthians that giving an offering, even a small one, requires one to *first* give oneself to the Lord. Indeed, it this giving of oneself that is most important to God. Many of us regularly give an offering to the work of the Church. We often do this gladly without coercion of any kind. But if we lack joy in this giving, perhaps we can learn from the Corinthians and spend some time giving *ourselves* to the Lord first. This may well be where joy is found.

Prayer

Grant us joy in our giving, Gracious Lord. Grant us the desire to be generous, especially when we are faced with siblings in Christ who lack basic necessities. Help us be joyful and generous, so that all may have what they need for life. We ask this in Jesus' name. AMEN.

Thursday

Luke 9:1–6

> Then Jesus called the twelve together and gave them power
> and authority over all demons and to cure diseases, [2] and he
> sent them out to proclaim the kingdom of God and to heal
> the sick. [3] He said to them, "Take nothing for your journey:
> no staff, nor bag, nor bread, nor money—not even an extra
> tunic. [4] Whatever house you enter, stay there, and leave from
> there. [5] Wherever they do not welcome you, as you are leaving
> that town shake the dust off your feet as a testimony against
> them." [6] So they departed and went through the villages, bring-
> ing the good news and curing diseases everywhere.

This command of Jesus to his disciples seems unthinkable to us in the modern Western world. We are so accustomed to individualism that we are aghast to think that Jesus would command his disciples to go out taking nothing for their journey: "No staff, nor bag, nor bread, nor money—not even an extra tunic." What Jesus is reflecting here is a different understanding of life, where every person is dependent on everyone else. This we see even today in non-Western cultures. I remember a friend of mine from Sudan telling me that there are no homeless people in their culture. Even if a family already has a houseful, if a member of the community is without shelter it is the obligation of the community to take them in. He told me that though he and his wife had 8 children, a man without a home had been living with them for several weeks. This is the kind of culture Jesus is reflecting here. He is saying to his disciples, "God will provide for you through the community of faith. Do not fear." We, who so often fail to recognize our mutual dependence on one another, could learn much from this.

Prayer

Thank you for the community of faith, Lord Jesus. Thank you for the way you use us to support those who bring the gospel to the world. Grant us generous hearts so that the work of the gospel might go forth with vigor. We ask this in your holy name. AMEN.

Friday

Acts 19:23–27

> About that time no little disturbance broke out concerning
> the Way. 24 A man named Demetrius, a silversmith who made
> silver shrines of Artemis, brought no little business to the ar-
> tisans. 25 These he gathered together, with the workers of the
> same trade, and said, "Men, you know that we get our wealth
> from this business. 26 You also see and hear that not only in
> Ephesus but in almost the whole of Asia this Paul has per-
> suaded and drawn away a considerable number of people by
> saying that gods made with hands are not gods. 27 And there is
> danger not only that this trade of ours may come into disrepute
> but also that the temple of the great goddess Artemis will be
> scorned, and she will be deprived of her majesty that brought
> all Asia and the world to worship her."

There is an old saying, known to preachers, that there is a difference between preaching and "meddling." I'm not sure where this comes from, but I know what it means. It means that preachers are welcome to preach anything as long as it doesn't threaten the livelihood or lifestyle of those to whom it is addressed. This is what the apostle Paul ran into in Ephesus. He was preaching that the household idols fashioned by a silversmith named Demetrius were not actually gods. That meant that they weren't worth purchasing, and therefore Demetrius and every other artisan like him were in danger of losing their business. Seeing this, they stirred up the crowd into a frenzied mob, hoping to run Paul and his companions out of town. Sometimes we are like the Ephesians, blinded to the fact that our "idols" are not worth worshipping. Let us pray that if and when the day comes that a preacher's words convict us of our need to leave our idols behind, we might be open to this call, repent, and walk in the way of truth.

Prayer

Forgive us for our idolatry, Lord of All. We know that there are no gods but you, Holy One, and yet we often find ourselves trusting the gods we can see and touch more than you. Forgive our wandering ways and lead us into the way of life. In your holy name we pray. AMEN.

The Eleventh Week After Pentecost

Monday

Ps 119:73–80

73 Your hands have made and fashioned me;
give me understanding that I may learn your commandments.
74 Those who fear you shall see me and rejoice,
because I have hoped in your word.
75 I know, O LORD, that your judgments are right
and that in faithfulness you have humbled me.
76 Let your steadfast love become my comfort
according to your promise to your servant.
77 Let your mercy come to me, that I may live,
for your law is my delight.
78 Let the arrogant be put to shame,
for they have subverted me with guile;
as for me, I will meditate on your precepts.
79 Let those who fear you turn to me,
so that they may know your decrees.
80 May my heart be blameless in your statutes,
so that I may not be put to shame.

Psalm 119 has 22 stanzas of 8 verses each. There is a stanza for each letter of the Hebrew alphabet. Clearly this is a memory device for students of the Hebrew Bible. The entire psalm is in praise of God's wisdom. Note the many names that are given to God's wisdom here: commandments, word, judgments, promise, law, precepts, decrees, and statutes—eight different names for God's wisdom. A person could meditate profitably on each of these verses, but several strike me. First, Verse 73: "Your hands have made and fashioned me; give me understanding." Here, the psalmist is remembering that God, as Creator, is the best source for wisdom on how to live. This makes sense. The Creator of life knows what best gives health and strength to that life. Next, Verse 75: "In your faithfulness you have humbled me." In this verse, the psalmist is thanking God for humbling him with God's judgments. In other words, he is thanking God for correcting him. I wonder how often we do this. If you have never done it, I encourage you to spend some time with Ps 119, meditating on each of these precepts. God's wisdom is there.

Prayer

We praise you for your wisdom, Holy One. We thank you for the gift of your Word and your people who have preserved this wisdom for us down through the generations. Help us to be good stewards of your Word and to live in its wisdom each day. In your holy name we pray. AMEN.

Tuesday

Josh 23:1–3, 6–8

> A long time afterward, when the Lord had given rest to Israel
> from all their enemies all around and Joshua was old and well
> advanced in years, 2 Joshua summoned all Israel, their elders
> and heads, their judges and officers, and said to them, "I am
> now old and well advanced in years, 3 and you have seen all that
> the Lord your God has done to all these nations for your sake,
> for it is the Lord your God who has fought for you. 6 Therefore
> be very steadfast to observe and do all that is written in the
> book of the law of Moses, turning aside from it neither to the
> right nor to the left, 7 so that you may not be mixed with these
> nations left here among you, or make mention of the names of
> their gods, or swear by them, or serve them, or bow yourselves
> down to them, 8 but hold fast to the Lord your God, as you
> have done to this day.

Joshua is an old man now. He has led the people of Israel through the time of conquest as they have entered the land and settled there. In his final speech to them, he reminds the people that God has fought for them and made this new home possible. As he is preparing to die, he exhorts them to steadfastly observe the precepts which his predecessor, Moses, taught them, and not get mixed up in the practices of the pagans with whom they live. "Hold fast to the Lord your God," he says. "Hold fast." This is a good word for us today, as well. We might be tempted to think that any success we have had in our lives is all our own doing. This is never the case. Even if we have worked hard, we are all indebted to parents, teachers, mentors, even strangers who have done for us what needed to be done so that we could find success. God is a part of all of this, too. The God who has made us is also the God who protects and sustains, encourages and supports us our whole life long. Given this, let us all heed the word of Joshua and "hold fast to the Lord our God."

Prayer

Thank you for your abundant blessings, O God. Thank you for health and strength, for minds and bodies that work, for colleagues that inspire, for mentors that teach, and for all those who have blessed us so that we might thrive. Grant us humility and gratitude each day, and the willingness to be used by you so that others may thrive as well. In your holy name we pray. AMEN.

Wednesday

Jas 2:14–23

> What good is it, my brothers and sisters, if someone claims to
> have faith but does not have works? Surely that faith cannot save,
> can it? [15] If a brother or sister is naked and lacks daily food [16] and
> one of you says to them, "Go in peace; keep warm and eat your
> fill," and yet you do not supply their bodily needs, what is the
> good of that? [17] So faith by itself, if it has no works, is dead.
>
> [18] But someone will say, "You have faith, and I have works." Show
> me your faith apart from works, and I by my works will show
> you faith. [19] You believe that God is one; you do well. Even the
> demons believe—and shudder. [20] Do you want to be shown,
> you senseless person, that faith apart from works is worthless?

> [21] Was not our ancestor Abraham justified by works when he offered his son Isaac on the altar? [22] You see that faith was active along with his works, and by works faith was brought to completion. [23] Thus the scripture was fulfilled that says, "Abraham believed God, and it was reckoned to him as righteousness," and he was called the friend of God.

It is well-known that Martin Luther called the book of James "an epistle of straw." He called it such because it contained no gospel word, but simply exhortations to do good works. One could conclude by this that Luther saw no value in good works. But on the contrary, Luther saw *great* value in good works and, in fact, insisted that true faith *always* produces good works. He insisted that faith always shows itself in love. Perhaps the way we can reconcile Luther's words and this passage from James is to say that faith that does not have works is not faith; it is something else. It is not merely a dead faith, but no faith at all. I like how the psalmist said it: "Trust God and do good." That is the whole package.

Prayer

Grant us true faith, Generous Lord. Grant us hearts that are open to your leading and responsive to your call. Forgive us whenever we do not live in love. Help us trust you and do good all our days. In the name of Jesus we pray. AMEN.

Thursday

Lev 19:1–4, 32–37

> The LORD spoke to Moses, saying:
>
> [2] "Speak to all the congregation of the Israelites and say to them: You shall be holy, for I the LORD your God am holy. [3] You shall each revere your mother and father, and you shall keep my Sabbaths: I am the LORD your God. [4] Do not turn to idols or make cast images for yourselves: I am the LORD your God.
>
> [32] "You shall rise before the aged and defer to the old, and you shall fear your God: I am the LORD.
>
> [33] "When an alien resides with you in your land, you shall not oppress the alien. [34] The alien who resides with you shall

> be to you as the native-born among you; you shall love the alien as yourself, for you were aliens in the land of Egypt: I am the LORD your God.
>
> [35] "You shall not cheat in measuring length, weight, or quantity. [36] You shall have honest balances, honest weights, an honest ephah, and an honest hin: I am the LORD your God who brought you out of the land of Egypt. [37] You shall keep all my statutes and all my ordinances and observe them: I am the LORD."

Leviticus is a book of laws. Chapter 19 is an example. There are dozens of laws here. Notice the phrase following each law: "I am the Lord your God." It is as though God is saying, "You must obey this law because of who I am. This law reveals my character to the nations. When you obey this law, you tell the world what God is like." So what do we learn about God from these laws? We learn that God holds parenting in high esteem. We learn that Sabbath-keeping is important to God. We learn that things that we make must not be our gods. We learn that God lifts up the aged and protects the alien in our midst. We learn that honesty and integrity in business practice is something God values highly. In this day and age, when politicians and profiteers regularly "play the God card," it is important to be discerning as to who exactly is following in the way of Christ and who is not. Perhaps the ancient book of Leviticus can be of some help.

Prayer

Thank you for your ancient wisdom, Holy One. Thank you for commandments which guide us and precepts that keep us from foolish living. Help us to heed your wisdom always and to lead our children in the way of life. In your holy name we pray. AMEN.

Friday

John 3:16–21

> "For God so loved the world that he gave his only Son, so that everyone who believes in him may not perish but may have eternal life.
>
> [17] "Indeed, God did not send the Son into the world to condemn the world but in order that the world might be saved through

> him. 18 Those who believe in him are not condemned, but those
> who do not believe are condemned already because they have
> not believed in the name of the only Son of God. 19 And this
> is the judgment, that the light has come into the world, and
> people loved darkness rather than light because their deeds were
> evil. 20 For all who do evil hate the light and do not come to the
> light, so that their deeds may not be exposed. 21 But those who
> do what is true come to the light, so that it may be clearly seen
> that their deeds have been done in God."

In the gospel of John, judgment is not something that will come in the future. Rather, it is the state in which one lives apart from Christ. In various places, John calls it either *darkness* or *blindness* or *lostness*. This is both terrifying and hopeful. It is terrifying because we realize that to live in total darkness or blindness or lostness is a terrible place to be, and none of us would wish to be there. It is hopeful in that we can be rescued from this place through the presence of Christ. We can discover places of light and hope and welcome as we experience the presence of Christ. Someone said that evangelism is simply one beggar telling another beggar where to go for food. Perhaps in John's parlance we might say that evangelism is simply one formerly lost soul shining the light into the darkness and showing others the way home.

Prayer

Lord Christ, embrace us, we pray. Keep us close to you lest we stray and find ourselves lost in the darkness. Use us to shine your light in the world, and bring all home to you. We pray this in your loving name. AMEN.

The Twelfth Week After Pentecost

Monday

Jas 2:1–7

> My brothers and sisters, do not claim the faith of our Lord Jesus Christ of glory while showing partiality. [2] For if a person with gold rings and in fine clothes comes into your assembly, and if a poor person in dirty clothes also comes in, [3] and if you take notice of the one wearing the fine clothes and say, "Have a seat here in a good place, please," while to the one who is poor you say, "Stand there," or, "Sit by my footstool," [4] have you not made distinctions among yourselves and become judges with evil thoughts? [5] Listen, my beloved brothers and sisters. Has not God chosen the poor in the world to be rich in faith and to be heirs of the kingdom that he has promised to those who love him? [6] But you have dishonored the poor person. Is it not the rich who oppress you? Is it not they who drag you into the courts? [7] Is it not they who blaspheme the excellent name that was invoked over you?

Showing partiality is something we all do. We naturally gravitate towards people like us—those who look like us, speak like us, and appear to have similar tastes. This is not wrong; it just is. What James reminds us is that partiality can become prejudice, when we not only gravitate towards those who are like us but put down those who are not like us. We may regard with less honor those we view as "less" than us by virtue of their financial wherewithal, their education, their ability or disability, or their physical appearance. If we notice ourselves slipping from partiality into prejudice, we need to stop and remember that God's children come in all shapes and sizes, colors, abilities, and identities. Regarding one as more deserving of honor than another is simply a failure to see people as God sees them.

Prayer

Forgive us, Lord, when our partiality turns nasty. Forgive us when we dishonor those we encounter by failing to see them as you do. Grant us gracious spirits, generous hearts, and eyes that see beyond appearances so that all might receive the honor they deserve as children of God. In your holy name we pray. AMEN.

Tuesday

Prov 19: 4, 6–7, 10, 17

[4] Wealth brings many friends,
but the poor are left friendless.
[6] Many seek the favor of the generous,
and everyone is a friend to a giver of gifts.
[7] If the poor are hated even by their kin,
how much more are they shunned by their friends!
When they call after them, they are not there.[
[10] It is not fitting for a fool to live in luxury,
much less for a slave to rule over princes.
[17] Whoever is kind to the poor lends to the LORD
and will be repaid in full.

It has been said that the Bible speaks about money more than any other subject, and certainly the book of Proverbs is full of wisdom sayings regarding money. In Chapter 19, we have some examples. We can laugh at the observation that the rich have many "friends" and the poor few, but just ask a lottery winner and they will tell you about the "friends" that suddenly showed up. The writer of Proverbs also reminds us that a fool with riches is often a disastrous combination. Great wealth brings with it the need for great wisdom, for great wealth is a fire that can burn out of control in a moment. Finally, the writer reminds us that God has an interesting lending policy. Whenever we are kind to the poor, we, in fact, are lending money to the Lord, and the Lord will repay us with interest. What a generous God we have!

Prayer

Give us wisdom, O Holy One, with our great wealth. We live in a land of plenty and all that we need is ever present. Give us grateful hearts, generous spirits, and a willingness to share our abundance with those in need, so that all may enjoy what you provide. In your holy name we pray. AMEN.

Wednesday

1 John 3:16–22

> [16] We know love by this, that he laid down his life for us—and we
> ought to lay down our lives for the brothers and sisters. [17] How
> does God's love abide in anyone who has the world's goods and
> sees a brother or sister in need and yet refuses help?
>
> [18] Little children, let us love not in word or speech but in deed
> and truth. [19] And by this we will know that we are from the
> truth and will reassure our hearts before him [20] whenever our
> hearts condemn us, for God is greater than our hearts, and he
> knows everything. [21] Beloved, if our hearts do not condemn
> us, we have boldness before God, [22] and we receive from him
> whatever we ask, because we obey his commandments and do
> what pleases him.

The first line in this passage says it all: we love because Christ first loved us. Our lives are simply a response to the love of God. Our giving is simply a response to God's generosity to us. Our willingness to forgive, to be steadfast in the face of challenges, to be patient even when we want to lash out—all this comes through modeling how God first dealt with us. *We* have been forgiven, so we forgive. *We* have been shown steadfast love, so we show steadfast love. God has been patient with *us*, so we are patient with others. Perhaps then, the best way to start each day is to simply meditate upon the ways God's love has been shown to us. This might set us up to mirror those acts of love in our own lives.

Prayer

We thank and praise you for your steadfast love, O God. We thank and praise you for the life Christ laid down on our behalf. Give us grateful hearts, and then use us to bring this steadfast love to the world. We are your servants. Use us for your glory, we pray. In the name of Christ. AMEN.

Thursday

Eccl 9:13–18

> [13] I have also seen this example of wisdom under the sun, and
> it seemed great to me. [14] There was a little city with few people
> in it. A great king came against it and besieged it, building
> great siegeworks against it. [15] Now there was found in it a poor
> wise man, and he by his wisdom delivered the city. Yet no one
> remembered that poor man. [16] So I said, "Wisdom is better
> than might; yet the poor man's wisdom is despised, and his
> words are not heeded."
>
> [17] The quiet words of the wise are more to be heeded
> than the shouting of a ruler among fools.
> [18] Wisdom is better than weapons of war,
> but one bungler destroys much good.

I have always been thankful for common folks who have uncommon wisdom. Churches are often filled with such people. I remember a man that my father used to talk about. This man could build anything, fix anything, and seemed able to tackle any problem. Even though he was a man without a college education, a man who lacked any of the sophistication you might regularly assume to be necessary to be wise, he was uncommonly wise. This is the kind of person that the wisdom writer was speaking about in this passage. This is the wise one whose quiet words are to be heeded more than the shouting of the ruling fool. I wonder if it isn't long past time for us to start listening again to the quiet voices amongst us—those who can easily get lost in the din of nonsense that assaults us so regularly—and hear what they have to say. It may be that they are the ones who will save the city.

Prayer

Thank you, God, for common people with uncommon wisdom. Thank you for common folk who see what is right and true and speak that truth. Thank you for common people who live amongst us who speak softly and lead us in the ways of wisdom. Give us ears to hear them, O God. Give us courage to follow their lead, trusting that you are guiding us. In your holy name we pray. AMEN.

Friday

Matt 25:31–40

> [31] "When the Son of Man comes in his glory and all the angels with him, then he will sit on the throne of his glory. [32] All the nations will be gathered before him, and he will separate people one from another as a shepherd separates the sheep from the goats, [33] and he will put the sheep at his right hand and the goats at the left. [34] Then the king will say to those at his right hand, 'Come, you who are blessed by my Father, inherit the kingdom prepared for you from the foundation of the world, [35] for I was hungry and you gave me food, I was thirsty and you gave me something to drink, I was a stranger and you welcomed me, [36] I was naked and you gave me clothing, I was sick and you took care of me, I was in prison and you visited me.' [37] Then the righteous will answer him, 'Lord, when was it that we saw you hungry and gave you food or thirsty and gave you something to drink? [38] And when was it that we saw you a stranger and welcomed you or naked and gave you clothing? [39] And when was it that we saw you sick or in prison and visited you?' [40] And the king will answer them, 'Truly I tell you, just as you did it to one of the least of these brothers and sisters of mine, you did it to me.'

In this well-known passage, we often concentrate on the words of the king who commended the person for their acts of charity. This is as it should be, but what is equally telling is the response of the faithful person. What do they say? They ask, "When did we see you hungry, thirsty, naked, or a stranger? And when did we see you sick or in prison?" They are completely unaware of their own acts of charity. They are blind to their own righteousness because they are so completely engaged in helping those in need. Martin Luther, in his commentary on the Magnificat, once said that it never enters the mind of the humble that they are humble because they are so completely consumed with humble acts. They are then always surprised by any honors bestowed on them, and indeed wonder what all the fuss is about. What all this points out is that true service is always outward centered, not inward looking. True service seeks the good of those served not the adulation that comes from service. As Jesus famously said, "Strive first for the kingdom of God and his righteousness, and all these things will be given to you as well."

Prayer

Grant us hearts that are fixed solely on serving you, Gracious One. Grant us eyes that see the needs before us and not our own reward. Grant us the faith to believe that when we seek your kingdom and righteousness all we require will be provided. In your precious name we pray. AMEN.

The Thirteenth Week After Pentecost

Monday

Ps 15

1 O LORD, who may abide in your tent?
Who may dwell on your holy hill?
2 Those who walk blamelessly and do what is right
and speak the truth from their heart;
3 who do not slander with their tongue
and do no evil to their friends
nor heap shame upon their neighbors;
4 in whose eyes the wicked are despised
but who honor those who fear the LORD;
who stand by their oath even to their hurt;
5 who do not lend money at interest
and do not take a bribe against the innocent.
Those who do these things shall never be moved.

Scholars believe that Ps 15 was conceived of as a liturgy. The first verse was what the priest said to the people: "O Lord, who may abide in your tent? Who may dwell on your holy hill?" This referred to the temple in Jerusalem, and simply asked what was required for a person to enter the temple for worship. The people provided the reply: "Those who walk blamelessly and do what is right!" The priest then might have asked again, "O Lord, who may abide in your tent and dwell on your holy hill?" And again the people reply: "Those who speak truth from their heart." And so it would go, through the whole psalm. What is noteworthy is that entrance to the temple is not based upon right sacrifices or right piety or belief, but on how one treats the neighbor. To live in solidarity with others, to refuse to take advantage of the weak or vulnerable, and to stand by your word even when it hurts: these are the things that please God. This is what we are still called to as God's people.

Prayer

Thank you, Holy God, for your people down through the ages who have been our teachers, the ones who have shown us the way of righteousness. Help us to live in ways that honor you and bring blessing to others. Grant us strength to live as people of integrity and compassion, knowing that all we have is from your hand. In your holy name we pray. AMEN.

Tuesday

Gen 12:10–20

10 Now there was a famine in the land. So Abram went down to Egypt to reside there as an alien, for the famine was severe
in the land. 11 When he was about to enter Egypt, he said to his wife Sarai, "I know well that you are a woman beautiful
in appearance, 12 and when the Egyptians see you, they will say, 'This is his wife'; then they will kill me, but they will let
you live. 13 Say you are my sister, so that it may go well with me because of you and that my life may be spared on your ac-
count." 14 When Abram entered Egypt the Egyptians saw that the woman was very beautiful.
15 When the officials of Pharaoh saw her, they praised her to Pharaoh. And the woman was
taken into Pharaoh's house. 16 And for her sake he dealt well with Abram, and he had sheep, oxen, male donkeys, male and female slaves, female donkeys, and camels.

17 But the LORD afflicted Pharaoh and his house with great plagues because of Sarai, Abram's wife.
18 So Pharaoh called Abram and said, "What is this you have done to me? Why did
you not tell me that she was your wife? 19 Why did you say, 'She is my sister,' so that I took her for my wife? Now then, here is
your wife, take her, and be gone." 20 And Pharaoh gave his men orders concerning him, and they set him on the way with his wife and all that he had.

This peculiar story shows the humanity of one of the patriarchs of the Old Testament, Abram. Even though we know him as a man of great faith, who on another occasion will be willing to sacrifice his son, Isaac, on an altar before God, on this occasion his fears get the best of him. He decides that telling a little "white lie" might be the best way to go. As we see, this little lie sets all sorts of things in motion that could have been avoided if he had been straightforward. This story is a good reminder to us whenever we are tempted to "massage the truth" a bit in order to protect our own interests. Lies always have a way of coming home to roost, and the more we tell, the more difficult it becomes to disentangle ourselves from the web we have spun. Better simply to be straightforward and let the chips fall where they may. After all, faith, as Abram will eventually demonstrate, is all about trusting that God will provide for and protect us all our days, come what may.

Prayer

Grant us faith, O God. Keep our fears from overwhelming us. Remind us that your will is always that we may have life and have it to the full. Lead us in the way of truth and peace all our days, we pray. In the name of Christ. AMEN.

Wednesday

Eph 3:14–21

14 For this reason I bow my knees before the Father, 15 from whom
every family in heaven and on earth takes its name. 16 I pray that,
according to the riches of his glory, he may grant that you may
be strengthened in your inner being with power through his
Spirit 17 and that Christ may dwell in your hearts through faith,
as you are being rooted and grounded in love. 18 I pray that you
may have the power to comprehend, with all the saints, what
is the breadth and length and height and depth 19 and to know
the love of Christ that surpasses knowledge, so that you may be
filled with all the fullness of God.

20 Now to him who by the power at work within us is able to
accomplish abundantly far more than all we can ask or imag-
ine, 21 to him be glory in the church and in Christ Jesus to all
generations, forever and ever. Amen.

This powerful prayer is one we could pray for one another every day. Look at what is being asked for: to be strengthened in the inner being, that Christ may dwell in our hearts through faith, that we may have the power to comprehend and know the love of Christ that surpasses knowledge. And why are these things being requested? So that we may be filled with all the fullness of God! Wow! Now there is a prayer worth praying. Notice that everything being prayed for here is in the innermost heart and mind of a person. What is being asked for is nothing less than a resilient faith that has the power to sustain us throughout all the tests and trials of this life. Do you know someone who is struggling with chronic pain or a terminal illness? Do you know someone whose work is difficult to the point of exhaustion? Do you know someone who is discouraged or disheartened because of events beyond their control? Perhaps this prayer might be the very thing you could be praying for them. Sending them a note reminding them of your concern might not hurt either. As Paul says here, that small act of concern could well have "the power to accomplish abundantly far more than you can ask or imagine."

Prayer

Gracious God, thank you for the strength you give us every day. Thank you for your Holy Spirit that inspires us and gives us faith. Thank you for your dear Son, Jesus, whose sacrifice sets us free from sin and death and gives us hope for this life and the next. Keep us always in the faith, we pray. In the name of Jesus. AMEN.

Thursday

Luke 8:4–8, 11–15

> 4 When a large crowd was gathering, as people were coming to
> [Jesus]from town after town, he said in a parable: 5 "A sower
> went out to sow his seed, and as he sowed some fell on a path
> and was trampled on, and the birds of the air ate it up. 6 Some
> fell on rock, and as it grew up it withered for lack of mois-
> ture. 7 Some fell among thorns, and the thorns grew with it
> and choked it. 8 Some fell into good soil, and when it grew it
> produced a hundredfold." As he said this, he called out, "If you
> have ears to hear, then hear!"

> [11] "Now the parable is this: The seed is the word of God. [12] The
> ones on the path are those who have heard; then the devil comes
> and takes away the word from their hearts, so that they may
> not believe and be saved. [13] The ones on the rock are those who,
> when they hear the word, receive it with joy. But these have no
> root; they believe only for a while and in a time of testing fall
> away. [14] As for what fell among the thorns, these are the ones
> who hear, but as they go on their way they are choked by the
> cares and riches and pleasures of life, and their fruit does not
> mature. [15] But as for that in the good soil, these are the ones who,
> when they hear the word, hold it fast in an honest and good
> heart and bear fruit with endurance.

In our Lutheran baptismal liturgy, we do something that is quite unique to us as people of God. We renounce three powers: "The devil and all the forces that defy God," "the powers of this world that rebel against God," and "the ways of sin that draw [us]from God." These three powers are the very things that Jesus points to in this parable that can cause God's word to die in our hearts. First, there is the devil that comes and takes the Word away. Second, there are the ways of sin—what we call "the flesh"—that fails in the time of testing. Finally, there are the powers of this world with all their allures of riches and pleasure that choke off the Word. Jesus knew full well what he was talking about when he warned his disciples about the need to hold fast to the Word. He also knew that when the Word falls into good soil it produces abundant fruit. Oh, that we *all* might be such soil!

Prayer

Gracious God, create in us a welcome place for your word. We know that we are so easily distracted by the things of this world, so busy with so many things, and so prone to forget what you have taught us, that we easily fall away. Forgive us, Lord, and work in us that faith that will bear fruit in the world. In the name of Christ, we pray. AMEN.

Friday

Exod 18:13, 17–24

> [13] The next day Moses sat as judge for the people, while the
> people stood around him from morning until evening. [17] Mo-
> ses's father-in-law said to him, "What you are doing is not
> good. [18] You will surely wear yourself out, both you and these

> people with you, for the task is too heavy for you; you cannot do it alone. [19] Now listen to me. I will give you counsel, and God be with you! You should represent the people before God and bring their cases to God. [20] Teach them the statutes and instructions and make known to them the way they are to go and the things they are to do. [21] You should also look for able men among all the people, men who fear God, are trustworthy, and hate dishonest gain; set them as officers over thousands, hundreds, fifties, and tens. [22] Let them sit as judges for the people at all times; let them bring every important case to you but decide every minor case themselves. So it will be easier for you, and they will bear the burden with you. [23] If you do this and God so commands you, then you will be able to endure, and all these people will go to their homes in peace." [24] So Moses listened to his father-in-law and did all that he had said.

This is a story of wise delegation. Moses, the leader of the Israelites, has somehow gotten himself into the situation where he is the sole arbiter of every dispute that comes up amongst the people. The writer tells us that the people come and make their case before Moses day after day, from morning until night. Moses's father-in-law, Jethro, happens to see this situation and offers him some wisdom. He basically says to Moses, "You must delegate. You are killing yourself." I wonder how many times this is a word we need to hear. Perhaps we too are quick to simply assume all the responsibility for every bake sale, every service project, every yard pickup, every committee at church and at school, and so on and so on. What happens, predictably, is that we burn out. We may even become bitter because of the whole experience and poison the waters when we leave. Jethro's words to Moses should be words we hear when we are in this situation: "What you are doing is not good." That's right. To be the *only one* doing good is *not* good, as strange as that may sound. We are created to live in community, and the sooner we remember to engage others in some of the leadership that is required, the better.

Prayer

Thank you for faithful leaders, Holy One. Thank you for people who go the extra mile, people who keep the candle burning late at night, and those who never tire of doing good. Thank you also for times of rest, for the community of the faithful who can lighten the burden for us all. Grant us wisdom in our use of time, and the freedom and faith to delegate to others according to your gracious will. In your holy name we pray. AMEN.

The Fourteenth Week After Pentecost

Monday

Ps 119:97–104

97 Oh, how I love your law!
It is my meditation all day long.
98 Your commandment makes me wiser than my enemies,
for it is always with me.
99 I have more understanding than all my teachers,
for your decrees are my meditation.
100 I understand more than the aged,
for I keep your precepts.
101 I hold back my feet from every evil way,
in order to keep your word.
102 I do not turn away from your ordinances,
for you have taught me.
103 How sweet are your words to my taste,
sweeter than honey to my mouth!
104 Through your precepts I get understanding;
therefore I hate every false way.

Psalm 119 is broken up into 22 sections of 8 verses each, all proclaiming the greatness of God's word. In this section the psalmist is reflecting on the *wisdom* in God's word, wisdom that has been important for people of faith down through the generations. Many of us can attest to the way that God's word, though ancient, continues to speak to us today. We find guidance, encouragement, and comfort there. We also find wisdom for being a good neighbor, for parenting, for aging, and even for healthy financial habits. Most of all, God's word proclaims God's everlasting love for us, shown most profoundly in the life, death, and resurrection of Christ. In Christ is true wisdom, and the way to the abundant life God wants for us all.

Prayer

We praise and thank you, Almighty God, for the gift of your word. Thank you that your word continues to speak to us, to guide and correct us, and to redirect us in the ways of life whenever we need it. Give us open ears and open hearts to hear and respond to your wisdom. In Christ's name we pray. AMEN.

Tuesday

1 John 2:1–6

> My little children, I am writing these things to you so that you
> may not sin. But if anyone does sin, we have an advocate with
> the Father, Jesus Christ the righteous, [2] and he is the atoning
> sacrifice for our sins, and not for ours only but also for the sins
> of the whole world.
>
> [3] Now by this we know that we have come to know him, if we
> obey his commandments. [4] Whoever says, "I have come to know
> him," but does not obey his commandments is a liar, and in such
> a person the truth does not exist; [5] but whoever obeys his word,
> truly in this person the love of God has reached perfection. By
> this we know that we are in him: [6] whoever says, "I abide in
> him," ought to walk in the same way as he walked.

In this, John's first letter, he is warning his people about folks who understood faith in Christ to be mostly an intellectual affair. These people were called Gnostics, which is rooted in the Greek word *gnosis*, meaning knowledge. These Christians believed that faith was a matter of knowing some secret spiritual knowledge, and if you had that secret knowledge you were saved. John wants to correct that. He says that faith is not about knowing but about loving. Faith is not about secret knowledge but public acts of mercy and justice. Faith is not about having some personal insight, but very much about living in community and sharing joys and sorrows with other people of faith. These days, more than ever, we as people of faith need to remember that "walking in the same way that [Jesus]walked" is absolutely essential. The world does not need people who claim to be followers of Jesus but live lives that are anything but Jesus-like. Luther said we are called to be "little Christs" for one another, and so we are.

Prayer

Gracious God, forgive us for sometimes "talking the talk" but not "walking the walk." Forgive us for claiming to follow you but failing to live that out. Convict us when we err. Show us the way forward. Strengthen us to live in Christlike ways this day and every day. In your strong name we pray. AMEN.

Wednesday

Deut 12:8–12

> 8 "You shall not act as we are acting here today, all of us ac-
> cording to our own desires, 9 for you have not yet come into
> the rest and the possession that the LORD your God is giving
> you. 10 When you cross over the Jordan and live in the land
> that the LORD your God is allotting to you, and when he gives
> you rest from your enemies all around so that you live in safe-
> ty, 11 then you shall bring everything that I command you to the
> place that the LORD your God will choose as a dwelling for his
> name: your burnt offerings and your sacrifices, your tithes and
> your donations, and all your choice votive gifts that you vow to
> the LORD. 12 And you shall rejoice before the LORD your God,
> you together with your sons and your daughters, your male and
> female slaves, and the Levites who reside in your towns (since
> they have no allotment or inheritance with you).

It's interesting that the first thing the people of Israel were to do when they entered the Promised Land was to give an offering. Not just burnt offerings, but tithes and other donations were also commanded. Was it because a tabernacle building addition was being considered? Perhaps. More likely, it was commanded simply because, having received a whole new land and life from the hands of Almighty God, this was "right and meet so to do." In other words, given the generosity of God, the only appropriate response was to be generous in return. This is the same for us today. We are also commanded to bring offerings to God's house. For members of a church, these offerings likely sustain and support a congregation and its mission goals, but more than that, they are a tangible way of expressing our gratitude to God. God has given us so much in Christ. We are free and forgiven. We are children of God, heirs of eternal life. We are recipients of God's Spirit that inspires us every day. How can we not express our gratitude to this generous God?

Prayer

Thank you, God of Life, for blessings beyond number. Your abundance is our constant supply. We have all we need and more than we need. We are assured of an eternal home. We have all things in Christ. Accept our grateful sacrifices and our offerings to you. In your holy name we pray. AMEN.

Thursday

Luke 8:22–25

> 22 One day [Jesus]got into a boat with his disciples, and he said
> to them, "Let us go across to the other side of the lake." So they
> put out, 23 and while they were sailing he fell asleep. A wind-
> storm swept down on the lake, and the boat was filling with
> water, and they were in danger. 24 They went to him and woke
> him up, shouting, "Master, Master, we are perishing!" And
> waking up, he rebuked the wind and the raging waves; they
> ceased, and there was a calm. 25 Then he said to them, "Where
> is your faith?" They were terrified and amazed and said to one
> another, "Who then is this, that he commands even the winds
> and the water and they obey him?"

Anyone who grows up on a lake knows how it is when the wind really comes up. The waves become whitecaps, and they are no longer harmless rollers, but heavy swells capable of swamping boats and even causing loss of life. Jesus certainly knew all about the wind and waves. Indeed, in Old Testament poetry, the wind and waves are a metaphor for chaos. The sea is considered a place of danger, filled with monsters and unknown perils. The sea is a place where a person is at the mercy of the elements. So, when Jesus said, "Where is your faith?" he was not simply asking the disciples about their present worries, but about his care of them generally. "Do you not trust me? Did you think I brought you out here to die? Do you not remember that I have come to give life?" These are questions that Jesus might ask *us* when we are in the stormy days of life, when we are tempted to say, along with the disciples, "Do you not care that we are perishing?" Yes, Jesus cares that we are perishing, and he has come precisely to save us from those violent waves of sin and death that would destroy us.

Prayer

Thank you, Jesus for saving us from sin and death. Thank you for saving us from those dangers that threaten us and those voices that accuse us. Thank you, Jesus for being able to quiet the raging storm around us and within us, and give us peace. Be near us always, and bring us to everlasting life, we pray. In your holy name. AMEN.

Friday

Col 2:16–23

> [16] Therefore, do not let anyone condemn you in matters of food or drink or of observing festivals, new moons, or Sabbaths. [17] These are only a shadow of what is to come, but the body belongs to Christ. [18] Do not let anyone disqualify you, insisting on self-abasement and worship of angels, initiatory visions, puffed up without cause by a human way of thinking, [19] and not holding fast to the head, from whom the whole body, nourished and held together by its ligaments and tendons, grows with a growth that is from God.
>
> [20] If with Christ you died to the elemental principles of the world, why do you live as if you still belonged to the world? Why do you submit to regulations, [21] "Do not handle! Do not taste! Do not touch!"? [22] All these regulations refer to things that perish with use; they are simply human commands and teachings. [23] These have indeed an appearance of wisdom in promoting self-imposed piety, humility, and severe treatment of the body, but they are of no value in checking self-indulgence.

Paul is taking on here what has sometimes been called "negative religion." Negative religion is epitomized by what Paul calls "regulations": "Do not handle! Do not taste! Do not touch!" On the surface, the concept of negative religion seems to make some sense. Boundaries, after all, are important and even healthy. But negative religion finally is a joyless expression of life in God's kingdom. It is joyless because it leaves out the essence of faith, which is love: love for God, love for neighbor, love for God's creation, and even love for our own selves. Negative religion finally is self-absorbed. It is all about our ability to keep rules, no matter how joyless and loveless they might be, and to be sure that we congratulate ourselves in this deadly task. Quite in contrast to this, God's will is for us to live freely, joyfully, fully in love with God and God's world in all of its expressions. This is a *positive* religion, one that Christ walked, and invites us to live out every day.

Prayer

Thank you, dear Lord, for inviting us into joy. Thank you for inviting us into a life of love. Grant us freedom from believing that life in you is all about rules. Lead us in the way of freedom, and help us to be a blessing to all we encounter. In Jesus' name, we pray. AMEN.

The Fifteenth Week After Pentecost

Monday

Esth 6:1–7, 10–11

On that night the king could not sleep, and he gave orders to
bring the book of records, the annals, and they were read to the
king. 2 It was found written how Mordecai had told about Big-
thana and Teresh, two of the king's eunuchs who guarded the
threshold and who had conspired to kill King Ahasuerus. 3 Then
the king said, "What honor or distinction has been bestowed
on Mordecai for this?" The king's servants who attended him
said, "Nothing has been done for him." 4 The king said, "Who
is in the court?" Now Haman had just entered the outer court
of the king's palace to speak to the king about having Mordecai
hung on the pole that he had prepared for him. 5 So the king's
servants told him, "Haman is there, standing in the court." The
king said, "Let him come in." 6 So Haman came in, and the king
said to him, "What shall be done for the man whom the king
wishes to honor?" Haman said to himself, "Whom would the
king wish to honor more than me?" 7 So Haman said to the king,
"For the man whom the king wishes to honor, 8 let royal robes
be brought, which the king has worn, and a horse that the king
has ridden, with a royal crown on its head " 10 Then the king said
to Haman, "Quickly, take the robes and the horse, as you have
said, and do so to Mordecai the Jew who sits at the king's gate.
Leave out nothing that you have mentioned." 11 So Haman took
the robes and the horse and robed Mordecai and led him riding
through the open square of the city, proclaiming, "Thus shall it
be done for the man whom the king wishes to honor."

This snippet from the book of Esther happens near the climax of the story where the evil henchman, Haman, who has planned the hanging of Mordecai (one of the heroes of the story), is forced instead to honor him. It is a delightful reversal of fortune, and whenever I read it, I think it would make a great movie. Great reversals are what Jesus is all about. He champions those to whom no one pays any attention, calling them children of God. He blesses those who are poor and hungry and gives warning to those are rich and sated. Again and again, he lifts up those whom the world ignores and ignores those whom the world adores. Whenever we are feeling lost or abandoned, battered and bruised, we can know that Jesus stands near. He is our Savior; he is the one who defies even death for us. After all, the Resurrection is the greatest reversal of all.

Prayer

Gracious Lord, Savior of us all, we thank and praise you for your care of us in our time of need. When all seems lost, you are our champion. When the world calls us cursed, you call us blessed. Grant us faith to hold onto you, even in our darkest hour, and to trust that you will bring us through. In your strong name we pray. AMEN.

Tuesday

Matt 5:43–48

> 43 "You have heard that it was said, 'You shall love your neighbor
> and hate your enemy.' 44 But I say to you: Love your enemies and
> pray for those who persecute you, 45 so that you may be children
> of your Father in heaven, for he makes his sun rise on the evil
> and on the good and sends rain on the righteous and on the
> unrighteous. 46 For if you love those who love you, what reward
> do you have? Do not even the tax collectors do the same? 47 And
> if you greet only your brothers and sisters, what more are you
> doing than others? Do not even the gentiles do the same? 48 Be
> perfect, therefore, as your heavenly Father is perfect.

Talk about a high bar! Be perfect even as your heavenly Father is perfect? C'mon! Get real, Jesus! If, however, we look at the context of what Jesus is saying, we might better understand this command. Notice that the whole passage is about love: loving neighbor, loving enemies, loving those who love you and those who don't, and greeting those you know and those you don't. Over and over, Jesus is exhorting us to love. Martin Luther says this happens "when I *let love move* along on the true middle course, treating everyone alike and excluding no one." Luther's language about letting love move in us is important. This means we allow Christ, who *is* love, free reign in our lives. We don't stifle the life of Christ within us, nor insist on trying to love on our strength alone. Certainly, this is futile. But when we allow Christ to reign in our hearts, his love for all people shines through us, and we, being filled with Christ's spirit, are given the ability to love even those whom we thought we could not. What a miracle this is!

Prayer

Come and live within us, Loving Lord. Send your Spirit into our small hearts and make them grow. Grant that our love for all people, even those with whom we struggle, might grow daily, until we are in some regard a reflection of you. We ask this in your strong name. AMEN.

Wednesday

Ps 49:1–6, 10–12

1 Hear this, all you peoples;
give ear, all inhabitants of the world,
2 both low and high,
rich and poor together.
3 My mouth shall speak wisdom;
the meditation of my heart shall be understanding.
4 I will incline my ear to a proverb;
I will solve my riddle to the music of the harp.
5 Why should I fear in times of trouble,
when the iniquity of my persecutors surrounds me,
6 those who trust in their wealth
and boast of the abundance of their riches?
10 When we look at the wise, they die;
fool and dolt perish together
and leave their wealth to others.

11 Their graves are their homes forever,
their dwelling places to all generations,
though they named lands their own.
12 Mortals cannot abide in their pomp;
they are like the animals that perish.

This psalm is called "The Folly of Trust in Riches." Trusting in riches is folly, according to this writer, because riches will not buy immortality; they will not even buy a lasting memory. I recall being in the Panthéon, a vast cemetery housing graves of many famous people, on a visit to Paris. Sure enough, we saw the graves of Alexander Dumas, author of "The Three Musketeers," Adolph Sax, inventor of the saxophone, and Nadia Boulanger, a famous teacher of many of the world's great composers. But the striking thing was, we had never heard of most of the people whose graves we walked by. Assumedly, if they were in the Panthéon, they were people of note, but we had no idea who they were. So it will be with us all. We might claim wealth, or genius, or even some measure of fame, but someday someone is likely to happen by our grave and say, "Who's that?" So says the wisdom of the psalmist: "Mortals cannot abide in their pomp; they are like animals that perish."

Prayer

God of the Living and the Dead, we praise you for your immortal wisdom. We praise you that, even though we perish, you do not. We praise you chiefly for your great love which extends to us even when we are dust. You are the God of the Resurrection; forgotten though we may be, you will not forget us but will raise us to new life, held forever in your embrace. All praise to you, Holy God. AMEN.

Thursday

Eph 4:17–24

17 Now this I affirm and insist on in the Lord: you must no longer
walk as the gentiles walk, in the futility of their minds; 18 they
are darkened in their understanding, alienated from the life of
God because of their ignorance and hardness of heart. 19 They
have lost all sensitivity and have abandoned themselves to

> licentiousness, greedy to practice every kind of impurity. [20] That
> is not the way you learned Christ! [21] For surely you have heard
> about him and were taught in him, as truth is in Jesus, [22] to put
> away your former way of life, your old self, corrupt and deluded
> by its lusts, [23] and to be renewed in the spirit of your minds, [24] and
> to clothe yourselves with the new self, created according to the
> likeness of God in true righteousness and holiness.

Do you like new clothes? I do not. Mainly I don't like the *feel* of them. New clothes always seem to me to be stiff and scratchy to the skin, unlike old clothes that feel soft and comfortable. Now, of course, all clothes began as new clothes at some point, but that process of "breaking in" a new shirt or a pair of pants is something I would love to avoid. I wonder if it's not like that for us and the old self that Paul talks about in Ephesians. He says that we need to put away the old self and be renewed in the spirit of our minds, clothing ourselves with the new self. New self or old self—which one is likely to feel more comfortable? Probably the old self. Yes, it's corrupt in some regard, maybe even in profound ways, but it's what we are used to. It's comfortable. Paul says to throw it in the garbage. The old self deludes us into thinking that following our desires (our lusts) is the way to life abundant. That's a lie. The new self, the one fashioned by the Great Tailor, is the one that will make us look our best. Indeed, clothed in Christ, everyone looks fabulous!

Prayer

Clothe us in your holiness, Lord Christ. Take away anything that would rob us of the authentic life you offer. Renew our minds by your Holy Spirit, and lead us in your wisdom all our days. In your holy name we pray. AMEN.

Friday

Mark 10:17–22

> [17] As [Jesus]was setting out on a journey, a man ran up and
> knelt before him and asked him, "Good Teacher, what must
> I do to inherit eternal life?" [18] Jesus said to him, "Why do you
> call me good? No one is good but God alone. [19] You know the
> commandments: 'You shall not murder. You shall not com-
> mit adultery. You shall not steal. You shall not bear false wit-
> ness. You shall not defraud. Honor your father and mother.'

> " [20] He said to him, "Teacher, I have kept all these since my youth." [21] Jesus, looking at him, loved him and said, "You lack one thing; go, sell what you own, and give the money to the poor, and you will have treasure in heaven; then come, follow me." [22] When he heard this, he was shocked and went away grieving, for he had many possessions.

The last line of this passage has always struck me: "He was shocked and went away grieving." Why? "For he had many possessions." This is not what we expect. Being rich *and* shocked and grieving just don't seem to go together. Why exactly was he shocked? Because Jesus had put his finger on a place of vulnerability for this young man. Why was he grieving? Because his possessions owned him, that's why. His grief indicates that he *wanted* to do what Jesus asked but simply *couldn't*. He couldn't let go. Or, perhaps more accurately, he couldn't break free of what was holding *him*. In the First Letter to Timothy, we read that "the love of money is the root of all kinds of evil." So it is. As the writer goes on to say, "In their eagerness to be rich some have wandered away from the faith and pierced themselves with many pains." Imagine that: the pursuit of wealth not only leads us away from the faith, but also ensures much pain. We are like this young man who encountered Jesus: we can pursue wealth, or we can follow Jesus. We must choose.

Prayer

Keep us near you, Lord of Life. Protect us from those beguiling spirits that would suggest that wealth is the equivalent of the abundant life you desire for us. Give us contentment with what we have and joy in sharing with others. We ask this in Jesus' name. AMEN.

The Sixteenth Week After Pentecost

Monday

Col 3:18—4:1

> 18 Wives, be subject to your husbands, as is fitting in the
> Lord. 19 Husbands, love your wives and never treat them
> harshly. 20 Children, obey your parents in everything, for this
> is your acceptable duty in the Lord. 21 Fathers, do not provoke
> your children, or they may lose heart. 22 Slaves, obey your
> earthly masters in everything, not with a slavery performed
> merely for looks, to please people, but wholeheartedly, fearing
> the Lord. 23 Whatever task you must do, work as if your soul
> depends on it, as for the Lord and not for humans, 24 since you
> know that from the Lord you will receive the inheritance as your
> reward; you serve the Lord Christ. 25 For the wrongdoer will be
> paid back for whatever wrong has been done, and there is no
> partiality. 4 1 Masters, treat your slaves justly and fairly, for you
> know that you also have a Master in heaven.

Clearly this passage supports the status quo in first century Mediterranean culture. That is to say, there is a clear hierarchy present, and the writer makes no suggestion that such an arrangement is unjust. Having said this, it is instructive in that *everyone* is reminded that they have "a Master in heaven." This is why husbands and fathers and masters of slaves—those who undoubtedly sat in the seats of power in this culture—were told in no uncertain terms that their positions of cultural privilege did not give them license to abuse their position. Quite the contrary: They are reminded that they will be held accountable to the One Master of All and it is required of them to live and act justly. In our day, hierarchies continue to exist;

perhaps that will always be the case. No matter the age we live in, those of us who hold positions of privilege and power do well to remember that the Lord Jesus is our example, who came "not to be served, but to serve and to give his life as a ransom for many."

Prayer

Gracious Master of us all, forgive us whenever we abuse the power we have. Forgive us for lording it over those whom we somehow deem less than us. Help us to see all people as worthy of honor, and to devote ourselves to lives of service for the sake of the world and for the glory of your holy name. We pray this through Christ our Lord. AMEN.

Tuesday

Eccl 12:1–7

> Remember your creator in the days of your youth, before the days of trouble come and the years draw near when you will say, "I have no pleasure in them"; [2] before the sun and the light and the moon and the stars are darkened and the clouds return with the rain; [3] in the day when the guards of the house tremble, and the strong men are bent, and the women who grind cease working because they are few, and those who look through the windows see dimly; [4] when the doors on the street are shut, and the sound of the grinding is low, and one rises up at the sound of a bird, and all the daughters of song are brought low; [5] when one is afraid of heights, and terrors are in the road; the almond tree blossoms, the grasshopper drags itself along, and the caper bud falls; because all must go to their eternal home, and the mourners will go about the streets; [6] before the silver cord is snapped, and the golden bowl is broken, and the pitcher is broken at the fountain, and the wheel broken at the cistern, [7] and the dust returns to the earth as it was, and the breath returns to God who gave it.

This narrative poem from the last chapter of Ecclesiastes is part of the wisdom literature associated with King Solomon. Here, the writer advises us to remember our creator in the days of our youth, before the days of trouble come. The writer then goes on to list the ways that troubles come, poetically describing the process of growing old. Finally, the writer describes death as the time when "the dust returns to the earth as it was, and the breath returns to God who gave it." These last words are reminiscent of the funeral service where we do both a commendation and a committal. The commendation is the final part of the funeral liturgy where we commend a person to God, or as the wisdom writer says here, "The breath returns to God." I often say to families who will be taking part in a funeral service for a loved one, "Here is where we say to God, "They are all yours now, God." The breath or spirit of a person returns to God. The committal, usually done at the burial site, recognizes the presence of the body. Here we say the words, "Earth to earth, ashes to ashes, dust to dust." This also is an acknowledgement that our bodies are from God as well, and they too return to God the Creator. We are, we confess, totally *from* God and we return totally *to* God.

Prayer

We thank you, Creator of All Things, that we are totally *from* you, and we will someday return totally *to* you. You promise to keep us all our days. You promise to walk with us through the troubles and joys of this life. You promise to grant us your eternal presence in death. Give us faith to believe these promises and to live in joy all our days. We ask this through Christ our Lord. AMEN.

Wednesday

Luke 12:22–31

> 22 Jesus said to his disciples, "Therefore I tell you, do not worry
> about your life, what you will eat, or about your body, what you
> will wear. 23 For life is more than food and the body more than
> clothing. 24 Consider the ravens: they neither sow nor reap, they
> have neither storehouse nor barn, and yet God feeds them. Of
> how much more value are you than the birds! 25 And which of
> you by worrying can add a single hour to your span of life? 26 If
> then you are not able to do so small a thing as that, why do you
> worry about the rest? 27 Consider the lilies, how they grow: they
> neither toil nor spin, yet I tell you, even Solomon in all his glory
> was not clothed like one of these. 28 But if God so clothes the
> grass of the field, which is alive today and tomorrow is thrown
> into the oven, how much more will he clothe you, you of little

> faith! [29] And do not keep seeking what you are to eat and what you are to drink, and do not keep worrying. [30] For it is the nations of the world that seek all these things, and your Father knows that you need them. [31] Instead, seek his kingdom, and these things will be given to you as well."

"Stop worrying," says Jesus. If only it were that easy! It's like saying to a person who is afraid of heights, "Relax." "Easy for you to say," they might say. And we might say the same to Jesus: "Easy for you to say, 'Stop worrying,' when you're the Son of God and all. As for me, I'm not all-powerful, all-knowing, and all-seeing, and I've got lots of good reasons to be worried!" But then Jesus changes the focal point of our gaze. He points out that worry comes from what we are *seeking, what we are focusing on.* I remember a woman I once knew who was always seeking deals. I visited her home once and she brought me to her basement where she had literally *hundreds* of cans of food that she had gotten "a deal" on. She was completely blind to the abundance she had because of her obsessive focus on getting deals. We can be like this too, living in abundance, yet continually seeking more. Jesus says, "Seek my kingdom. I will see that you have enough. Seek to live a life of love and compassion. I will take care of you. Seek to bring joy to others. I will bring joy to you." It's all about what we are seeking.

Prayer

Gracious Lord of All, grant us faith in you. Grant us the ability to let go of our fears and anxieties and seek those things that will bring your kingdom a little closer in this world. We know that we often worry about things that you have promised to provide for us. Release us from such worry, and give us the joy of seeking the kingdom. We ask this in Jesus' name. AMEN.

Thursday

Ps 33:13–22

> 13 The LORD looks down from heaven;
> he sees all humankind.
> 14 From where he sits enthroned he watches
> all the inhabitants of the earth—
> 15 he who fashions the hearts of them all

and observes all their deeds.
16 A king is not saved by his great army;
a warrior is not delivered by his great strength.
17 The war horse is a vain hope for victory,
and by its great might it cannot save.
18 Truly the eye of the LORD is on those who fear him,
on those who hope in his steadfast love,
19 to deliver their soul from death
and to keep them alive in famine.
20 Our soul waits for the LORD;
he is our help and shield.
21 Our heart is glad in him
because we trust in his holy name.
22 Let your steadfast love, O LORD, be upon us,
even as we hope in you.

The scene here is of the Lord looking down from heaven and observing the goings on of humankind. It comes as no surprise to the Lord that people are seen trusting in power and might. Kings trust in their armies, warriors in their great strength, and war horses in their great might. It is as if all creatures, great and small, trust in their own strength. This is foolish, says the psalmist. Our only hope is God. God alone is our help and shield. God alone will make our hearts glad. We are no different today. Wars still rage and tyrants still rule. And all the world assumes that the one with the biggest weapons will win. Of course, in our day and age that could include nuclear weapons, which if used, could be the end of all humanity. How much better to trust in the God to whom Jesus pointed, the One who said, "Blessed are the peacemakers, for they shall be called children of God."

Prayer

Your way is the way of life, Dear Lord. Your way is the way of peace. Bring us into a right mind that we might see the insanity of trusting in armies and armaments and instead begin trusting in your wisdom and guidance. Make us into peacemakers and give courage and resolve to all who seek peace. In Christ's name we pray. AMEN.

Friday

Matt 6:19–24

[19] "Do not store up for yourselves treasures on earth, where moth
and rust consume and where thieves break in and steal, [20] but
store up for yourselves treasures in heaven, where neither moth
nor rust consumes and where thieves do not break in and
steal. [21] For where your treasure is, there your heart will be also.

[22] "The eye is the lamp of the body. So if your eye is healthy, your
whole body will be full of light, [23] but if your eye is unhealthy,
your whole body will be full of darkness. If, then, the light in you
is darkness, how great is the darkness!

[24] "No one can serve two masters, for a slave will either hate the
one and love the other or be devoted to the one and despise the
other. You cannot serve God and wealth.

A friend of mine used to say, "The more stuff you have, the more tending it takes." That simple phrase reminds us that whatever we accumulate makes demands on us. When we sell our starter home and move into a bigger one, we soon find out that more square footage means more time cleaning and repairing things. When we buy that long-dreamed-of lake home, we find we have an extra lawn to mow, another roof to repair, and all the other tasks that go with owning a second home. When we decide to collect keepsakes or artwork or any other fine things, we soon learn that all those things need tending, and on it goes. Jesus does not say fine things are a hindrance to faith, but he does remind us that treasures finally demand something from us, and we need to be cognizant of this. We cannot serve God and wealth. Only one master is possible. Better to serve the master who is gracious and forgiving.

Prayer

You are the Gracious Master of us all, Dear Lord. You are the one who gives us life and sustains us all our days. Grant us wisdom with our wealth, and a firm faith in you, all our days. In your precious name we pray. AMEN.

The Seventeenth Week After Pentecost

Monday

Ps 89:5–11

5 Let the heavens praise your wonders, O Lord,
your faithfulness in the assembly of the holy ones.
6 For who in the skies can be compared to the Lord?
Who among the heavenly beings is like the Lord,
7 a God feared in the council of the holy ones,
great and awesome above all who are around him?
8 O Lord God of hosts,
who is as mighty as you, O Lord?
Your faithfulness surrounds you.
9 You rule the raging of the sea;
when its waves rise, you still them.
10 You crushed Rahab like a carcass;
you scattered your enemies with your mighty arm.
11 The heavens are yours; the earth also is yours;
the world and all that is in it—you founded them.

As I sit down to write this week, Hurricane Ian is bearing down on the Gulf Coast of Florida. With winds nearing 150 miles per hour accompanied by torrential rains, catastrophic damage is predicted. Few natural phenomena rival the power of this storm. We pray for all in its ferocious path. The psalmist certainly knew of the power of nature. The deserts and mountains and seas of Israel were not strangers to wind and rain. Yet the psalmist says these powers are no match for the power and majesty of God. "You rule the raging of the sea; when its waves rise, you still them," says the writer. "The heavens are yours; the earth also is yours." In other words, though these storms are powerful beyond compare, there is One whose power makes even these storms seem puny. What a great and mighty God we have! There is none to compare. What a faithful and generous God we have! Again, there is none to compare.

Prayer

We praise you, Mighty God, for your great power and faithfulness. We praise you for the powers of nature that bring life to the world. Have mercy on those whose lives are impacted so greatly by powers of nature unleashed. Have mercy too, on the creatures and vegetation who have little defense against such powers. Give us faith to believe in you and the resolve to do all we can to protect and support all life. In your holy name we pray. AMEN.

Tuesday

2 Chr 33:9–13

> [9] Manasseh misled Judah and the inhabitants of Jerusalem, so that they did more evil than the nations whom the LORD had destroyed before the people of Israel.
>
> [10] The LORD spoke to Manasseh and to his people, but they
> gave no heed. [11] Therefore the LORD brought against them
> the commanders of the army of the king of Assyria, who took
> Manasseh captive in manacles, bound him with fetters, and
> brought him to Babylon. [12] While he was in distress, he en-
> treated the favor of the LORD his God and humbled himself
> greatly before the God of his ancestors. [13] He prayed to him,
> and God received his entreaty, heard his plea, and restored
> him again to Jerusalem and to his kingdom. Then Manasseh
> knew that the LORD indeed was God.

Scholars differ in their assessment of the reign of King Manasseh, who reigned as king of Judah for 55 years. Some say he was the most corrupt king Judah ever had. They note that not only did he encourage idol worship amongst the people, but he even erected idols *in the temple of the Lord* and encouraged their worship there! Other historians, specifically the chroniclers of ancient Judah, had another take, however. While they admit that King Manasseh misled the people, they blame *the people* for the wickedness that emerged. Furthermore, they remembered Manasseh's repentance and announced that, after his exile, Manasseh learned his lesson and "knew that the Lord indeed was God." We could pray for such repentance and enlightenment for some of the leaders in our country. We have elected officials in America who repeatedly mislead the people, trafficking in lies they know to be false. As a result, many good people are led into patterns of thinking and living that are hurtful and dangerous. This is not how God would have us live. We must be led by those who are loyal to the truth.

Prayer

We pray for our country and our leaders, O Lord. We pray that wisdom and righteousness, justice and compassion, would prevail. We pray that those who use their power only to steal and destroy, only to create fear and division, would be thwarted in their plans and brought to repentance. Protect us and guide us, gracious Lord. In your holy name, we pray. AMEN.

Wednesday

Heb 11:1–7

> Now faith is the assurance of things hoped for, the conviction of
> things not seen. [2] Indeed, by faith our ancestors received ap-
> proval. [3] By faith we understand that the worlds were prepared
> by the word of God, so that what is seen was made from things
> that are not visible. [4] By faith Abel offered to God a more ac-
> ceptable sacrifice than Cain's. Through this he received approval
> as righteous, God himself giving approval to his gifts; he died,
> but through his faith he still speaks. [5] By faith Enoch was taken
> so that he did not experience death, and "he was not found,
> because God had taken him." For it was attested before he was
> taken away that "he had pleased God." [6] And without faith it
> is impossible to please him, for whoever would approach God
> must believe that he exists and that he rewards those who seek
> him. [7] By faith Noah, warned by God about events as yet unseen,
> respected the warning and built an ark to save his household; by

> this he condemned the world and became an heir to the righteousness that is in accordance with faith.

These well-known verses from Heb 11 have long been the definition of faith: "the assurance of things hoped for, the conviction of things not seen." Faith is not, as American satirist, H. L. Mencken once quipped, "An illogical belief in the occurrence of the improbable." Rather, faith is being convinced that what God has promised will come to pass. Faith is living out the hope we have in Christ, where all things are made new. Faith is trusting in the mercy and justice of God and living all our days in the peace that such trust gives. I sometimes wonder if faith isn't simply part of the human condition. I do not mean faith in God, per se, but faith in *something*. It seems impossible to live if one doesn't believe in *something*, in some goal, or some pattern of meaning, or some purpose to life. Perhaps one of our jobs as people of faith is to remind one another, and whomever we might encounter, that faith is what gives one hope, and hope is what one needs to get out of bed in the morning.

Prayer

Gracious and Faithful God, thank you for your great promises. Thank you for your declaration of everlasting love, for the example of Jesus, and for your Holy Spirit that inspires us. Grant that we might live in faith and hope all our days and inspire others to do the same. Through Christ our Lord. AMEN.

Thursday

Luke 12:42–48

> 42 And the Lord said, "Who, then, is the faithful and prudent
> manager whom his master will put in charge of his slaves, to
> give them their allowance of food at the proper time? 43 Blessed
> is that slave whom his master will find at work when he ar-
> rives. 44 Truly I tell you, he will put that one in charge of all his
> possessions. 45 But if that slave says to himself, 'My master is
> delayed in coming,' and begins to beat the other slaves, men
> and women, and to eat and drink and get drunk, 46 the mas-
> ter of that slave will come on a day when he does not expect
> him and at an hour that he does not know and will cut him in
> pieces and put him with the unfaithful. 47 That slave who knew

> what his master wanted but did not prepare himself or do what
> was wanted will receive a severe beating. 48 But the one who did
> not know and did what deserved a beating will receive a light
> beating. From everyone to whom much has been given, much
> will be required, and from the one to whom much has been
> entrusted, even more will be demanded.

This severe parable ends with a memorable sentence that could be a mantra for any of us who are fortunate enough to have lived in abundance all our lives. Though most of us who live in the United States would not call ourselves rich, it is undeniable that most of the world would. Many of us have received a long and rich educational experience. We have benefited in innumerable ways as citizens of a country where laws and norms of behavior that benefit all are regularly in place. We have enjoyed an infrastructure that other nations can only dream of: medicine, finance, transportation, commerce, education, public works, and voting rights, to name a few. In short, we are those "to whom much has been given." And as such, God says, "From you much is required." This is only fair. Even a child knows that if one playmate has five pieces of candy and another playmate has one, fairness requires that the playmate with five pieces of candy shares more than the playmate with one. More is required of us who have more. How much more peaceful our world would be if we all understood and abided by this simple rule.

Prayer

Lord Jesus, grant to those of us who have much the grace to do all that is required of us. Forgive us when we fail to see our abundance and do not do what justice requires. We are your people. We wish to be faithful. Inspire us, we pray. In Christ's name. AMEN.

Friday

Josh 7:1–7

> But the Israelites broke faith in regard to the devoted things: Achan son of Carmi son of Zabdi son of Zerah, of the tribe of Judah, took some of the devoted things, and the anger of the LORD burned against the Israelites.
>
> 2 Joshua sent men from Jericho to Ai, which is near Beth-aven,
> east of Bethel, and said to them, "Go up and spy out the land."

> And the men went up and spied out Ai. [3] Then they returned to Joshua and said to him, "Not all the people need go up; about two or three thousand men should go up and attack Ai. Since they are so few, do not make the whole people toil up there." [4] So about three thousand of the people went up there, and they fled before the men of Ai. [5] The men of Ai killed about thirty-six of them, chasing them from outside the gate as far as Shebarim and killing them on the slope. The hearts of the people melted and turned to water.
>
> [6] Then Joshua tore his clothes and fell to the ground on his face before the ark of the LORD until the evening, he and the elders of Israel, and they put dust on their heads. [7] Joshua said, "Ah, Lord God! Why have you brought this people across the Jordan at all, to hand us over to the Amorites so as to destroy us? Would that we had been content to settle beyond the Jordan!

This is the beginning of the story of the Sin of Achan, who, following the defeat of Jericho, took some of the spoils of war for himself, even though there were strict orders forbidding it. As a result of his dishonesty, God refused to continue championing the armies of Israel, and they were defeated at the battle of Ai. When Joshua, the leader of Israel, heard of this defeat, he cried out to God, "Why has this happened?" He did not yet know that Achan had disobeyed the explicit command to take none of the plunder. What Achan's sin highlights is how one person's sinful pattern can become a devastating poison that spreads through the whole community. We all know this. It can happen in workplaces, in neighborhoods, in churches, and in whole communities. One destructive person can create havoc with an entire ecosystem. It turns out we are all connected, for better or for worse. How much better to be that leaven of kindness, that fragrance of generosity, and that spirit of helpfulness that make communities into healthy, happy places for all. Surely this is what God wills for us all.

Prayer

Give us wisdom, Holy God, to live as people who understand how connected we are, one to another. Forgive us when we forget this and act as though our misdeeds have no effect on anyone else. Protect our communities from division and wickedness, and give to all those who lead a clear understanding of what is required for all to flourish. In the name of Jesus we pray. AMEN.

The Eighteenth Week After Pentecost

Monday

Ps 82

1 God has taken his place in the divine council;
in the midst of the gods he holds judgment:
2 "How long will you judge unjustly
and show partiality to the wicked?
3 Give justice to the weak and the orphan;
maintain the right of the lowly and the destitute.
4 Rescue the weak and the needy;
deliver them from the hand of the wicked."
5 They have neither knowledge nor understanding;
they walk around in darkness;
all the foundations of the earth are shaken.
6 I say, "You are gods,
children of the Most High, all of you;
7 nevertheless, you shall die like mortals
and fall like any prince."
8 Rise up, O God, judge the earth,
for all the nations belong to you!

It may not be immediately obvious, but God is talking to heavenly beings here, presumably angels. Notice what is in quotes. God is calling the angels to account for showing partiality to the wicked and for failing to provide justice to the vulnerable. This is interesting because we often assume that angels are beyond sin; apparently not. Notice also that God pronounces judgment upon them in verse 6: "You are gods [but, because of your sins] . . . you shall die like mortals." This scene reminds me of Jesus' response to the rich young ruler in Matt 19: "Why do you ask about what is good? There is only one who is good." Clearly the only one who is good is the Triune God. All other beings, both earthly and heavenly, stand in need of God's grace. This certainly expands our view of what Jesus meant when he said he died for *all*.

Prayer

Merciful God, how thankful we are for your ever-expanding grace which comes to all creatures. We thank you for your desire that none be lost, but that all come to know the truth of the Gospel and hear the word of forgiveness. Give us open hearts to receive your forgiveness and tongues to confess you as Lord and Savior of all. In your holy name we pray. AMEN.

Tuesday

1 Sam 5:1–5

> When the Philistines captured the ark of God, they brought it
> from Ebenezer to Ashdod; [2] then the Philistines took the ark
> of God and brought it into the house of Dagon and placed it
> beside Dagon. [3] When the people of Ashdod rose early the next
> day, there was Dagon, fallen on his face to the ground before
> the ark of the LORD. So they took Dagon and put him back
> in his place. [4] But when they rose early on the next morning,
> Dagon had fallen on his face to the ground before the ark of
> the LORD, and the head of Dagon and both his hands were
> lying cut off upon the threshold; only the trunk of Dagon was
> left to him. [5] This is why the priests of Dagon and all who enter
> the house of Dagon do not step on the threshold of Dagon in
> Ashdod to this day.

The ark of God was the visible sign of God's covenant with Israel. In the days of the wilderness wanderings, it was housed in the tabernacle, a tent-like sanctuary serving this nomadic people. In later years such as the days of Samuel, it was housed in Shiloh, in a modest temple. In a superstitious attempt to win a battle against the Philistines, the army of Israel took the ark with them into battle, as though by its very presence, they were assured of victory. This was not to be, and, along with being defeated, Israel lost control of this sacred object. What happened next was a testimony to God's jealous rage. God would not abide having the ark in the temple of Dagon, the god of the Philistines. On two subsequent days, the idol was found fallen on its face before the ark, as if to say, "I know who is the One True God. It is the Lord." In an ironic twist, it was the idol who bore witness to God's power. Martin Luther, in the *Large Catechism,* said that "Whatever your heart clings to and confides in, that is really your God." It is good to remember that our Lord will not abide other gods. Indeed, all bow to this Lord.

Prayer

Keep us from false gods, O Lord. Open our hearts to cling only to you and to confide only in you. Forgive us when we fail to worship you as Lord of All. We are your people. We wish to be found faithful. In your holy name we pray. AMEN.

Wednesday

1 John 4:1–6

> Beloved, do not believe every spirit, but test the spirits to see
> whether they are from God, for many false prophets have gone
> out into the world. 2 By this you know the Spirit of God: every
> spirit that confesses that Jesus Christ has come in the flesh
> is from God, 3 and every spirit that does not confess Jesus is
> not from God. And this is the spirit of the antichrist, of which
> you have heard that it is coming, and now it is already in the
> world. 4 Little children, you are from God and have conquered
> them, for the one who is in you is greater than the one who is
> in the world. 5 They are from the world; therefore what they say
> is from the world, and the world listens to them. 6 We are from
> God. Whoever knows God listens to us, and whoever is not
> from God does not listen to us. From this we know the spirit
> of truth and the spirit of error.

The error that John was writing about in this letter was the heresy of *Gnosticism.* This word comes from the Greek word for knowledge. Gnosticism taught that our flesh, and by logical extension, our earthly life, was of no concern to God; the only thing God cared about was right *knowledge.*

Christians were thought to be those who possessed the right knowledge, and this knowledge was of the spiritual sort, available only to the chosen. John insisted that this was an error. God did very much care about our earthly life and especially how we treated one another. He said that *love,* not knowledge, was the true test of a follower of Jesus. He also insisted that Jesus had indeed come in the flesh and died in the flesh, for to say otherwise was to undermine the whole notion of Jesus' sacrifice. Finally, John reminded his readers that the spirit of the antichrist, the final opponent of God, was not to be feared, for the Spirit that lives within us, is "greater than the one who is in the world." All of this is tremendously good news. We are called to a life of love, we are assured that Christ died for us, and the Spirit within us is stronger than any spirit in the world.

Prayer

We praise you, Sovereign Lord, for your mighty Spirit that resides in each of us. We praise you that your power is greater than any antichrist, and your victory over death and the devil is already won. Give us faith in the redemption given to us in Christ, and lead us in the way of love. We ask this through Christ our Lord. AMEN.

Thursday

Luke 19:41–48

41 As [Jesus]came near and saw the city, he wept over it, 42 say-
ing, "If you, even you, had only recognized on this day the
things that make for peace! But now they are hidden from your
eyes. 43 Indeed, the days will come upon you when your enemies
will set up ramparts around you and surround you and hem you
in on every side. 44 They will crush you to the ground, you and
your children within you, and they will not leave within you one
stone upon another, because you did not recognize the time of
your visitation from God."

45 Then he entered the temple and began to drive out those who
were selling things there, 46 and he said, "It is written,

'My house shall be a house of prayer,'
    but you have made it a den of robbers."

[47] Every day he was teaching in the temple. The chief priests, the
scribes, and the leaders of the people kept looking for a way to
kill him, [48] but they did not find anything they could do, for all
the people were spellbound by what they heard.

Years ago, I knew a pastor who served at a church where fundraising was a constant presence. They had bake sales and rummage sales, car washes and dinners, service auctions and raffles; you name it, they had it. Their whole life together seemed to be about raising money for the church. This disturbed my friend for a number of reasons, but primarily because it seemed that selling stuff was what the church was known for. One day he told me, "I am going to tell the Church Board, 'If you don't call a halt to all this fundraising and get back to the business of ministry, I'm leaving.'" He didn't really know what they would say. As it turned out, this passage from Luke was critical in their decision. They decided that they had indeed made the house of God into a house of commerce, and they changed their ways. What a joy for my friend. The Word of God had convicted them, they had cleaned house, ended their practice of selling things, and had gotten back to the reason for their existence: proclaiming and living out God's love. We do well to remember that as disciples of Christ we are called always to ministry. Yes, fundraising has its place, but only to the extent that it furthers the mission of Christ. We must keep God's work our priority.

Prayer

Let your house of prayer be forever a house of prayer, O Lord. Keep us from falling into patterns that do not honor you. Keep us from being distracted by money and all of its allure, and lead us in the way aright. We ask this in Jesus' name. AMEN.

Friday

Acts 17:16–21

[16] While Paul was waiting for them in Athens, he was deeply
distressed to see that the city was full of idols. [17] So he argued
in the synagogue with the Jews and the devout persons and also
in the marketplace every day with those who happened to be
there. [18] Also some Epicurean and Stoic philosophers debated

> with him. Some said, "What does this pretentious babbler want to say?" Others said, "He seems to be a proclaimer of foreign divinities." (This was because he was telling the good news about Jesus and the resurrection.) 19 So they took him and brought him to the Areopagus and asked him, "May we know what this new teaching is that you are presenting? 20 It sounds rather strange to us, so we would like to know what it means." 21 Now all the Athenians and the foreigners living there would spend their time in nothing but telling or hearing something new.

The description of the folks living in Athens who spent their time "in nothing but telling or hearing something new" sounds like a very modern situation. Today we find people pursuing all kinds of exotic spiritual practices in hopes of connecting with God, but somehow overlooking the fact that classic spiritual practices like prayer, meditation, journaling, Bible reading, and acts of devotion have sustained people for centuries. It's almost as if people feel that unless the practice is "new," it's not relevant. And predictably, when this newest thing doesn't work out, they have to move on to the next "new" thing. Finding new ways of connecting with God is, of course, laudable; however, it seems wise to continue the ancient practices as well since they are tried and true. As the writer to the Hebrews said, "Jesus Christ is the same yesterday and today and forever."

Prayer

Thank you, Almighty and Ever-living God, that you are the same from one age to another. Thank you also for your continual invitation to come into your embrace. Grant us your presence each day, that we might be filled with joy, knowing that you are our God today and tomorrow and forever. In your holy name we pray. AMEN.

The Nineteenth Week After Pentecost

Monday

Neh 13:15–18

> [15] In those days I saw in Judah people treading winepresses on the Sabbath and bringing in heaps of grain and loading them on donkeys, and also wine, grapes, figs, and all kinds of burdens that they brought into Jerusalem on the Sabbath day, and I warned them at that time against selling food. [16] Tyrians also, who lived in the city, brought in fish and all kinds of merchandise and sold them on the Sabbath to the people of Judah in Jerusalem. [17] Then I contended with the nobles of Judah and said to them, "What is this evil thing that you are doing, profaning the Sabbath day? [18] Did not your ancestors act in this way, and did not our God bring all this disaster on us and on this city? Yet you bring more wrath on Israel by profaning the Sabbath."

Nehemiah was a very unlikely reformer, and yet a reformer he was. He was not a priest, nor a prophet, but a layperson, a servant of the Persian King Artaxerxes. While serving as a cupbearer in the court, he heard tales of his people in Israel living in disarray and dysfunction, and his sorrow over their state was such that the king asked him what was wrong. After Nehemiah described the reason for his anguish, the king gave him leave to go back home and see what he could do to help. In various ways Nehemiah then began to lead a renaissance and reform movement in Israel. As one of his final acts he even began to suggest reforms in piety, such as Sabbath practice, highlighted in this text. As we approach Reformation Sunday, it is good to remember that the Church of Christ has always been in need of reforming. We get off track, we forget what is really important, we become engaged in pointless debates or fruitless quarrels. Faithful people like Nehemiah, courageous, hard-working, and lovers of God and God's people, will always be needed in the Church. It is the way God continues to lead us in life-giving ways.

Prayer

Thank you, Gracious God, for courageous reformers. Thank you for people who will take risks to say things that get our attention and cause us to reevaluate our priorities. Thank you for people who challenge us in love and who hold us close even while they lead us in truth. Guide us each day, we pray. In Christ's name. AMEN.

Tuesday

Heb 3:7–14

7 Therefore, as the Holy Spirit says,
"Today, if you hear his voice,
8 do not harden your hearts as in the rebellion,
as on the day of testing in the wilderness,
9 where your ancestors put me to the test,
though they had seen my works 10 for forty years.
Therefore I was angry with that generation,
and I said, 'They always go astray in their hearts,
and they have not known my ways.'
11 As in my anger I swore,
'They will not enter my rest.' "

12 Take care, brothers and sisters, that none of you may have an evil, unbelieving heart that turns away from the living God. 13 But exhort one another every day, as long as it is called "today," so that none of you may be hardened by the deceitfulness of sin. 14 For we have become partners of Christ, if only we hold our first confidence firm to the end.

These verses in Hebrews remind us that we are dependent upon one another to remain faithful to Christ. "Going astray in our hearts" is how the writer describes what happens when we drift away from the faith. Perhaps this means that our desires change, or our priorities and commitments change, and suddenly, without meaning to, we are drifting away from the community of faith. When this happens and we are no longer connected regularly to other followers of Christ, we can enter into an even more precarious place, "hardened by the deceitfulness of sin." The antidote for this is for each of us to be vigilant in staying connected with our siblings in Christ. Have you noticed that someone hasn't been around church for a while? Give them a call and tell them they are missed. Have you noticed that a person who went through a difficult time like the death of a loved one, a job loss, or a major disappointment, has been seen only seldom in worship? Drop them a card and tell them you are thinking about them. These acts of compassion and love can make all the difference in keeping a person as part of the Body of Christ. We are keepers, one of another.

Prayer

God of Love and Compassion, we thank you for the people of God, your Church. We thank you for those who love us and listen to us, celebrate with us and console us. We could not be the people we are without them. Give us hearts that love and listen, celebrate and console, that all your people may be found ever close to you. In your precious name we pray. AMEN.

Wednesday

Luke 6:6–11

> 6 On another Sabbath [Jesus]entered the synagogue and taught,
> and there was a man there whose right hand was withered. 7 The
> scribes and the Pharisees were watching him to see whether he
> would cure on the Sabbath, so that they might find grounds
> to bring an accusation against him. 8 But he knew what they
> were thinking, and he said to the man who had the withered
> hand, "Come and stand in the middle." He got up and stood
> there. 9 Then Jesus said to them, "I ask you, is it lawful to do good
> or to do harm on the Sabbath, to save life or to destroy it?" 10 Af-
> ter looking around at all of them, he said to him, "Stretch out
> your hand." He did so, and his hand was restored. 11 But they
> were filled with fury and began discussing with one another
> what they might do to Jesus.

In the movie *Chocolat*, a young mother and her daughter move into a quiet French town and open a chocolate shop. Her chocolates prove to be more than mere delicacies, however; they are life-giving. It turns out that the townspeople are held in moral bondage by a mayor who somehow believes that strict piety will lead to the abundant life. In this restrictive culture, simple chocolate treats become a threat to that system. A few of the townspeople, some of them withering under the regulations imposed upon them, boldly step out of their moral cages and begin to come alive as they experience the freedom they have longed for. Other townspeople simply find joy in these new delicacies. Finally, the mayor himself succumbs to their allure. In his new-found freedom he finally sees life in all of its fullness and begins to lead the people in a new and joyful way. In much the same way, Jesus was showing humanity a new way. He made sure we knew that saving life and doing good were far more important than any piety. He showed us that compassion rather than adherence to rules must be our concern. He showed us that sacrifice for the sake of the neighbor was more important than any offering we could ever give. He showed us the path of life.

Prayer

Life-giving Christ, forgive us when we start to believe that rules lead to life. Forgive us when we act as though judging others is our main task. Remind us that love will always be our guide, and your compassion and sacrifice are our call. In your holy name we pray. AMEN.

Thursday

Ps 112

1 Praise the LORD!
Happy are those who fear the LORD,
who greatly delight in his commandments.
2 Their descendants will be mighty in the land;
the generation of the upright will be blessed.
3 Wealth and riches are in their houses,
and their righteousness endures forever.
4 They rise in the darkness as a light for the upright;
they are gracious, merciful, and righteous.

5 It is well with those who deal generously and lend,
who conduct their affairs with justice.
6 For the righteous will never be moved;
they will be remembered forever.
7 They are not afraid of evil tidings;
their hearts are firm, secure in the LORD.
8 Their hearts are steady; they will not be afraid;
in the end they will look in triumph on their foes.

This psalm is remarkable in its promises to those who delight in God's commandments. At the outset we hear that they are *happy*. Then we hear that their descendants will be *blessed*. We learn that their good deeds will *endure*; in other words, they will be remembered. They are *a light*, a guide perhaps, for others. Things *go well* with them and they are *steady*, immovable. They are also *not living in fear* nor anxious about the days to come. Finally, they will look in *triumph* on those who oppose them. Do you know people like this? I can remember more than one faithful church member I have known whom this describes. It is true; they are unforgettable, steady, happy, immovable, and non-anxious. All of these characteristics are theirs. They do not fear death and, even as they have grown old, they continue to bear fruit and be a blessing to others. Perhaps this really is a recipe for the abundant life—to delight in God's commandments.

Prayer

God of All Life, you have blessed us in many ways: with your Church, with your Word, with your Spirit, with your provision for all we need from day to day. How can we ever thank you? Give us hearts that delight in your commandments that we might always be found in your peace and joy. We pray this in Jesus' name. AMEN.

Friday

Prov 18:1–8

The one who lives alone is self-indulgent,
showing contempt for all sound judgment.
2 A fool takes no pleasure in understanding,

but only in expressing personal opinion.
3 When wickedness comes, contempt comes also,
and with dishonor comes disgrace.
4 The words of the mouth are deep waters;
the fountain of wisdom is a gushing stream.
5 It is not right to be partial to the guilty
or to subvert the innocent in judgment.
6 A fool's lips bring strife,
and a fool's mouth invites a flogging.
7 The mouths of fools are their ruin,
and their lips a snare to themselves.
8 The words of a whisperer are like delicious morsels;
they go down into the inner parts of the body.

These verses from Proverbs are some of my favorites, but none more so than the second verse: "A fool takes no pleasure in understanding, but only in expressing personal opinion." Perhaps there have always been people whom this describes, but it seems that today, in our media-saturated world, we are flooded with voices who are not interested in understanding anything, but only in spouting off. How wearisome this is. Conversely, how refreshing it is when we encounter a person who is actually seeking understanding and trying to find out the truth about one thing or another. The writer of these verses also goes on to say what the lips of fools produce: strife, ruin, and a snare. These, too, seem to be characteristics of people who have no pleasure in understanding. They do indeed cause problems and ruin wherever they go. We must commit ourselves to be people of humility and grace, ever listening for true wisdom and true insight, helped by others and helpful to others for the sake of the world.

Prayer

Grant us wisdom, God of All. Grant us discernment so that when we encounter voices that sound authoritative but actually know little, we shall know them for who they are. Give us leaders who will lead us humbly and with grace, ever learning, ever listening to hear the way you are leading them for the sake of the world. In Christ's name we pray. AMEN.

The Twentieth Week After Pentecost

Monday

1 Pet 4:7–11

> [7] The end of all things is near; therefore be serious and discipline yourselves for the sake of your prayers. [8] Above all, maintain constant love for one another, for love covers a multitude of sins. [9] Be hospitable to one another without complaining. [10] Like good stewards of the manifold grace of God, serve one another with whatever gift each of you has received. [11] Whoever speaks must do so as one speaking the very words of God; whoever serves must do so with the strength that God supplies, so that God may be glorified in all things through Jesus Christ. To him belong the glory and the power forever and ever. Amen.

Scholars have, for years, recognized that Christians in the first century of the Church very much expected Christ to return in their lifetime. They truly thought "the end of things" was near. In today's world most of us do not think in those terms. We believe that the End will come, but few of us expect it in our lifetime. Indeed, we tend to dismiss people who spend a lot of time announcing that the End is near, perhaps pegging them as mentally unstable or even deranged. In Peter's letter, however, we see the notion of the imminent end of the world being taken very seriously. But notice what Peter exhorts the believers to do as a matter of first priority: "*Maintain constant love* for one another, for love covers a multitude of sins." Isn't that interesting. The most important thing we can do as we await the second coming of Christ is to maintain constant love for those in the faith community. Why? Because this love "covers a multitude of sins." In other words, mutual love makes up for the fact that we are all sinners, all the time, which means we do and say things that are hurtful to one another. So that's our agenda as we look forward to Christ's coming: we love one another.

Prayer

Loving God, give us your loving spirit. Forgiving God, give us your forgiving spirit. Compassionate God, give us your compassionate spirit. We are so prone to be unloving, even though we wish to be otherwise. Help us in our weakness, we pray. In the name of Jesus. AMEN.

Tuesday

Matt 20:20–28

> 20 Then the mother of the sons of Zebedee came to him with her
> sons, and kneeling before him, she asked a favor of him. 21 And
> he said to her, "What do you want?" She said to him, "Declare
> that these two sons of mine will sit, one at your right hand and
> one at your left, in your kingdom." 22 But Jesus answered, "You
> do not know what you are asking. Are you able to drink the cup
> that I am about to drink?" They said to him, "We are able." 23 He
> said to them, "You will indeed drink my cup, but to sit at my
> right hand and at my left, this is not mine to grant, but it is for
> those for whom it has been prepared by my Father."
>
> 24 When the ten heard it, they were angry with the two broth-
> ers. 25 But Jesus called them to him and said, "You know that
> the rulers of the Gentiles lord it over them, and their great ones
> are tyrants over them. 26 It will not be so among you; but who-
> ever wishes to be great among you must be your servant, 27 and
> whoever wishes to be first among you must be your slave; 28 just
> as the Son of Man came not to be served but to serve, and to
> give his life a ransom for many."

I remember playing King of the Mountain as a kid. It usually happened after school in the winter when there were huge snow piles around town. We'd scramble to the top of one of those big piles and attempt to be the one who stayed on top. Of course, everyone else's job was to throw us off. For some reason the disciples of Jesus had this notion of life in Christ's kingdom. They thought being king of the mountain was part of their calling. "Not so much," said Jesus. And Jesus says the same thing to us. When we start to believe that our place as disciples of Christ is to take the best seats at the table, and the most honored positions in the community, and receive the most acclaim for our efforts, Jesus says, "Not so much." He reminds us that as he came *not* to be served but to serve, so that is our calling too. We find that such service is actually where life and joy are found.

Prayer

Thank you for showing us the joy of being a servant, Lord Christ. Thank you for calling us into service, and for equipping us for it every day. Thank you for people who serve joyfully and show us the way. Help us all to be joyful servants of yours. In your holy name we pray. AMEN.

Wednesday

Ps 119:63–72

63 I am a companion of all who fear you,
of those who keep your precepts.
64 The earth, O LORD, is full of your steadfast love;
teach me your statutes.
65 You have dealt well with your servant,
O LORD, according to your word.
66 Teach me good judgment and knowledge,
for I believe in your commandments.
67 Before I was humbled I went astray,
but now I keep your word.
68 You are good and do good;
teach me your statutes.
69 The arrogant smear me with lies,
but with my whole heart I keep your precepts.
70 Their hearts are fat and gross,
but I delight in your law.
71 It is good for me that I was humbled,
so that I might learn your statutes.
72 The law of your mouth is better to me
than thousands of gold and silver pieces.

In this section of Ps 119, the writer mentions more than one time that he learned wisdom by being humbled. I don't know about you, but that's not my favorite way of learning wisdom. Nevertheless, it really works. Years ago, I was in the market for my first car. I had seen an ad in a magazine for a French make of car, Peugeot, and I had fallen in love with that car. When I went car shopping, my dad advised me to buy a new car with a warranty, a small, sporty car that would serve me without problems. But I saw a used Peugeot on the lot and said, "No new car for me. I want that Peugeot." So I bought it. Talk about learning wisdom by being humbled! That car was in the shop more than it was on the road. Meanwhile, the car my dad wanted me to buy was so popular that I could have sold it three years later for more than I paid for it! Ouch. Being humbled is no fun, but there's no doubt that it can lead to some lessons well learned. It can also lead to life.

Prayer

God of all wisdom, thank you for your desire to guide us in the way of truth all our days. Thank you for wise teachers, mentors, and leaders who lead us in your way. Thank you, also, for humbling us now and then to teach us well. Help us to listen so that we might gain the wisdom that leads to life. In your holy name we pray. AMEN.

Thursday

Isa 2:12–17

12 For the LORD of hosts has a day
against all that is proud and lofty,
against all that is lifted up and high;
13 against all the cedars of Lebanon,
lofty and lifted up;
and against all the oaks of Bashan;
14 against all the high mountains,
and against all the lofty hills;
15 against every high tower,
and against every fortified wall;
16 against all the ships of Tarshish,
and against all the beautiful craft.

17 The haughtiness of people shall be humbled,
and the pride of everyone shall be brought low;
and the LORD alone will be exalted on that day.

Gerhard Forde, a longtime professor of systematic theology at Luther Seminary, used to talk about our "upward rebellion" against God. By this he meant that we are always trying to be like God. That first temptation in the Garden of Eden, when the tempter said to Eve, "God knows that when you eat of [the tree of knowledge]your eyes will be opened, and you will be like God," is still with us. We want so much to be all-knowing, and yet our knowledge is incomplete. We want so much to be all-powerful, and yet our powers are limited. We want so much to be immortal, but our bodies are in a constant state of decay. All of our limits as mortals are a source of frustration to us and so we rebel against God, crying out, "I want more!" The prophet Isaiah recognized this too. He saw upward rebellion in everything from the cedars of Lebanon to the ships of Tarshish. Wherever the creation was prone to declare itself mighty, the prophet said, "Remember that there is but One who is to be exalted." Humility is the garment that suits us best, not pride.

Prayer

Forgive us, Lord, for our upward rebellion. Forgive us for our desire to be in control of all things. We know that would be a disaster, and yet it is our desire. Grant us humility and the grace to live humbly in joy all our days. In the Name of Christ we pray. AMEN.

Friday

Isa 57:17–21

17 Because of their wicked covetousness I was angry;
I struck them, I hid and was angry;
but they kept turning back to their own ways.
18 I have seen their ways, but I will heal them;
I will lead them and repay them with comfort,
creating for their mourners the fruit of the lips.
19 Peace, peace, to the far and the near, says the LORD;
and I will heal them.

[20] But the wicked are like the tossing sea
that cannot keep still;
its waters toss up mire and mud.
[21] There is no peace, says my God, for the wicked.

"There's no rest for the wicked," is a phrase one might hear just about anywhere these days. A boss is working late and a co-worker comes by and says, "No rest for the wicked, eh?" Or a homeowner is busy cutting the grass or painting or doing some other household chore and the neighbor calls across the lawn, "I can see there's no rest for the wicked." It's a phrase we use in jest in many situations. The prophet Isaiah was not jesting, however. He meant it. The wicked have no peace, but are like the tossing sea, he said, tossing up mire and mud. Perhaps this means that the wicked are stirring up trouble for themselves and others, or that their speech is continually tearing others down, what we call mudslinging. Peace, however, comes to those whom the Lord draws near, says the prophet. Peace and healing come to those whom God embraces and comforts. Peace comes to those who quit their wicked ways and allow God to show them the way. Peace comes to those who confess sin and hear the word of God's forgiveness. Rest comes to the forgiven.

Prayer

Grant us peace, dear Lord. Help us to let go of patterns of life that stir up trouble for ourselves and others. Give us good and faithful friends who will support us in the ways of goodness and life. In all things, be near us and guide us we pray. In Christ's name. AMEN.

The Twenty-first Week After Pentecost

Monday

Ps 1

[1] Happy are those
    who do not follow the advice of the wicked
or take the path that sinners tread
    or sit in the seat of scoffers,
[2] but their delight is in the law of the Lord,
    and on his law they meditate day and night.
[3] They are like trees
    planted by streams of water,
which yield their fruit in its season,
    and their leaves do not wither.
In all that they do, they prosper.
[4] The wicked are not so
    but are like chaff that the wind drives away.
[5] Therefore the wicked will not stand in the judgment
    nor sinners in the congregation of the righteous,
[6] for the Lord watches over the way of the righteous,
    but the way of the wicked will perish.

There is a pair of Burr Oaks that stand in the park just outside the east windows of our home. I am always amazed at how fruitful and resilient they are. In the spring they look like they are dead, compared to other trees, as they are late to come out of their winter slumber and acquire greenery. In the summer they are green and strong, no matter the amount rain. Now, in the fall, their leaves have turned a brilliant yellow, but they will not drop as other trees do. They will remain hanging on through the winter until the new green sprouts push through in the spring. The psalmist says that God's faithful people are like these trees. They bear fruit in season and do not wither even when winds and storms assail them. They know that the Lord watches over them, and living in that promise, they retain their commitment to service and experience the attendant joy. In all things they stand as a testament to God's undying faithfulness. How good it is to know that God's faithfulness endures and, because of that, God's people endure as well.

Prayer

We thank you, Ever-living God, that your faithfulness is everlasting. We thank you that, because of your active Spirit in our lives, we can stand tall and bear fruit all our days. Enable each of us to live in faith, to take joy in you and in one another, and to finally find our rest in you, our Savior and Lord. AMEN.

Tuesday

Deut 7:12–16

> [12] "If you heed these ordinances by diligently observing them,
> the Lord your God will maintain with you the covenant loyalty
> that he swore to your ancestors; [13] he will love you, bless you,
> and multiply you; he will bless the fruit of your womb and the
> fruit of your ground, your grain and your wine and your oil, the
> increase of your cattle and the issue of your flock, in the land
> that he swore to your ancestors to give you. [14] You shall be the
> most blessed of peoples, with neither sterility nor barrenness
> among you or your livestock. [15] The Lord will turn away from
> you every illness; all the dread diseases of Egypt that you experi-
> enced, he will not inflict on you, but he will lay them on all who
> hate you. [16] You shall devour all the peoples that the Lord your
> God is giving over to you, showing them no pity; you shall not
> serve their gods, for that would be a snare to you.

The promises in this chapter are given to the Israelite people as they are preparing to enter the land of Canaan. It has been many years since their escape from slavery in Egypt; indeed, nearly the entire generation that left Egypt has passed away. Now Moses is reminding the people that the Lord has made a covenant with them, and that covenant must be the basis for their life together. Moses stresses the fact that blessings follow the keeping of this covenant, but serving other gods is nothing but a snare for them. We also live in a covenant with our God, a covenant sealed in the waters of baptism. At our baptism, we or our parents or sponsors promised to faithfully live out the calling which is ours. At the affirmation of baptism—a rite we call confirmation—we once again affirm our intention to "continue in the covenant God made with us in Holy Baptism," to live, hear, share, proclaim, serve and strive according to God's will for our lives. Once again, we affirm that, as long as we live in this covenant, we are blessed. God is the same today and yesterday and tomorrow.

Prayer

As you made covenant with Israel so many years ago, so you have made covenant with us in our baptism, O God. We thank and praise you for this marvelous covenant with all its gifts. Grant us your Spirit so that we might be inspired each day to live faithfully, following in the footsteps of Christ, who showed us the way of justice, peace, and love. We ask this through Christ our Lord. AMEN.

Wednesday

Matt 10:34–39

> 34 "Do not think that I have come to bring peace to the earth; I
> have not come to bring peace but a sword.
> 35 For I have come to set a man against his father,
> and a daughter against her mother,
> and a daughter-in-law against her mother-in-law,
> 36 and one's foes will be members of one's own household.
>
> 37 "Whoever loves father or mother more than me is not worthy
> of me, and whoever loves son or daughter more than me is not
> worthy of me, 38 and whoever does not take up the cross and

> follow me is not worthy of me. [39] Those who find their life will lose it, and those who lose their life for my sake will find it.

These strident words were spoken by Jesus to the twelve disciples as he sent them out on their first mission. He was making clear to them what discipleship meant. Of course, all of them were Jews, and so following Jesus would inevitably find them in conflict with the traditions of their elders. Jesus reminded them that finally *his* claim on them was superior to even that of their families'. That must have been a bitter pill to swallow. As we continue to heed the call to discipleship, we too are left with choices. When family or career or leisure activities or even seemingly noble causes threaten to pull us away from Christ, we must choose: will we continue to follow Christ in this circumstance or not? Sometimes the choices are neither simple nor easy. In all this we must remember that Christ's way is the way of *life*, and his call is meant neither to estrange us from others nor to rob us of joy. Quite the contrary, when we follow Christ, we experience life in all of its fullness.

Prayer

Discipleship is often tough for us, dear Lord. We hear the call to sacrifice, and we falter. We hear the call to leave behind people and things that pull us away from you, and we struggle. Help us to trust that your way for us is the way of life. Grant us faith, we pray. In your precious name. AMEN.

Thursday

2 Kgs 17:24–28

> [24] The king of Assyria brought people from Babylon, Cuthah,
> Avva, Hamath, and Sepharvaim and placed them in the cities of
> Samaria in place of the people of Israel; they took possession of
> Samaria and settled in its cities. [25] When they first settled there,
> they did not worship the LORD; therefore the LORD sent lions
> among them that killed some of them. [26] So the king of Assyria
> was told, "The nations that you have carried away and placed in
> the cities of Samaria do not know the law of the god of the land;
> therefore he has sent lions among them; they are killing them
> because they do not know the law of the god of the land." [27] Then
> the king of Assyria commanded, "Send there one of the priests
> whom you carried away from there; let him go and live there and

> teach them the law of the god of the land." [28] So one of the priests whom they had carried away from Samaria came and lived in Bethel; he taught them how they should worship the LORD.

Isn't this an interesting passage? Following the defeat of Israel by the Assyrian army and the subsequent exile of many of Israel's leaders, the king of Assyria sent citizens of his country to live in Israel. As they settled there, they necessarily brought with them their pagan gods and worship practices. When this idolatry proved to be a curse to them, they cried out to the king who commanded that the transplanted Assyrians be taught in the ways of "the god of the land." And so, the Assyrians were taught to worship the Lord. In this way these Assyrians were given a glimpse into life as a covenant nation. I wonder if we ever do this. Do we see people who are floundering in their religious practice and offer them the experience of life in Christ? Do we know people for whom the life of faith is only burden and guilt and offer them a glimpse of grace? Perhaps this story reminds us of the blessing that is ours in our life with Christ, and urges us on to extend this blessing to others.

Prayer

You are the God of All People, Holy One. You are the creator of all things. We give you all honor and praise for your wonderful works. Help us to share generously with others the blessing we have received as your people. Keep us from fear and doubt. Remind us that you are calling all people to yourself. In your holy name we pray. AMEN.

Friday

1 Tim 4:6–10

> [6] If you put these instructions before the brothers and sisters, you will be a good servant of Christ Jesus, nourished on the words of the faith and of the sound teaching that you have followed. [7] Have nothing to do with profane and foolish tales. Train yourself in godliness, [8] for, while physical training is of some value, godliness is valuable in every way, holding promise for both the present life and the life to come. [9] The saying is sure and worthy of full acceptance. [10] For to this end we toil and suffer reproach, because we have our hope set on the living God, who is the Savior of all people, especially of those who believe.

Some of us have a workout routine. We go to the gym, or we lift weights at home, or we have a regular time at the racquetball court. Our goal is to get in good physical shape, or perhaps to stay in some semblance of physical shape. This is important work, and we are told that such training will likely give us a better quality of life, especially as we age. The elder who wrote to Timothy also recognized the value of physical training, but he insisted that training in godliness is of even greater value, as it holds promise for "both the present life and the life to come." That's true. Training in godliness *does* provide blessings right now *and* it provides blessings for the life to come. How do we train in godliness? A routine of prayer, scripture reading, listening to God, serving others, worship, and fellowship with other believers are just a few ways that God's people, down through the ages, have trained in godliness. As you find your own way, you will be blessed.

Prayer

We wish to be strong in faith and love, O God. Train us. We wish to be faithful in the Word and in prayer. Sustain us. We wish to be servants to others, a source of encouragement and hope, always bearing testimony to the life of Christ within us. Fill us. We pray all this in the name of Jesus our Savior. AMEN.

The Twenty-second Week After Pentecost

Monday

2 Kgs 19:1–7

> When King Hezekiah heard it, he tore his clothes, covered himself with sackcloth, and went into the house of the LORD. 2 And he sent Eliakim, who was in charge of the palace, and Shebna the secretary, and the senior priests, covered with sackcloth, to the prophet Isaiah son of Amoz. 3 They said to him, "Thus says Hezekiah: This day is a day of distress, of rebuke, and of disgrace; children have come to the birth, and there is no strength to bring them forth. 4 It may be that the LORD your God heard all the words of the Rabshakeh, whom his master the king of Assyria has sent to mock the living God, and will rebuke the words that the LORD your God has heard; therefore lift up your prayer for the remnant that is left." 5 When the servants of King Hezekiah came to Isaiah, 6 Isaiah said to them, "Say to your master: Thus says the LORD: Do not be afraid because of the words that you have heard, with which the servants of the king of Assyria have reviled me. 7 I myself will put a spirit in him so that he shall hear a rumor and return to his own land; I will cause him to fall by the sword in his own land."

Prior to this passage, the king of Assyria had sent a message to King Hezekiah, saying, "Do not let your God on whom you rely deceive you by promising that Jerusalem will not be given into the hand of the king of Assyria." This is the ultimate insult to God, that God would deceive God's people. It reminds us of the words of the serpent in the Garden who said to

Eve when he heard that God had said she and Adam would die if they ate of the tree in the middle of the garden: “You will not die; for God knows that when you eat of it . . . you will be like God.” The serpent, you see, was suggesting that God was deceiving them. This voice can also come to us. When we, like King Hezekiah, face daunting odds, perhaps when we face grave illness or injury for ourselves or a loved one, or when catastrophe or tragedy strikes, we too might hear this voice that says, “God has deceived you. God has no care of you.” Whenever we hear this voice, we must remember the words of Jesus: “I am the Good Shepherd. I am the Bread of Life. I am the Way, the Truth and the Life.” The Deceiver will not have the last word as we turn our gaze to Jesus and hear him say, “I am with you always, even to the close of the days.”

Prayer

Give us faith, dear Lord, especially in those days that are difficult. When we are grieving, comfort us. When we are weak, strengthen us. When we are lonely, embrace us. When we are hungry, feed us. Fill us with your Spirit every day, so that, come what may, we might be found faithful and joyful. In your precious name we pray. AMEN.

Tuesday

Luke 18:18–27

> 18 A certain ruler asked him, “Good Teacher, what must I do to
> inherit eternal life?” 19 Jesus said to him, “Why do you call me
> good? No one is good but God alone. 20 You know the com-
> mandments: ‘You shall not commit adultery. You shall not mur-
> der. You shall not steal. You shall not bear false witness. Honor
> your father and mother.’ ” 21 He replied, “I have kept all these
> since my youth.” 22 When Jesus heard this, he said to him, “There
> is still one thing lacking. Sell all that you own and distribute the
> money to the poor, and you will have treasure in heaven; then
> come, follow me.” 23 But when he heard this, he became sad, for
> he was very rich. 24 Jesus looked at him and said, “How hard it
> is for those who have wealth to enter the kingdom of God! 25 In-
> deed, it is easier for a camel to go through the eye of a needle
> than for someone who is rich to enter the kingdom of God.”

[26] Those who heard it said, "Then who can be saved?" [27] He re-
plied, "What is impossible for mortals is possible for God."

We find both Law and Gospel in this passage. On one hand, we hear the warning regarding wealth. There is no doubt that Jesus is warning us that wealth can short circuit our relationship with God. We can become so distracted by and focused on our accumulated wealth that we find God is no longer our center, our Rock. Our bank account becomes that center instead. As Luther said in his *Large Catechism,* "Whatever your heart clings to and confides in, that is *really* your God." On the other hand, there is a promise in this passage as well: "What is impossible for mortals is possible for God." This promise reminds us that wealth need not ensnare us and rob us of a rich relationship with God. God's Spirit can free us to live generously, to focus on the Giver and not the gifts, and to be faithful stewards of all God gives. The fact is, there will always be wealthy people amongst God's people. It is no sin to be wealthy. We must simply be vigilant to listen to the words of Jesus that continually say, "Follow me. I am the way to abundant life."

Prayer

Good Creator, thank you for the abundance you have poured on your people. Thank you for abundant resources to use to serve others and bring glory to you. Help us always to live our lives freely, generously, and faithfully, reminded that you are the Source of all things, and as we live in you, we experience life in all of its abundance. In your holy name we pray. AMEN.

Wednesday

Ps 51:1–4

[1] Have mercy on me, O God,
according to your steadfast love;
according to your abundant mercy,
blot out my transgressions.
[2] Wash me thoroughly from my iniquity,
and cleanse me from my sin.
[3] For I know my transgressions
and my sin is ever before me.

> [4] Against you, you alone, have I sinned
> and done what is evil in your sight,
> so that you are justified in your sentence
> and blameless when you pass judgment.

These opening words of King David are thought to be his confession following his encounter with the prophet Nathan, who made known his adulterous and murderous affair with Bathsheba (recounted in 2 Sam 12). What David understood, and what we often fail to understand, is that sins not only hurt us and other people, they also hurt God. David, in fact, claims that his sin was done against *God alone*, for his sin was done in secret. No one, with the exception of Bathsheba, knew that David had had Bathsheba's husband killed and taken her for himself. David's sin and guilt were his alone, or so he thought. With Nathan's rebuke, he understood that nothing that he had done was a secret to God. All was known to God. It is good for us to remember this, too. Our secret sins may be things *others* fail to see or suspect about us, but God knows. God knows everything about us, and certainly God knows our sins. We can learn from David and say with him, "Against you, you alone, O God, have I sinned and done what is evil in your sight." When we do this, we are assured of God's forgiveness, for as the psalmist says, "As far as the east is from the west, so far will I remove your transgressions from you."

Prayer

Thank you for your forgiveness, Merciful God. Thank you also for your Spirit of rebuke that calls us to repentance. Keep us from deceiving ourselves, thinking you do not see or know us. Remind us of your love and your desire that we be wholly yours. Grant us your peace, O God. In the Name of Jesus we pray. AMEN.

Thursday

1 Tim 1:1–7

> Paul, an apostle of Christ Jesus by the command of God our Savior and of Christ Jesus our hope,
>
> [2] To Timothy, my true child in the faith:

> Grace, mercy, and peace from God the Father and Christ Jesus our Lord.
>
> 3 I urge you, as I did when I was on my way to Macedonia, to remain in Ephesus so that you may instruct certain people not to teach different teachings 4 and not to occupy themselves with myths and endless genealogies that promote speculations rather than the divine training that is known by faith. 5 But the aim of such instruction is love that comes from a pure heart, a good conscience, and sincere faith. 6 Some people have deviated from these and turned to meaningless talk, 7 desiring to be teachers of the law without understanding either what they are saying or the things about which they make assertions.

These opening words to Timothy are instructive to us even in this modern age. Paul says, "Do not occupy yourselves with myths and endless genealogies that promote speculations." In other words, as disciples of Christ, we are not to occupy ourselves with endless chatter about things that lead us nowhere. Martin Luther was of much the same mind. It is reported that when asked what God was doing before God made the world, Luther replied, "God was making hell for people who ask such questions!" In other words, don't spend your time wondering about such things; it leads nowhere. Paul says that instead we should spend our time in "divine training," which has as its aim "love that comes from a pure heart, a good conscience, and sincere faith." We can see immediately that these are aims that bear fruit in our lives. Paul says elsewhere that faith, hope, and love are the greatest gifts. This godly training leads us there.

Prayer

Thank you, Divine Teacher, that you guide us in faith. Thank you for your word that is a "lamp to our feet and a light to our path." Help us to be attentive students, ready to receive the divine training that leads to life. Grant that we too might lead others, so that all might know the life that is truly life. In your holy name we pray. AMEN.

Friday

Gen 8:1–7

> But God remembered Noah and all the wild animals and all the domestic animals that were with him in the ark. And

> God made a wind blow over the earth, and the waters subsid-
> ed; 2 the fountains of the deep and the windows of the heavens
> were closed, the rain from the heavens was restrained, 3 and
> the waters gradually receded from the earth. At the end of one
> hundred fifty days the waters had abated, 4 and in the seventh
> month, on the seventeenth day of the month, the ark came
> to rest on the mountains of Ararat. 5 The waters continued to
> abate until the tenth month; in the tenth month, on the first
> day of the month, the tops of the mountains appeared. 6 At the
> end of forty days Noah opened the window of the ark that he
> had made 7 and sent out the raven, and it went to and fro until
> the waters were dried up from the earth.

The Hebrew verb that opens this chapter seems curious to us. The writer says that God "remembered" Noah and all the animals. Does that mean God that had forgotten about them for a time? Actually, the meaning of the word is more precisely that God "turned God's attention to" them once again. That is to say, God's attention had been elsewhere for a while and now God was again focused on Noah and the rest of creation. God then gets to work causing a wind to blow, the waters to subside, the rains to cease, and the waters to recede from the earth. When God's attention turns toward something, things happen—dramatic things. This is important to remember. We may not be riding an ark through a deluge, but there are times in our lives when the sea is rough. We might be encountering bouts of depression or anxiety or fear. We might be battling an illness or enduring a long recovery from an injury, and it feels like we shall never be whole again. We can call out to God as the thief on the cross near Jesus did, "Jesus, remember me." When we do so, we can be sure that God's attention will be drawn to us once again.

Prayer

Thank you, Merciful God, for your loving attention to your whole creation. Thank you for the beasts and plants, for the mountains and seas, for the rain and sun. Thank you for your people whom you have made to give you praise. Give us ears to hear you when you speak. Give us hearts open to your will. Give us faith to trust you all our days. We ask this in the name of Christ. AMEN.

The Twenty-third Week After Pentecost

Monday

John 10:11–16

[11] "I am the good shepherd. The good shepherd lays down his
life for the sheep. [12] The hired hand, who is not the shepherd
and does not own the sheep, sees the wolf coming and leaves
the sheep and runs away, and the wolf snatches them and scat-
ters them. [13] The hired hand runs away because a hired hand
does not care for the sheep. [14] I am the good shepherd. I know
my own, and my own know me, [15] just as the Father knows
me, and I know the Father. And I lay down my life for the
sheep. [16] I have other sheep that do not belong to this fold. I
must bring them also, and they will listen to my voice. So there
will be one flock, one shepherd.

When Jesus spoke these words, he was speaking to the people about spiritual guides—teachers and members of the hierarchy charged with the spiritual care of the people. He clearly states the difference between a good shepherd and a bad one. While these words could well be directed at pastors today, I wonder if they might not also apply to elected officials. In the wake of our recent election might this description of a good shepherd serve well as the description of a faithful elected leader? A person of courage, integrity, and compassion, willing to sacrifice for the sake of the flock? Martin Luther was very clear that public officials have the same responsibilities before God as do spiritual leaders. Indeed, he insisted that each person, regardless of their station in life, has the duty to see to the bodily and spiritual welfare of the community, and the ordained person and the layperson differ only in function, not in standing before God. In short, we are all keepers, one of another, and this is as true for leaders in the government as it is in the Church.

Prayer

Thank you for faithful leaders, Gracious God. Thank you for people of courage, integrity, and compassion. Thank you for leaders who have been elected who are now serving or will soon serve in important roles in our government. Protect them from wicked and dangerous voices. Give them keen ears to hear your guiding voice. Bless us all, we pray. In your holy name. AMEN.

Tuesday

Ps 73:21–26

21 When my soul was embittered,
when I was pricked in heart,
22 I was stupid and ignorant;
I was like a brute beast toward you.
23 Nevertheless, I am continually with you;
you hold my right hand.
24 You guide me with your counsel,
and afterward you will receive me with honor.
25 Whom have I in heaven but you?
And there is nothing on earth that I desire other than you.
26 My flesh and my heart may fail,
but God is the strength of my heart and my portion forever.

The 73rd psalm is worth reading in its entirety. It is the struggle of a person who is envious of the arrogant rich. He sees their wickedness and their prosperity and wonders why God allows such as these to prosper. But, at some point, he realizes that wickedness and riches are a dangerous combination that lead inevitably to ruin. Finally, looking at his own situation, he says, "I am blessed. Even though I am not rich, I am continually with you, O God. You guide me and honor me. You are my strength and portion forever." What the psalmist realizes is that the treasures he enjoys are *eternal*, secure for all time, while the treasures of wicked prosperity are anything but secure. The treasures God provides sustain us and lead us to joy, while ill-gotten gains only lead to misery and corruption. We do well to remember the words of St. Paul who said, "I have learned to be content with whatever I have. I know what it is to have little, and I know what it is to have plenty. In any and all circumstances I have learned the secret of being well-fed and of going hungry, of having plenty and of being in need. I can do all things through [Christ]who strengthens me" (Philippians 4:11–13).

Prayer

We thank you, God, for the treasures we have in Christ. We thank you that these treasures are eternal, secure in your hands forever. Grant that whatever riches we may gain in this life, we might keep our eyes forever focused on that which is eternal, living in peace and joy all our days. In Christ's name we pray. AMEN.

Wednesday

Jon 3:4–10

> 4 Jonah began to go into the city, going a day's walk. And he cried
> out, "Forty days more, and Nineveh shall be overthrown!" 5 And
> the people of Nineveh believed God; they proclaimed a fast, and
> everyone, great and small, put on sackcloth.
>
> 6 When the news reached the king of Nineveh, he rose from his
> throne, removed his robe, covered himself with sackcloth, and
> sat in ashes. 7 Then he had a proclamation made in Nineveh:
> "By the decree of the king and his nobles: No human or animal,
> no herd or flock, shall taste anything. They shall not feed, nor
> shall they drink water. 8 Humans and animals shall be covered
> with sackcloth, and they shall cry mightily to God. All shall
> turn from their evil ways and from the violence that is in their
> hands. 9 Who knows? God may relent and change his mind;
> he may turn from his fierce anger, so that we do not perish."
> 10 When God saw what they did, how they turned from their evil
> ways, God changed his mind about the calamity that he had said
> he would bring upon them, and he did not do it.

This story about the repentance of a pagan city is a parable for any of us, who, like Jonah, might assume there are people whose corruption is so deep God could never reach them. Not so, says this parable. Yes, there are people who seem beyond help, but nothing is impossible with God. We see this sometimes in prisons where people who have been convicted of infamous crimes come to faith. We are often skeptical of such "jailhouse conversions;" perhaps, like Jonah, we are not even willing to rejoice in such conversions or even consider them sincere. But God's compassion and forgiveness is far beyond ours. God's word is clear, "If we confess our sins, God is faithful and just and will cleanse us from all unrighteousness" (1 John 1:9). This is no less true for people serving criminal sentences. As Jesus said, "With God all things are possible."

Prayer

Forgive us, Gracious Lord, when we doubt the faith of others. Forgive us when we claim a measure of your grace, but refuse that grace for others. Forgive us when we believe that some sins are beyond forgiving and some people are beyond saving. Give us generous hearts, willing that none be lost, but all come to know the truth of the Gospel. In the name of Christ, we pray. AMEN.

Thursday

Luke 22:31–33, 54–62

[31] "Simon, Simon, listen! Satan has demanded to sift all of you like wheat, [32] but I have prayed for you that your own faith may not fail, and you, when once you have turned back, strengthen your brothers." [33] And he said to him, "Lord, I am ready to go with you to prison and to death!" [34] Jesus said, "I tell you, Peter, the cock will not crow this day until you have denied three times that you know me."

[54] Then they seized him and led him away, bringing him into the high priest's house. But Peter was following at a distance. [55] When they had kindled a fire in the middle of the courtyard and sat down together, Peter sat among them. [56] Then a female servant, seeing him in the firelight, stared at him and said, "This man also was with him." [57] But he denied it, saying, "Woman, I do not know him." [58] A little later someone else, on seeing him, said, "You also are one of them." But Peter said, "Man, I am not!" [59] Then about an hour later still another kept insisting, "Surely this man

> also was with him, for he is a Galilean." 60 But Peter said, "Man,
> I do not know what you are talking about!" At that moment,
> while he was still speaking, the cock crowed. 61 The Lord turned
> and looked at Peter. Then Peter remembered the word of the
> Lord, how he had said to him, "Before the cock crows today, you
> will deny me three times." 62 And he went out and wept bitterly.

What must Peter have felt like when the Lord turned and looked at him? Can you imagine the shame and guilt he felt after his betrayal? He had boasted that he was ready to go to prison and even die for Jesus, but when push came to shove, he could no more stand up for Jesus than a blade of grass can stand up to the wind. He toppled like the house of cards he was. Peter's story is a familiar one, of course. It is one we fear we could easily replicate. Would *we* be willing to stand up to persecution and threat for the sake of our confession of Christ if it came to that? We don't know. Most of us have never had to confront that scenario. There are times, however, when our faithfulness to Christ is challenged in common ways. We make choices every day about how we will spend our time and money, who our friends will be, where our loyalties will lie, and what kind of culture we will embrace. We do well to look at the face of Jesus and remember that he calls us to confess him in all times and places, no matter the cost.

Prayer

We are not courageous disciples, O God. We are so much like Peter, wanting to be faithful, but faltering at the first threat. Give us courage. Give us faith. Grant us a measure of your Spirit so that when we are called upon to confess your name, we might do it boldly, trusting in your abiding presence. In the name of Christ we pray. AMEN.

Friday

Rom 8:31–39

> 31 What then are we to say about these things? If God is for us,
> who is against us? 32 He who did not withhold his own Son but
> gave him up for all of us, how will he not with him also give us
> everything else? 33 Who will bring any charge against God's elect?
> It is God who justifies. 34 Who is to condemn? It is Christ who
> died, or rather, who was raised, who is also at the right hand of

> God, who also intercedes for us. [35] Who will separate us from
> the love of Christ? Will affliction or distress or persecution or
> famine or nakedness or peril or sword? [36] As it is written,
>
> "For your sake we are being killed all day long;
> we are accounted as sheep to be slaughtered."
>
> [37] No, in all these things we are more than victorious through
> him who loved us. [38] For I am convinced that neither death,
> nor life, nor angels, nor rulers, nor things present, nor things to
> come, nor powers, [39] nor height, nor depth, nor anything else in
> all creation will be able to separate us from the love of God in
> Christ Jesus our Lord.

There are few passages in the Bible more comforting than these grand words of St. Paul: "Nothing in all creation is able to separate us from God's love!" What a promise. Yes, we suffer at times. Yet, we are loved by God. Yes, we are threatened by forces around us at times. Yet, we are held by God. Yes, we are accused falsely, betrayed, and even slandered because of our fidelity to Christ. Yet, we are never abandoned by God. Even spiritual forces, things beyond us in every way, are no threat to us, because we are victorious through Christ who loves us. In these tumultuous days, when partisan politics, pandemics, the war in Ukraine, famine in Somalia, and hurricanes in Florida fill the headlines, we sometimes wonder how much more we can endure. Yet, through it all, we know that God's love is firm. We are held in God's embrace. Christ's death on the Cross seals it. *Nothing* can separate us from God's love.

Prayer

We praise you, Loving God, for your infinite love, your eternal embrace, and your never-ending faithfulness. When we are weak in faith, strengthen us. When we suffer, come to our aid. When we are discouraged, build us up. We live by your grace. Walk with us each day, we pray. In Christ's name. AMEN.

The Final Week After Pentecost

Monday

Ps 113

1 Praise the LORD!
Praise, O servants of the LORD;
praise the name of the LORD.
2 Blessed be the name of the LORD
from this time on and forevermore.
3 From the rising of the sun to its setting,
the name of the LORD is to be praised.
4 The LORD is high above all nations
and his glory above the heavens.
5 Who is like the LORD our God,
who is seated on high,
6 who looks far down
on the heavens and the earth?
7 He raises the poor from the dust
and lifts the needy from the ash heap,
8 to make them sit with princes,
with the princes of his people.
9 He gives the barren woman a home,
making her the joyous mother of children.
Praise the LORD!

This psalm is traditionally sung by Jewish families as they gather for the Passover observance. It is a hymn of praise that acknowledges that our God is unlike any other god, "high above all nations, whose glory is in the heavens." As we soon make plans to be with family on Thanksgiving Day, this psalm might be a great way to begin the meal together. Even children could be encouraged to participate by thanking God for something for which they are grateful. Giving praise to God is always appropriate, and even more so when we gather as God's people to give thanks for God's blessings.

Prayer

There is none like you, Holy One. You are seated on high, and yet you come to be amongst us in the person of Jesus. You are without sin and yet you come to be with us who are sinful. You are immortal and yet you come and dwell with us who are dust. How can we ever thank you, O God? There are not words to express your greatness. We praise you and thank you this day for all your greatness and love. AMEN.

Tuesday

Mark 12:41–44

> 41 [Jesus]sat down opposite the treasury and watched the crowd
> putting money into the treasury. Many rich people put in large
> sums. 42 A poor widow came and put in two small copper coins,
> which are worth a penny. 43 Then he called his disciples and said
> to them, "Truly I tell you, this poor widow has put in more than
> all those who are contributing to the treasury. 44 For all of them
> have contributed out of their abundance, but she out of her pov-
> erty has put in everything she had, all she had to live on."

When we read this familiar story we sometimes wonder how good Jesus is at math. We are told that rich people put large sums in the offering and the widow only gave two copper coins, yet Jesus says that the widow gave the most. How can that be? The answer is in the last line. We are told she put in "all she had to live on." A better translation might be "her whole life." What Jesus is teaching us here is that giving one's life to God far outweighs any monetary gift we might give. When we give our life to God, we are giving God first place in our life; we are declaring our ultimate loyalty to

God; we are saying that nothing is more precious to us than our relationship with God. That's what the widow did. It's true that she gave very little money, but she gave her whole self to God. Often overlooked is that all of us, no matter how much wealth we have or how little, are invited to do the same. We are invited every day to give our whole self to God, living in the joy and freedom of that relationship.

Prayer

Give us open hearts, O God. Give us hearts that are willing to put our whole lives into your hands. Help us to release into your safe-keeping all that we treasure and to trust you for all that we need to live and grow. We pray this in the name of Jesus. AMEN.

Wednesday

Prov 14:12–20

12 There is a way that seems right to a person,
but its end is the way to death.
13 Even in laughter the heart is sad,
and the end of joy is grief.
14 The perverse get what their ways deserve,
and the good, what their deeds deserve.
15 The simple believe everything,
but the clever consider their steps.
16 The wise are cautious and turn away from evil,
but the fool throws off restraint and is careless.
17 One who is quick-tempered acts foolishly,
and the schemer is hated.
18 The simple are adorned with folly,
but the clever are crowned with knowledge.
19 The evil bow down before the good,
the wicked at the gates of the righteous.
20 The poor are disliked even by their neighbors,
but the rich have many friends.

In this section of Proverbs, the writer talks about "wearing" wisdom and folly. In other words, others can see them. The simple ones—that is, fools—"are adorned with folly." Their foolishness is obvious. The clever ones—those who live wisely—"are crowned with knowledge." Again, the world can see their wisdom, and it is a sign of royalty. One of my school teachers while I was growing up would sometimes recite this quote: "You can fool all the people some of the time, and some of the people all of the time, but you can't fool all of the people all of the time." The wisdom writer of Proverbs would agree: eventually it will be known whether we are fools or wise ones.

Prayer

Give us wisdom, Creator of All. Give us clear minds and faithful counselors as we live our days. There is so much foolishness in the world. Keep us from its snares. Keep us faithful to you all our days. In your holy name we pray. AMEN.

Thursday

Deut 26:1–4, 8–11

> "When you have come into the land that the LORD your God is
> giving you as an inheritance to possess and you possess it and
> settle in it, 2 you shall take some of the first of all the fruit of the
> ground, which you harvest from the land that the LORD your
> God is giving you, and you shall put it in a basket and go to the
> place that the LORD your God will choose as a dwelling for his
> name. 3 You shall go to the priest who is in office at that time and
> say to him, 'Today I declare to the LORD your God that I have
> come into the land that the LORD swore to our ancestors to give
> us.' 4 When the priest takes the basket from your hand and sets
> it down before the altar of the LORD your God, 5 you shall make
> this response before the LORD your God:
>
> 8 The LORD brought us out of Egypt with a mighty hand and an
> outstretched arm, with a terrifying display of power, and with
> signs and wonders; 9 and he brought us into this place and gave
> us this land, a land flowing with milk and honey. 10 So now I
> bring the first of the fruit of the ground that you, O LORD, have
> given me.' You shall set it down before the LORD your God and
> bow down before the LORD your God. 11 Then you, together

with the Levites and the aliens who reside among you, shall celebrate with all the bounty that the LORD your God has given to you and to your house.

This passage is a part of the First Reading appointed for Thanksgiving Day. As I read it, I cannot help but think that those early settlers in North America, people we sometimes call the Pilgrims, might well have thought of these words as they sat down to their first harvest meal in this new land. While much has been said about that first Thanksgiving, some of it historically accurate and some of it legend, there is no doubt that these early settlers were Christians who came to America seeking freedom from persecution. Their practices and beliefs did not match well with those of their fellows in their homeland, and so they left for parts unknown. It is not hard to imagine that, as they lived through the hardship of that first year in a new land, stories from the Bible about the Israelites in the wilderness would have resonated with them. The Lord had brought them through a difficult time to a land "flowing with milk and honey." They had survived. They would continue. They knew their life was a gift of God. Our lives, too, are a gift from God. As we celebrate this Thanksgiving Day, let us remember that the bounty that we enjoy comes from the Lord's hand.

Prayer

God of Abundance, we thank you this day for all your blessings to us: family, friends, home, work, health, and faith. We live by your grace. Give us grateful hearts on this and every day, and make us agents of your generosity to all we meet. In Christ's name we pray. AMEN.

Friday

1 Cor 9:19–23

[19] For though I am free with respect to all, I have made myself
a slave to all, so that I might gain all the more. [20] To the Jews I
became as a Jew, in order to gain Jews. To those under the law
I became as one under the law (though I myself am not under
the law) so that I might gain those under the law. [21] To those
outside the law I became as one outside the law (though I am
not outside God's law but am within Christ's law) so that I might
gain those outside the law. [22] To the weak I became weak, so that

> I might gain the weak. I have become all things to all people, that I might by all means save some. [23] I do it all for the sake of the gospel, so that I might become a partner in it.

In this passage, we hear St. Paul giving voice to his determination to "keep the first things the First Thing." He says that he has all sorts of identities that he could claim: a freeman, a Jew, a person living under Jewish law, etc. Finally, however, those identities don't matter as much as the fact that he is an ambassador for Christ. He has been called to bring the Gospel to the world, and if that means abandoning some of his identities for a short time, then so be it. The Gospel is worth it. This is a challenge to us. We are often tempted to make unimportant things the First Thing. Maybe it's money or our status or our preferences around lifestyle. Whatever it may be, if we let these secondary things become the First Thing, they threaten our call to be ambassadors for Christ. We will need to learn to live with an open hand with some of our identities, so that we might be, as St. Paul says, "all things to all people" for the sake of the Gospel. It is what God calls us to do.

Prayer

Use us in your service, dear Lord. Keep us from selfishness or stubbornness that limits how you can use us. Let us live freely, trusting that when we keep our relationship with you central in our life, life is lived in all of its fullness. We pray this in your holy name. AMEN.